The Ripple Effects of College Prison Programs

The Ripple Effects of College Prison Programs

Hope, Humanity, and Transformation

Taffany Lim, EdD

BLOOMSBURY ACADEMIC
NEW YORK • LONDON • OXFORD • NEW DELHI • SYDNEY

BLOOMSBURY ACADEMIC
Bloomsbury Publishing Inc, 1385 Broadway, New York, NY 10018, USA
Bloomsbury Publishing Plc, 50 Bedford Square, London, WC1B 3DP, UK
Bloomsbury Publishing Ireland, 29 Earlsfort Terrace, Dublin 2, D02 AY28, Ireland

BLOOMSBURY, BLOOMSBURY ACADEMIC and the Diana logo are trademarks of
Bloomsbury Publishing Plc

First published in the United States of America 2025

Cover art by Kitona Paepule

Bloomsbury Publishing Inc does not have any control over, or responsibility for, any
third-party websites referred to or in this book. All internet addresses given in this
book were correct at the time of going to press. The author and publisher regret any
inconvenience caused if addresses have changed or sites have ceased to exist, but can
accept no responsibility for any such changes.

ISBN: HB: 978-1-5381-9579-6
PB: 978-1-5381-9580-2
ePDF: 979-8-7651-5523-3
eBook: 978-1-5381-5981-3

Typeset by Deanta Global Publishing Services, Chennai, India
Printed and bound in the United States of America

For product safety related questions contact productsafety@bloomsbury.com.

To find out more about our authors and books visit www.bloomsbury.com
and sign up for our newsletters.

Brief Contents

Contents

Preface

My first introduction to the students who would make up Cal State LA's Cohort 1 at California State Prison, Los Angeles County (LAC), was in May 2016. Twenty-five students had taken one or two credit-bearing courses with Cal State LA's Dr. Bidhan Roy long before I met them, but my role that day was to tell them that they were now officially part of the only face-to-face bachelor's degree program for incarcerated students in the state of California. The Cal State LA Prison BA Graduation Initiative had acquired pilot funding, and the degree would be in communication with an emphasis on organizational communication.

It turns out that the students had already assumed the identity of proud Golden Eagles. They had conjured a rallying cry they thought befitting of their mascot ("Caw Caw!"). They had called their mothers and written the university thank-you notes. They were looking forward to their next class.

When our first meeting was over, they lined up to introduce themselves, shake my hand, and offer their gratitude and thanks many times over. They shared stories. Darren told me that as a newly enrolled college student, he was no longer the "low man on the totem pole" in his family. Instead, he was a role model who was inspiring his nieces and nephews to go to college. Jesse told me that his sister was thinking about going back to school because if he could do it, so could she. Tin said his mother cried when he told her he was in college and that she would do whatever it took to attend his graduation (which she did twice—for both his bachelor's and his master's degrees).

Dortell was one of the last to come up. He had waited patiently for the crowd to thin. In his soft, distinctive voice, he said:

"I will never forget what you said."

"Errrr—what did I say?"

"You said that you believed in us. You said that you know we can do this. That you have our back."

"Well, yes. I did say those things. And I mean them."

"But, you see—most of us in here? We're like forty years old plus and no one has ever said that to us before. No one has ever told us that they believe in us. More than 90 percent of us in this room have experienced some kind of trauma in our lives. No one has ever told us that they had confidence in us before. Thank you."

What Dortell and his classmates told me then, and now, is that they believe the true power of higher education is that it builds self-efficacy. Resilience. Hope. Critical thinking. Transformation. A ripple effect. They basked in the honor of being college students.

So I keep saying it: I am proud of you. You are inspiring. Look at how far you've come! You are amazing.

Who knew that this is what education could do?

Until I walked onto a prison yard, I don't think I truly understood what the absence of hope looks like, or how profound it is to call someone by their first name. Until I met our students, I don't think I believed that true transformation is possible, and yet now I bear witness to it every day.

Through the students, I am learning that the true gift of education is about connecting with ourselves and each other in our humanity. It is an honor to have been entrusted with their stories of challenge and triumph in this book so that we may all share in this gift.

Figure 0.1 Cohort 1 and 2 graduates on A Yard, October 6, 2021. Photo by R. Huskey, 2021. Courtesy of California State University, Los Angeles Center for Engagement, Service, and the Public Good.

Acknowledgments

I am forever grateful for all of the students in Cohorts 1 and 2, who persisted in their college education, even when it was incredibly rocky and unpredictable. You plowed new ground, and because of you, the field of higher education in prison is thriving all across the United States. I am humbled by your dedication and commitment to change your lives and awe-inspired by your success and persistence. I am deeply moved by those of you who volunteered to share your stories for this compilation. I am so touched that you offered these precious pieces of yourself with candor and courage. Your stories are a gift that will create a lasting ripple effect for us all. I am so proud of you!

None of this work would have ever happened if a bachelor's degree completion program in prison did not speak to the values and mission of Cal State LA. With the backing of former president Bill Covino and executive vice president Jose Gomez, the university was able to make great strides in a short amount of time.

It was never my intention to become involved on the forefront of the return of higher education in prison (who knew it was even a thing?), but I have Bidhan Roy to thank for introducing me to the field and partnering with me during the crazy first several years of the journey. I am also grateful to David Olsen, who cheerfully wandered into the unknown with us, recruiting and supporting an amazing group of faculty members who are all excellent in their field, student-centered, and flex-o-mistic: Frances Chee, Angela Cooke-Jackson, Greg Langner, Tina McDermott, Elisabeth Houston, Amad Jackson, Sharoni Little, Luis Martinez, Owynn Lancaster, Oscar Mejia, Nina O'Brien, Cynthia Wang, and Mu Wu. Special thanks to Sarah Black, for always going above and beyond, and to Kamran Afary, who has taught us all about being trauma-informed practitioners and who inspires faculty, staff, and students alike by leading with kindness, compassion, and a generosity of spirit.

There were many other staff and administrators who willingly threw themselves into this work on top of all of their other responsibilities. Thank you to Eric Bullard, Harkmore Lee, Tom Lau, Kathryn Martinez, Jean Cruz, Victor Iglesias, Jimmy Solis, and Evelyn Espinoza for your patience and fortitude.

None of this would have happened without the seed funding of support from the Opportunity Institute's Renewing Communities fund. Thank you to Debbie Mukamal for being an early cheerleader when it felt so impossible. And I will always appreciate Rebecca Silbert for asking the hard questions since the first day we met, for unapologetically advocating on behalf of Cal State LA, and for personally offering wisdom and guidance during some of my toughest days. I am so grateful for the best grant writing partner ever, Chris Bourdon, who always knows how to tell the story just right.

I am in awe of my colleagues from the California Department of Corrections and Rehabilitation. California would not be where it is today without the vision and advocacy of Brant Choate and the tireless championship of Shannon Swain. Thank you to Ronald Underwood for your belief in the men and your stalwart support of higher education and to Crystal Wood for making it all happen. I am endlessly grateful for J. D. Hughes, who has never stopped advocating for the men and stands by them always. Our students and I will never forget the exceptional kindness of Correctional Officers Keith Junior and Clinton Cody. Thank you to Lt. Karla Graves, who helped organize the first graduation during some extremely challenging conditions. Special thanks to Troy Tenhet and Jill Lollis for your leadership and tireless work behind the scenes.

I am so grateful to my dissertation co-chairs, Susan Tracz and Christian Wandeler, who provided clarity, guidance, and encouragement during my initial foray into these key research topics, especially Dr. Tracz, who on more than one occasion told me that the dissertation read like a book. Thanks to Gena Lew Gong, who was one of my earliest readers and who provided a quiet and relaxing writer's retreat, complete with lots of snacks and homemade desserts. Warm and special thanks to Ray Pun, who generously introduced me to his publisher just when I realized I needed to be somewhere new.

Thank you, Becca Beurer and Bloomsbury, for being so responsive and supportive from the very start.

Thank you to Vic Liptak, my favorite walking companion and fabulous copy editor who now knows these stories better than anyone else. Thank you, Vic, for your enthusiasm and insightfulness and for helping with all of the tedious details that so easily bog me down. I am so glad we finally found a chance to work together.

I am grateful for my parents, Martin and Janet Lim, who supported my early collegiate interests and endeavors even though they worried that a psychology and social work major would never earn any money. Thanks to my brother, Mark Lim, for always being curious and asking for updates up to the very end. Much love to Neil Rutman, who has borne the brunt of my time away during my graduate studies, long hours at the prison, and endless weekends spent researching and writing.

To Mason and Tong Tong: It is my deepest hope that you, too, will benefit from the ripple effects of this work and that we are able to leave this world a slightly better place because of it.

Introduction

I wasn't aware of how higher education possessed the power and capability for one to change their perspective of self and of the world (J. Keaton, Cohort 2, pers. comm., 2018).

California State Prison, Los Angeles County (LAC) is a desolate place. Lancaster is a maximum security prison for men in the high desert of Los Angeles, a ninety-minute drive from the Cal State LA main campus. It can be finger-numbingly cold in the winter months or so hot in the summer it feels as if your skin is crisping off your body. At any time of year, the winds can whip up so strongly that sand will scratch your eyeballs and fill your coat pockets when you walk across the yard.

In 2016, LAC's A Yard (also known as the Honor Yard or the Progressive Programming Facility) was a small oasis in the desert, a different place than most prison yards. In the heat and the dust of A Yard, among the men grouped around the chin-up bars and concrete benches, there were dog trainers in CDCR (California Department of Corrections and Rehabilitation) denim, leading dogs of every shape, size, and breed as part of the esteemed Paws for Life program. There were men heading to self-help classes created and facilitated by their peers. Some men waved cheerfully as they headed to the art room, a cool and quiet reprieve stocked full of self-funded art supplies and staggering talent. The college students sauntered toward the education building, books tucked into the crook of one arm while the other hand balanced a cup of coffee or a cellophane-wrapped sandwich and an apple, making their way to the classroom where, for three hours a day, they forgot where they were.

As a cofounder of the Cal State LA Prison BA Graduation Initiative (now known as the Prison Graduation Initiative, or PGI), I was on one of my

1

monthly visits to check in with the students before classes started. Allen Burnett, a student in the first cohort, walked into class early, probably because he needed to take advantage of the computer lab to finish typing up a paper, but I instantly waylaid him with questions. He had often used the term "ripple effect" when talking about the benefits of a college education in prison, and this was my chance to understand his theory better.

Allen was an excellent student, thoughtful and introspective, confidently soft-spoken, a critical thinker and a strong writer. He was a leader inside and outside the classroom. He was also on his twenty-fifth year of a life without parole (LWOP) sentence. He had thought about dropping out of college. He had recently had an unsuccessful hearing with the parole board. He thought he might die in prison.

In fact, more than 90 percent of our first cohort had life or LWOP sentences, and they, too, expected to spend the rest of their lives in prison. Yet, when they started the bachelor's degree program, these same students reported that education was making them feel hopeful for the first time since they had come to prison, and that they were starting to feel like human beings again. In addition to the startling changes they were feeling within themselves, almost all of the students had stories of how being in college was causing unexpected changes for their family and friends. Suddenly, these incarcerated college students were no longer viewed as the family embarrassment or black sheep but were being touted as good role models for their nieces and nephews. Their mothers bragged about them, and their children imagined that they, too, would go to college one day. Siblings wanted to compare report cards and competed for good grades. Allen called this the ripple effect.

On the day of my classroom visit, Allen stood thoughtfully at the whiteboard, juggling a couple of brittle dry-erase markers, then drew a stick figure of himself in the middle of the board. He drew a series of waves that went down to the lower corner of the board, each wave hitting another stick figure. These waves at the bottom of the board represented Allen's negative ripple effect. His crime, he explained, had destroyed his victim but also had a negative ripple effect on his victim's family, friends, and society at large. The world had lost out on all of the positive contributions that his victim, a young college student, was preparing to make but no longer could. Allen pointed at the other stick figures that were hit by waves. His mother, his aunt, his ex-wife, his stepchildren, his nieces and nephews—all suffered a negative ripple effect from his crime and throughout his incarceration.

Moving diagonally up from his central figure, Allen drew another set of waves that drifted upward and intersected with more stick figures. He explained that just as he had caused a negative ripple effect as a result of his crime, he was starting a positive ripple effect by being in college. His aunt was proud of him. His stepchildren were inspired to stay in school and enroll in college. Other men on the yard were asking him how they could enroll in college, too. Family and friends on the outside were calling and asking for his advice. Allen was serving life without parole, and yet he was having a huge ripple effect. He had become a positive influence just by being a college student in prison. He had become an inspirational role model in the community, even if he might never come home.

In the early days, when Cal State LA was the only university in California to offer an in-person bachelor's degree completion program for incarcerated students, people on the outside expressed mild curiosity or maybe thought it was cool. Often, there was a perverse fascination of what it was like to work among, as people would say, "criminals" and "felons." ("Aren't you afraid you'll get hurt when you're in there?" No. "What kind of criminals are in the program?" I don't know. I never asked.) Much more rarely, I encountered people who believed offering a bachelor's degree to incarcerated people was unfair and that the only free thing criminals should get in prison was bread and water. Occasionally, a correctional officer would sneeringly ask if he should instruct his kid to commit a felony so he could go to college, too. Naysayers typically rallied around the myth that incarcerated college students were taking their tax dollars from "more deserving" students. Their ultimate complaint: What is the point of providing a college education to someone who may never get out? If college is about finding gainful employment and having a meaningful career, what good is a bachelor's degree if no one will ever hire them anyway? And what does a bachelor's degree do for someone with LWOP who is probably never coming home?

Shortly after the Prison BA Graduation Initiative's kick-off in 2016, I began receiving a lot of mail from the students. They sent copies of their reflection papers, handwritten note cards, and typed letters. One student gifted a painting to me, but not before scores of other men (not all of them PGI students) scribbled heartfelt thank-you notes on the back of the canvas.

The students' letters and notes shared common refrains about the benefits of education. One student wrote, "Every class I take heals a broken part of me" (Anonymous, pers. comm., 2018). Although the sheer volume of letters I received was overwhelming, I faithfully stored each missive in a large metal drawer in my office, noting that even the simplest and shortest messages were generous, grateful, kind, and profound. Additionally, their messages were consistent: Pursuing a college degree in prison reconnected them to their humanity and elicited gratitude, hope, and, ultimately, their own transformation.

[T]his educational journey invokes optimism and a sense of pride that I can accomplish my goals and dreams despite my imprisonment. I look forward to a brighter future because of my educational opportunities. (M. Lindsey, Cohort 2, pers. comm., 2018)

Under the tutelage of Professor Kamran Afary, who incorporates the use of drama therapy in almost all the classes he teaches at Lancaster, the students wrote plays in which they reflected upon and reimagined some of their most poignant childhood memories and traumatic life experiences. They collaborated on scripts that described intimate details of their lives, which were produced into animated shorts by students on the Cal State LA main campus and then looped on the institutional television channel for everyone to see. They submitted journal articles and creative writing essays that delved into their pasts and fantasized about their futures. Unsolicited, they shared stories of sexual abuse and molestation and being abandoned on the streets in Mexico. They recalled parents who called them stupid and parents who died of drug overdoses in their own beds. They shared stories of being bullied and harassed and finding comfort and safety in gangs. The students recognized—well before I understood it myself—that the most dangerous part about trauma is that it is cyclical. As Bessel Van der Kolk says in *The Body Keeps the Score*, "Trauma breeds further trauma; hurt people hurt other people" (Van der Kolk 2014, 350).

What I have learned from the students in the past ten years of doing this work is that the value of earning a bachelor's degree in prison is much more than the classes that were taught or the theories that were reviewed. If you ask the PGI students what they remember the most from their college career, none of them will refer to a single activity or even a book that has stuck with them. What they talk about is how their critical thinking sharpened, their ability to write and articulate their ideas became more organized, and their confidence grew. What they remember is how it felt to be called by their first name and to have a professor shake their hand.

The men who were fortunate enough to be enrolled in the Cal State LA PGI program embraced the Golden Eagle mascot and saw themselves as students who gained in ways they never thought possible. Rather than internalizing the belief that the value of a college degree in prison is best measured by reducing the risk of recidivism or increasing their employability after coming home, the students focused their writings, presentations, interviews, and everyday interactions on the connections between higher education and renewed self-esteem, rehabilitation, transformation, and hope. They understood that they were role models with a far-reaching ripple effect. They showed that even on the most desolate yard, in a most desolate place, there is hope.

THE CHANGING LANDSCAPE

Sixty years ago, the United States was rich with college opportunities for incarcerated students. The Higher Education Act of 1965 gave rise to more than 700 college-in-prison programs in over 1,200 facilities across the country at the program's peak in the early 1990s. Thousands of incarcerated students at the time were enrolled in credit-bearing college courses and vocational programs (Sawyer 2019). Support for higher education in prison began to decline in 1992, when incarcerated students sentenced to life without parole (LWOP) or death were deemed ineligible for federal Pell Grants. After President Bill Clinton signed the Violent Crime Act in 1994, eliminating Pell Grant funding for all incarcerated students, prison education programs disappeared overnight. By 1997, only eight higher education in prison (HEP) programs forged on, largely through the help of private giving, or, as in the case of the highly regarded Prison University Project (now known as Mount Tamalpais College) at San Quentin Prison in California, a dedicated pool of volunteer instructors. The 1994 crime bill also fueled mass incarceration by licensing states to pass their own tough-on-crime laws and imprisoning more people for longer amounts of time. In 2013, RAND researchers published a seminal and highly influential report, "Evaluating the Effectiveness of Correctional Education" (Davis et al. 2013), contending that there are distinct societal benefits to offering prison education, most notably that students who participated in education while in prison had 43 percent lower odds of recidivating than those who did not. The researchers concluded that receiving education in prison reduces the likelihood that someone will return to prison; that the chances of gainful employment post-incarceration are higher; and that education in a correctional facility is a cost-effective deterrent to recidivism. An analysis of the RAND findings prepared for a 2019 Senate bill estimated that every dollar spent on correctional education saved taxpayers four to five dollars on reincarceration costs (Schatz 2019).

The RAND study has had a profound impact on state and federal policies, accelerating the rejuvenation and development of HEP programs for the past decade. In early 2015, Debbie Mukamal, Rebecca Silbert, and Rebecca M. Taylor (2015) jointly published the report *Degrees of Freedom,* which leveraged the RAND study to organize an unprecedented collaboration between the State of California and funders with national and local profiles to create the Renewing Communities initiative. Renewing Communities invested in an impressive and diverse group of seven prison education and reentry programs, including Cal State LA, with three years of pilot funding.

As a result, the landscape of prison education in California changed rapidly. While in 2014 California had just one prison with a face-to-face community college program, by 2017, there were thirty-four, enrolling approximately 4,500 unique students at a time (Mukamal and Silbert 2018). As a Renewing Communities grantee, Cal State LA piloted the first and (at the time) only in-person bachelor's degree completion program for incarcerated students in the state. As of September 2024, there were eight in-person bachelor's degree programs.

The RAND report spurred bipartisan support for prison education and campus-based reentry programs around the country. The Obama administration launched the Second Chance Pell Experimental Site program in 2015, providing Pell Grants to incarcerated students enrolled in one of sixty-seven higher education institutions selected to participate in the pilot. Cal State LA was one of the first universities accepted into the initial cohort of Second Chance Pell sites and one of only thirteen bachelor's degree programs. The FAFSA (Free Application for Federal Student Aid) Simplification Act signed in 2020 builds upon the collective experience of Second Chance Pell, officially extending Pell Grant eligibility to incarcerated students who enroll in eligible prison education programs (PEPs). PEPs are required to meet specific standards for approval, reporting, oversight, and evaluation as implemented by the US Department of Education. It is estimated that the number of incarcerated college students will have more than doubled in 2024, ballooning to more than 70,000 unique students enrolled in more than 200 prison education programs in the United States. Prison education is having another heyday.

In contrast, colleges and universities across the country are facing steep declines in full-time student enrollment, teetering on the edge of the long-anticipated enrollment cliff. Those who have been immersed in the field of HEP for a long time worry that some institutions will start catering to incarcerated Pell-eligible students to boost their enrollment numbers without considering how hard, complicated, and expensive it is to offer quality programming to system-impacted students both inside and outside of prison.

Impactful, meaningful degree programs in prisons require more than merely replicating classes and assigning instructors because of the many unique challenges and considerations that differ vastly from degree attainment on the outside. Bringing degree programs effectively and successfully into prisons requires mutual respect, creativity, resilience, and persistence among all partners. In Cal State LA's experience, the Pell Grant program may cover student tuition but is not nearly enough to absorb the significant costs associated with the development and administration of a college degree in prison. A college or university's reasons for doing this work must be driven by more than money and should reflect the institution's values and mission.

THE PRISON BA GRADUATION INITIATIVE (PGI)

Bidhan Roy was a tenure-track English professor at Cal State LA when he began volunteering in 2015 at Lancaster State Prison. He started with basic writing lessons out in the middle of the exercise area of A Yard, then grew his program to give the men the same reading and writing assignments as his students back on campus. He facilitated discussions between the incarcerated and the nonincarcerated students by setting up an anonymous pen pal system. The men at Lancaster and the students on the main campus compared and contrasted their ideas and reactions via handwritten reflections scrawled on lined notebook paper. The volunteer activity gave rise to a humanities-based program, WordsUncaged, which continues today.

The men on Lancaster's A Yard gathered faithfully every week, sitting on concrete benches surrounded by chin-up and dip bars, but they were frustrated. Most of the men had been encouraging each other for years, first earning their GEDs in prison, and then progressing together to community college. They each had accumulated more than ninety community college credits through accredited correspondence programs and by creating a self-support system of buying and sharing textbooks, but they had no way to progress to a bachelor's degree. The students were aware that California's SB 1391, which was signed in 2014 and effective January 2015, authorized California's community college system of 114 campuses to begin offering prison-based associate's degree programming at no charge to the students, but still, they saw no pathway to a higher degree. Around the same time, Cal State LA's leadership advisory board members, alerted to the lack of bachelor's degree options for incarcerated students, encouraged the university president and executive vice president to explore possibilities of filling the educational gap for incarcerated students.

The university's executive vice president, Jose Gomez, and Bidhan Roy connected with me separately, but at roughly the same time, to request my involvement in developing a bachelor's degree for incarcerated students. I had been on the campus for several years as an occasional lecturer, associate director of Cal State LA's Pat Brown Institute of Public Affairs, and most recently, the founding director of the Center for Engagement, Service, and the Public Good. The Center was a hub for innovative community engagement and service learning, blending community and university interests into mutually beneficial projects. As a longtime program developer who enjoys the challenge of the new and unknown, I was at first mildly intrigued by prison education. Then in the blink of an eye, I became so impassioned by the work and the students that I hardly realized I'd spent nearly seven years as the unofficial program lead. A reporter from a public television station observed me at work for many hours over several days and eventually concluded that my role was something in between "a school principal and a mom" (a mantle which I only just recently began to begrudgingly accept). My job at the time was to make things happen, which is what, I suppose, moms do best.

I did not have firsthand knowledge about incarceration nor a carceral family history. What I do have is a passion for college students and the energy and persistence to make things happen, which any prison program leader will tell you is needed in spades. I have been fortunate enough to blend my personal values of social justice and service with strong program administration and fund development skills throughout my career trajectory, so the work of starting up the first face-to-face bachelor's degree completion program for incarcerated students in the state of California was compelling and exciting to me.

When we started offering credit-bearing courses, the only money we had was a commitment from the President's Office that instructors would be paid for the classes they taught. Shortly after offering our first official class, we received the three years of pilot funding from the Renewing Communities initiative, and soon thereafter, we were honored to be recognized as one of sixty-seven institutions included in the inaugural Second Chance Pell Pilot—which meant that our university could receive federal tuition reimbursement for eligible matriculated incarcerated students. My frequent refrain at the time, and even now, is that financially "Pell is not enough" to start and sustain the earliest days of a degree-granting program in prison. Developing and implementing an accredited college program in a carceral setting is a demanding and time-intensive endeavor from the degree-granting institution and all of its associated departments (such as enrollment, admissions, financial aid, and advising) and faculty, in addition to the department of corrections, prison staff, community college partners, and the students themselves.

Despite the support from the top of our university, there was quiet resistance, too. My own supervisor at the time was patronizing and discouraging, telling me that I would face too much resistance within the prisons and that stackable certificates in practical fields would be more advisable. Frustrated and annoyed, I ignored his advice and blatantly worked around him. (He has since apologized for his pessimism and congratulated me on our success.)

Although PGI had always enjoyed the unflagging support of the Communication Studies Department chair and faculty, programmatic support from other campus entities came more slowly. Other Cal State LA staff and departments were so overburdened and understaffed that adding something totally new and inherently complicated was challenging, if not unwelcome, especially since there were no resources or compensation for those who took on additional responsibilities. And then there were those who just refused to help. In the first year of the program, I invited a new fund development associate to lunch, and I remember her stirring uncomfortably in her seat while I enthusiastically described the bachelor's degree program at Lancaster. Finally, she said, "I don't think I can fundraise for this. I don't feel right about prisoners getting a college degree. It isn't fair and I don't believe in this program." After getting over my initial shock (but not my anger), I assumed all fund development activity and was fortunate enough to garner awards and major gifts from large and small philanthropies, the Bureau of Justice Assistance, and private donors. Jose Gomez and I also advised the California Department of Corrections and Rehabilitation on the 2022–2023 Budget Act to establish an annual allocation in the state budget specifically for bachelor's degree in prison programs offered by California State Universities.

Often, when I attend prison education convenings across the country to network with others in the field, I am reminded that California is unique. Not only does the state provide unprecedented support for bachelor's degrees in prison, but the California Community College system also currently provides twenty-two in-person associate degree programs at thirty-one out of thirty-four prisons at no cost to the students. California also invests in scholars returning home from prison who wish to complete their college degree. The state generously supports campus-based reentry programs in our public community colleges, the California State University (CSU) system, and the University of California. As a state, however, California lacks centralized coordination and organization, unlike other states, such as Tennessee, North Carolina, and New Jersey, which balance strong relationships with their corrections departments in conjunction with their community colleges and four-year universities.

Cal State LA's Prison BA Graduation Initiative was officially launched in 2016 with an inaugural cohort (Cohort 1) of twenty-five students. Our first classroom was crowded with old-fashioned chair-desk combos like you would see in any high school, a tight squeeze for almost any college student, especially for these men, many of whom towered over six feet tall. At our first meeting, the students were bubbling with excitement and enthusiasm, their eyes shining and big grins on their faces. After years of accumulating community college credits through various correspondence programs, sharing textbooks, and tutoring each other in math, they could hardly believe they were finally on a path to a bachelor's degree. In fact, many of them confessed throughout their Cal State LA journey that there was always a small piece of their hearts that they protected because in prison, there is always the risk that a good thing can be taken away. They had known disappointment before.

I learned, largely from Bidhan Roy, how important it was to protect the students from that tiny kernel of fear. If the program was going to be successful, we would have to build trust. Follow-through and keeping promises were critical. If I said I was going to be at the prison, I showed up early. If I promised to look into something, I would do the research and report back within forty-eight hours. If they had questions I could not answer (which was often), I sought out those who knew. We had to work together to overcome unexpected setbacks, challenges, and what felt like insurmountable policies and procedures just for the first cohort to become matriculated Cal State LA students. Together, we learned how to climb out of loan defaults, to complete selective service forms (a mystery for those who had been incarcerated as teens) to be eligible for a Pell Grant, to dig up transcripts from college classes attended more than twenty years ago. We learned that despite their accumulation of credits, they had avoided taking statistics (a requirement for transfer to a Cal State University), and by virtue of taking correspondence programs in prison, most had never had the benefit of taking a science course with a required lab.

On May 5, 2016, the class presented me with a carefully typewritten letter of gratitude, which still hangs in my office today. After class, they clustered around me to shake my hand and introduce themselves, and then to share small stories of wonder. "I'm not the black sheep anymore," Darren said, shaking his bearded chin in disbelief. Tin told me his mother was already anticipating graduation, saying that she would take the bus all the way to Lancaster if she had to. Incredulous, Dortell exclaimed, "You said you believe in us! You're proud of us!?"

PGI was envisioned as an in-person bachelor's degree completion program in communication with an emphasis on organizational and applied communication. This is not what the students originally wanted. In fact, when these same students were surveyed by the local community college a year before Cal State LA started offering classes, most of them had voted for a business degree because they assumed that would be the most utilitarian pathway for someone who would be entering the work world as previously incarcerated. Cal State LA reasoned that a communication degree would also help them to be successful entrepreneurs in the work world by building essential skills like critical thinking, leadership, and psychosocial and emotional intelligence. Although many in the cohort had never heard of communication studies and were initially hesitant, in the end, they enjoy referring to each other as "Comm Scholars" and appreciate what they learned from the degree program and their faculty. As a small pilot program, Comm Studies at LAC did not have the capacity to offer a selection of classes or options. Students in the first and second cohorts were offered two classes a semester, including summers, for a total of six classes per year; it took them nearly five years to complete the degree.

Cal State LA's communication studies faculty were impressive for their skill in front of the classroom, their incredible dedication, and their unwavering commitment to education. They didn't fuss when they realized that there was no Wi-Fi, that most of their materials would be machine copied and handed out at the start of class, and that the most sophisticated equipment available to them in the prison was a projector and a touch screen. Instead of lamenting their technological challenges, the Cal State LA faculty chose instead to focus on the students. Each instructor established a classroom culture that was founded upon deep mutual respect and the honoring of each other's humanity. Because PGI was taught primarily by tenured and tenure-track professors and not a separate pool of lecturers hired to teach only in the prison, faculty continued to mentor and advise students even after they were released from prison and continued their studies on the main campus.

During the initial years of the program, the students worried that faculty pitied them and that they were receiving a watered-down version of lectures and expectations. The evaluation data, however, showed that the students at Lancaster outperformed students taking the same classes on the main campus and that students who continue their education immediately following their release from prison have no problem stepping into the college classroom and keeping up with the other students, most of whom are much younger than the men returning from Lancaster.

Like most prison educators across the country, Cal State LA faculty routinely reported that the prison classroom offered some of the most meaningful teaching experiences in their career. This was often attributed to fewer outside distractions such as cell phones, but also because the Lancaster students took their studies so seriously. In a survey comparing the critical thinking skills of Cal State LA students on the main campus with those incarcerated at Lancaster, faculty offered insightful perspectives on the difference between students. One instructor said, "When compared to campus-based students, LAC students' critical thinking skills are higher. They read a lot and they easily make connections between readings they have done in other classes, and theoretical questions that show they are thinking deeply about the material studied." Another instructor reflected on their ability to better tie theories and readings to their own lived experiences. "I find the LAC students particularly adept at drawing connections across topics, theories, and across contemporary issues and challenges. Their engagement with the material is deep and allows them to really push the material in new directions. I find their critical thinking sharp, as well as creative, even brave."

The start of any new program is expected to be rocky, and the PGI pilot at Lancaster State Prison was no exception. Students in the first cohort good-naturedly warned that if our program was going to be successful, we would need to collectively beef up our practice of being "flex-o-mistic," that is, our ability to be both flexible and optimistic at the same time. As partners in the first in-person BA program in the state of California, Cal State LA, community colleges, CDCR, and our students seemed to encounter new and unexpected hurdles every day, and I myself often teetered between my ability to embrace a flex-o-mistic attitude and feeling hopelessly embattled and profoundly discouraged. There were small procedural challenges like figuring out how students could complete and submit their FAFSA and Cal State LA applications without access to any kind of technology or if faculty could bring in PowerPoint presentations and videos using encrypted flash drives. Lancaster students were also obligated to have jobs, which, despite the shocking hourly pay range of only nine cents to nineteen cents per hour, often allowed them opportunities and freedom they would not otherwise experience in prison. Students worked their job assignments in the morning, and Cal State LA faculty willingly accommodated the students by offering classes during "third watch," or midafternoon to not conflict with work schedules.

I have often heard jokes that incarcerated students should be the best students because they have nothing else to do but study. Jesse Crespin from Cohort 1, however, dispelled that myth, noting that for PGI students, there are a lot of competing interests. "Sometimes it's hard to make time. We're surrounded by the stresses of our environment. There's all kinds of craziness going on. You have to juggle other people who aren't on the same page as you but also staff who have to enforce the safety of the institution. There is a misconception that we have a lot of time, but we're busy all the time" (J. Crespin, pers. comm., 2019). In addition to school and work, many of the students also were dog trainers with Paws for Life, involved in charitable activities such as crocheting hats and blankets for hospitalized children, and participated in self-help groups, band, softball, and church.

In comparison, the other challenges felt more menacing. We had some wardens who were minimally engaged and others who feigned ignorance when correctional officers (COs) were deliberately obstructionist. Some of the COs could barely hide their disdain in front of the faculty and openly taunted the students before and after class. There were officers who hazed the faculty by rifling through their papers or refusing to let them carry in a jacket despite the brittle desert chill that would set in once the sun went down. One student was so bullied and harassed by a correctional officer for being in college that he quit the program after the first semester and asked to be transferred to another facility for his mental health. Another student was abruptly transferred to another prison after class one day, even though enrolled students had an explicit hold to keep them at Lancaster until the completion of the degree. I was so enraged that I called a high-level director at CDCR headquarters and demanded that the student be returned or we would stop the program. Later, after the director made an impressive move to have the bus turned around midroute to bring the student back to Lancaster, he half-jokingly chided that I had acted as if my "hair was on fire."

Higher education in prison, as the name implies, marries two distinct bureaucratic entities—a department of corrections and a college partner—each of which is notorious for being slow moving, risk averse, inefficient, and unimaginative. Negotiating between the two institutions to launch something new and groundbreaking, which was my role for seven years, is often frustrating and lonely work. I also learned then organizations foster a culture that is resistant to change, it is sometimes hard to know who has your back and who is preparing to stab you in the back.

However, even though the CDCR director was clearly irritated by my demand to return the student to Lancaster, his responsiveness and decisive action reminded me that we would have never gotten the degree program off the ground without an unflinching team of supporters and allies like him. Associate Warden Crystal Wood, who was a captain when she began championing us, was a cheerful, enthusiastic advocate who confidently cleared the way for the start of the BA program even though she didn't have a degree herself. Our early day-to-day logistics were made possible by the educational coordinator, Ronald Underwood, who selflessly came in on Saturdays and stayed many hours past his regular workday to make our teaching days run smoothly. Mr. Underwood effortlessly used the honorific "Mister" in tandem with students' last names and led by example when referring to the students as "men" rather than "inmates." Mr. Underwood recruited a retired CO and parole agent, J. D. Hughes, to help us navigate the early logistics and internal hurdles of the program, and he continues to help us today, smoothing students' paths to reentry and ensuring they are immediately placed into safe and clean transitional housing upon coming home. J. D. had known many of the men at Lancaster decades ago as a correctional officer and, over time, has fully embraced the belief that lasting rehabilitation is possible. During the first several years of the program, we were fortunate to have two very kind and generous correctional officers working in the education building, Keith Junior and later Clinton Cody, who treated the students and faculty with unfailing respect and kindness.

HEP programs frequently identify technology as the primary hurdle that limits their ability to provide a quality education in prison. We have made great strides in the field to address some of our earliest struggles, although progress is slow and not uniform across the country. When PGI began in 2016, there were no computers to be seen, and only a handful of lucky students had the means to acquire a prison-regulated personal typewriter. When we first started the program, the students asked me if I would buy them all typewriters, never imagining that in just a few years, everyone would be assigned their own laptop computer. Students without a typewriter submitted 1,000-word essays written with a black Bic pen on yellow legal pads. The CSU college application and the FAFSA were printed out on campus, brought to the prison to be completed by hand, and then mailed with fingers crossed via the US Postal Service.

It was not until the COVID stay-at-home orders in March 2020 that CDCR expedited the installation and utilization of Wi-Fi technology in correctional facilities, starting with Lancaster. The pandemic swept through the prison yards, forcing lockdown situations that left men stuck in their cells for days and weeks at a time. Individuals who got sick at Lancaster were taken to the prison gym, which they were responsible for cleaning and maintaining regardless of how sick they were. Cal State LA students wrote regularly, reporting on their boredom, anxiety, and fears. They wrote impassioned letters begging to continue with their studies because they said it was the only way to feel hopeful during the darkest of times. While nationwide many college programs in prison stopped completely during COVID, Cal State LA partnered with Lancaster's principal, Troy Tenhet, to figure out a way to keep the college students engaged. We dropped off instructional packets at the prison, then waited for their individual assignments and essays to arrive in chaotic spurts via traditional mail. We tried to maintain contact with the students as much as possible; one faculty member produced instructional videos and lectures for his class that were aired repeatedly on CDCR's institutional television for anyone to see. In January 2021, the Cohort 1 patriarch, Terry D. Evans, passed away due to complications from COVID. The students became even more depressed.

Shortly before Terry passed, CDCR and Cal State LA combined forces to secure two dozen student laptops for bachelor's degree students. Lancaster activated Wi-Fi routers in the classrooms and the housing units. CDCR stretched itself to the limit by piloting Canvas, the cloud-based learning management system used throughout the CSU system, enabling limited student access to the internet.

Suddenly, our students were learning how to navigate Wi-Fi, discussion boards, video conferencing, and submitting homework electronically. Even now, it is mind-boggling to see the students walking around the yard, clutching their very own laptops. They described how classmates gathered in the mornings at the cold metal tables in their housing units, laptops open and paper cups of lukewarm coffee at hand. In those moments, they said they felt like real college students studying at Starbucks.

THE STUDENTS

A lot of new faculty report feeling nervous before their first visit to Lancaster State Prison, their imaginations filled with frightening images of what incarcerated people are supposed to be like. Jimmie Gilmer from Cohort 1 joked that most people are anxious before coming to the prison. "But not Mama T. She walked in with so much confidence that we were afraid of *her*!" I am sure that I had a lot of stereotypes about what the incarcerated students would be like, too, but I no longer remember them because even at my first visit, I was immediately aware that each student was an individual who brought his own unique story and experiences to the classroom. I was struck by the ethnic and racial diversity of the class, their outgoing friendliness, and their jocularity with each other. Even in the earliest stages of the cohort, they called each other "brother," hugged, and told each other "I love you."

Later, I would come to understand that the atmosphere in the classroom was a reflection of Lancaster's Honor Yard. Kenneth Hartman had been incarcerated for more than twenty years of his LWOP sentence when he led other lifers in organizing a yard that focused on positive programming and rehabilitation. Men who opted to live on the Honor Yard signed a commitment to forgo gang affiliation, promote racial integration, and abstain from drugs. The ultimate goal of the Honor Yard was to foster rehabilitation and create a safe, less dangerous prison environment. The PGI graduates interviewed for this book attributed much of their success and that of the bachelor's degree program to the unique culture that was nurtured on the Honor Yard, which allowed them to freely pursue their studies without having to worry about their personal safety.

The PGI degree program utilized a cohort model, meaning the students started and finished the program as a group. The cohort model not only made the Prison BA Graduation Initiative functionally easier to manage, but it also leveraged the foundation of the Honor Yard's familial sense of brotherhood, camaraderie, and support to create a unified classroom experience. Even after graduation, the students maintained a strong affinity to their cohort and good-natured rivalry with the others.

The first two cohorts of students were racially and ethnically diverse, and their average age hovered in the early to mid-forties. Although I did not fully understand the ramifications at the time, more than half of the students were serving life or LWOP sentences. Most had been incarcerated for fifteen to twenty-five years each, and they shared a common fear that they would never be released. When they started the PGI program, they fully expected to die in prison (commonly known as "death by incarceration" in the LWOP community), and prior to their enrollment in the bachelor's degree program, some students explained to me that people with LWOP sometimes refer to themselves as the "the walking dead."

Current state and federal prison education policies, however, prioritize potential college students who will be released from prison within five years. In 2016, Second Chance Pell expressly forbade LWOP students and any students without a release date from receiving Pell funding, a policy which Cal State LA and CDCR partnered together to refute because LWOPs in California were, in fact, coming home. For Cal State LA, the issue was not complicated: Serving incarcerated students, including those with LWOP, was and is consistent with Cal State LA's values as a public university and our mission to improve the social and economic mobility of our entire student population through higher education.

When Cal State LA started the Prison Graduation Initiative in 2016, our president at the time, Bill Covino, would often visit the students at Lancaster, and he would always say, "Once a Golden Eagle, always a Golden Eagle," meaning that if they did not finish their degree on the inside, we would ensure a seamless transition for them to graduate from Cal State LA on the outside.

At the time, the president may not have realized the depth of what he was promising. After all, more than 90 percent of our students were serving life or LWOP sentences, and when the bachelor's degree program started, the students did not expect to be coming home. When the president made his promise to the students, however, it was not lost on them. They became proud Golden Eagles who would "Caw! Caw!" to each other on the prison yard and in the classroom. They imagined what Cal State LA looked like and daydreamed about what it would be like to walk around campus, surrounded by students, as college students themselves.

Our first student to come home mid-degree was Bradley "Woody" Arrowood. Woody's LWOP sentence was commuted by Governor Jerry Brown, and he came home in fall 2018 after serving twenty-five years in prison. He was midway through his bachelor's degree and was excited to be the first PGI student to graduate from the main campus. At the time of Woody's homecoming, I oversaw the Center for Engagement, Service, and the Public Good's small, campus-based reentry program for formerly incarcerated scholars, Project Rebound. Project Rebound had started at our sister campus, San Francisco State University, in the 1960s, when a formerly incarcerated professor noted that system-impacted students needed extra care, connections, and resources to have a successful academic life.

When Woody came home, Project Rebound at Cal State LA found him in transitional housing at a sober living home within walking distance from campus (and has now established a great relationship with this transitional home so that all our returning students have a safe place to live with free room and board for the first six to nine months of their transition). We worked with the registrar's office to transfer him from the "Lancaster campus" to the main campus, connected him with financial aid, and offered him a federal work-study job working in our Project Rebound offices. Woody met one-on-one with an amazing academic advisor who facilitated a fairly seamless transition so that he could continue his studies uninterrupted. Woody, who was over fifty years old at the time, was a proud and engaged student in the classroom who openly talked about the role education had played in his transformation. Woody, who struggled to adapt to cell phones and technology when he came home, was amused when his younger classmates fondly referred to him as "Ice Man," as if to say he'd been trapped in a glacier the past twenty-five years.

I knew nothing about reentry at the time of Woody's arrival, but I had to learn fast because between 2018 and 2023, fifteen more students from the Prison Graduation Initiative at Lancaster were released and came straight to Cal State LA. Most of the students who came home during this time period, like Woody, had LWOP sentences that had been commuted. All but one had served more than twenty years when they came to Cal State LA as proud Golden Eagles, eager to complete their bachelor's degrees.

What I learned from Woody and, a few months later, our second PGI student to come home, Jeff Stein, is that the successful reentry of college students is specialized because it requires both attentive academic support as well as a cocoon of supports and services to help our students have productive and fulfilling lives. This means addressing basic needs—helping returning students obtain their driver's licenses and IDs, open bank accounts, and have a safe place to live. It also means ensuring that they continue to feel connected to the Cal State LA family and campus, through paid work experience, mental health support, and a warm place to hang out and grab a bottle of water or some snacks. It means setting students up for independence by helping them with cell phones and technology and having hard conversations when things aren't going well. Reentry support for formerly incarcerated scholars is relationship- and time-intensive work. Now that colleges and universities are rushing to become official PEPs (Prison Education Programs) to benefit from Pell reinstatement, they must also consider how they will ensure persistence and student success when their scholars come home.

All sixteen of the PGI students who came home between 2018 and 2023 have earned their bachelor's degrees in communication; three have even gone on to earn their master's, and four more are currently enrolled in graduate school. A few started successful small businesses, and the others ultimately found community work that was meaningful and allowed them to pay it forward. All of the alumni are thriving. They have not recidivated. They have overcome what appeared to be insurmountable challenges to provide inspiration and leadership in their own families and communities. Every student who was released has maintained connection with Cal State LA and each other, staying in touch through lively, meme-filled text threads, emails, and social gatherings. On any given day, two or three PGI students and alumni will hang out in my office or meet me for lunch. Sometimes, I'm still surprised to run into them on campus, backpacks slung over one shoulder, neat and sharp in their street clothes, grinning happily. On the weekends, they send me pictures of themselves catching up on everyday life, attending football games, hanging out at amusement parks, taking trips to the beach—their daydreams come true.

The graduation rate of released PGI students is 100 percent. The recidivism rate of released students is zero.

HOPE, TRANSFORMATION, AND THE RIPPLE EFFECT

The field of higher education in prison still takes its cues from the 2013 RAND study, using recidivism rates as the benchmark for programmatic success. I noticed that PGI graduates, however, never mention recidivism when they reflect on the benefits they gained from college in prison. Recidivism data does not tell the story of how the alumni are thriving, how they've stretched beyond what they had ever imagined for themselves, how they have battled their demons to embrace the future, how they maintain their humility while leveraging their academic achievements in combination with their lived experiences, how they remain accountable and responsible, how they are determined to exert positive change in communities they ruefully acknowledge they once helped to destroy. These are the stories that they want to tell.

Thirteen PGI graduates volunteered to share their personal stories and to reflect upon how earning a bachelor's degree has impacted their life's trajectory. Their stories are raw, harrowing, and painful in their honesty. They made themselves vulnerable to explore their childhood traumas and divulge the shame of their poorest choices and decisions. They chose to disclose the traumatic layers of their pasts to provide context for their journeys, not as excuses for the crimes they committed. They also offered the details of their criminal histories, not to sensationalize or romanticize their violent pasts, but to illustrate the dramatic shift in their mindsets and behavior as a result of a college education. Their stories tell us how earning a bachelor's degree in prison offered something much more meaningful and powerful than merely reducing the risk of recidivism. Instead, our college grads tell us how education can transcend prison walls to create deep and lasting transformation and a ripple effect that extends well beyond themselves to reach friends, family, and community.

As Billy G. explained in a group Zoom discussion that included Thaisan Nguon and Allen Burnett, the ability to candidly share their stories is an exercise that allows them to differentiate between the past and the present and to identify the key role education played in their maturation, which includes being accountable for their pasts and to the victims of their crimes. Billy says, "Honoring the people I harmed by being the person I am today is the complete opposite of when I was a kid, when I was taking from others. Now, when I'm going into situations, I'm leaving them better than when I arrived."

I have been inspired by their growth; moved by their candor; awed by the way they are finding their way, giving back to society, and living their lives as transformed human beings, creating powerful ripple effects wherever they go. They all believe that education has helped to shape the trajectory of their lives in powerful and meaningful ways and helped them to become better people for their families and for society.

The bachelor's program helped us to get on a path where we learned more about ourselves. We actually became engaged and interested in who we were as human beings. It doesn't mean that we didn't already have a certain level of interest, but it certainly heightened it. It certainly re-sensitized me to my concept of self and where I was and where I fit in the world. It helped me figure out what I wanted to do with myself and how I could accomplish those goals and move forward in my life in a meaningful way. So the bachelor's program was a catalyst and a source of information for me to be able to do all of that work that I want to do. To start understanding what it's going to require. And how I'm gonna move in that direction. (D. Whitlow, Cohort 1, pers. comm., March 12, 2020)

In September 2024, I traveled with Thaisan Nguon (Cohort 2 graduate) and Allen Burnett (Cohort 1 graduate, MA Communication Studies, 2023) to Jackson, Mississippi. We had been invited to speak to a convening of Mississippi community colleges, universities, nonprofits, and department of corrections staff about creating successful degree programs in prison and campus-based reentry programs for incarcerated and formerly incarcerated students with LWOP. They shared their experiences with touching candor and profound emotional depth. When the panel concluded an hour later, the audience instantly rose to their feet, giving them a heartfelt standing ovation. The moment was astonishing for how improbable it once was. Eight years earlier, Allen had illustrated his theory of ripple effects by drawing stick figures on a whiteboard in prison. Now, Allen and his PGI brothers are three-dimensional human manifestations of that theory in action in their communities and the world; the rest of this book shares their stories of the power of hope and education to transform.

QUESTIONS TO CONSIDER

- How does higher education in prison intersect with your field(s) of inquiry?
- What preconceived ideas about incarcerated people and the prison system do you bring to reading this book?
- What are your expectations for the personal stories that follow?
- Do you believe it is possible for people to transform themselves? Why or why not?
- In what ways, if any, do you think the motivation to pursue higher education is different for incarcerated scholars from your own?

Chapter 1

Samual Nathaniel Brown

Name: Samual Nathaniel Brown
Age: Forty-six[1]
Race/Ethnicity: Black
Sentence: Life without parole
Years Incarcerated: Twenty-two
Released: June 2022
Year Graduated: 2021
Interview: May 5, 2023[2]

Sam arrives for the interview with a small posse—two other African American men who are also formerly incarcerated. The first friend, Aaron, follows Sam through the door of my office, boisterous and jovial. Aaron was recently released from San Quentin, and he is full of stories and jokes. Sam has brought Aaron with him today because he's interested in being a sports announcer, and they are seeking a connection to the Cal State LA athletics department. The second friend, Brandon, quietly brings up the rear, clutching a Rubik's Cube he says he has been struggling to solve. Brandon and Sam were cellies in New Folsom many years ago and have stayed in touch now that they are both free men. Brandon retires to a nearby conference room to work on his Rubik's Cube for the duration of the interview, but before he steps out, he nods his head at Sam. "He saved my life," Brandon says. "He helped me think of things in new ways."

This is the Sam Brown I've known since 2017, organizing and connecting diverse people to help improve conditions and resources for currently and formerly incarcerated men and women. Sam can also be brash and opinionated, which sometimes put him at odds with his fellow Cal State LA students.

His mind is constantly whirling and generating new ideas for songs, product lines, or statewide policy changes, just as it did when he was a student inside.

Sam has been busy since the day he got out of prison, so we haven't seen each other in several months. He takes a moment to show me the new clothing logo he designed to promote family unity while skillfully dancing around the topic of his own marital relationship. He interrupts the interview to take a phone call from his mother, who is currently residing in Texas and struggling to send pictures through her email. Sam patiently tries to guide her through the process, reassuring her several times that the photos are not lost. I met his mother and his older sister at Sam's on-campus graduation in May 2022. Like Sam, they are both forces to contend with, but both have been recently hospitalized due to unexpected health issues, and this preoccupies Sam as well.

Sam started working on several projects immediately out of prison. He is rapping and producing music. He's been leading the charge for Assembly Constitutional Amendment 8, the "End Slavery in California Act," which will eradicate the phrase "involuntary servitude except as a punishment to crime" from California's constitution. He is bringing his 10P self-help program to prisons all over the state to promote self-growth and rehabilitation, including the yards at Lancaster, where he spent the last several years of his sentence.

Ultimately, Sam is a storyteller. And he has far more stories to tell than could be captured in this chapter. He has, I believe, his own book to write.

EARLY YEARS

Sam grew up in the Ninth Ward of New Orleans and says that, as a child, "I loved school. I loved to learn," which is still true for him today. As the third child of six siblings, he took comfort and companionship from books. His mother would allow him to order books from a mail catalog, and he would read on the stoop after school until an older brother or sister would get home to let him in the house. His mother impressed upon all the children that attendance at school and church were their jobs, and Sam knew that doing well in school was a way for him to make his mother proud. "My mom was *hard serious* about education."

Up until the second grade, he also loved school because it was an escape from the domestic violence he witnessed in his family life. Sam's father, who had done two tours in Vietnam before Sam was born, had developed a neighborhood reputation as a "killer," a "fighter," and as someone "off his damn rocker" (Brown 2018, 24). At home, his father's mind deteriorated, progressing from terrifying nightmares to paranoia, to putting a gun into his wife's mouth and threatening to kill her in front of Sam. His mother, a devout Christian, tried to stay in the marriage for three more years after the incident until she couldn't take it any longer. During a particularly violent argument, she clocked Sam's father in the head with an iron, and while he lay on the floor unconscious with blood gushing from his forehead, she threw the kids and one bag of belongings into the car and peeled off (Brown 2018, 21).

Sam's mother worked three jobs at a time to support the family, and when she wasn't working, she was attending church six days a week. Sam missed the regular attention of his mother, and in the seventh and eighth grades, he stopped enjoying school the way he once did. He still did well academically because he enjoyed learning, but he struggled to understand the meaning and higher purpose of education beyond satisfying his mother. He started getting into fights with other students and verbally sparring with his teachers in the classroom. He was suspended and then expelled. Sam surmises that all of the violent and difficult years leading up to his mother leaving his father, along with all of the subsequent challenges the family faced, caught up with him, expressed as unadulterated rage.

> In my theory of emotional-illiteracy-based criminality [a concept he would develop in prison under the tutelage of Dr. Angela Cooke-Jackson] . . . nobody's born bad. Nobody's born evil. But people with criminality have [developed] a coping mechanism for unprocessed traumas. . . . So you asked me when did it change [for me]? I became emotionally illiterate. I stopped expressing myself. I stopped talking. I didn't ask anybody for help. My main expression became anger.

In 1989, when Sam was fourteen and about to enter the tenth grade, his mother moved him and the younger siblings from New Orleans to Sacramento, California, which Sam resented. Sam had watched enough Hollywood movies that he assumed there would be a lot of gang activity in California, and that as the oldest male in the house, it would be his responsibility to protect the family. In New Orleans, he had grown up in a community where everyone was Black, but in Sacramento, he was exposed to White people for the first time. Sam was so shocked by the demographic differences that he rarely spoke to anyone during his first year in Sacramento.

His mother moved the family often, always assuring the kids they were moving to a better neighborhood, but much to their frustration, each move was still within walking distance of the housing projects. As a teenager, Sam would ride his bike to explore the city, straying from the familiarity of the housing projects. During one of these rides, Sam had his first encounter with police officers, who would continue to harass him throughout his life all the way up until his LWOP sentence. It was also the first time he would be called a n**ger by law enforcement.

I realized my affinity for running from the police and all that stuff didn't start with my criminal behavior, right? It didn't even start with when I was [doing something] wrong. It started with this fool calling me a n**ger and threatening me. [This same officer] was also bringing so much dope into my neighborhood, people were getting killed over that. I decided then I was going to be cool with the cats in my neighborhood [rather than] the police. So that's when I took my block over.

Sam used his considerable charisma to start the G-Parkway gang, named after the street on which he lived. Although Sam always had a soft spot for the neighborhood children and old folks, he became infamous for fighting, shooting, stealing, and robbing. Sam, who was arrested multiple times but never convicted, spent countless hours studying White criminals.

I was studying the politicians. I was studying the White folks. The mob. I studied the Mafia. I studied the president. On the one hand, they look all clean cut; on the other hand, they were corrupt gangsters. It was the American way. That was what I looked up to growing up.

Sam's love of learning helped him persist through high school, although he hated doing homework and was rarely on campus. His primary interests, other than being accepted by his peer group, were being independent, rap music, and money.

Money was important. Changing the reality of my family was important. It wasn't just the money. I was tired of the poverty. Tired of being broke. Tired of struggling. Tired of dead bodies and arguments and all that shit.

At the age of seventeen, Sam was fully immersed in criminality, and he surrounded himself with individuals facing challenges similar to his own.

I didn't have a father in my house. I had a mom who worked a lot. I had a lot of trauma I was dealing with and I didn't know how to talk about anger and angst. Almost everyone that I talked to and clicked with outside of my household was in the exact same situation as me.

So, what looked like a gang was truly a bunch of people bonding around our traumas. "He has his mama missing." "His daddy was gone." "Somebody in his house was getting molested or abused." "Somebody's doing drugs." So, when we come out and meet at the park—*I'm not judging you. I'm not gonna molest you. I'm not calling you stupid. In fact, I think you're great. I think you're cute. I think you're live* [emphasis added].

Next thing you know, we smoke weed together and it makes us all feel good. We drink together. And we're kids so we don't have money. So, now we need money to get out. The truth is, me and those guys, we bonded in our traumas.

This is the image I created for myself to run from my vulnerability. I was overcompensating, extremely. I didn't want anybody to know it. I didn't want anybody to know I just wanted a dad to throw a ball with. I didn't want you to know I thought I was ugly, and dirty and stinky, how I really felt about myself. So rather than just tell you that, I say, "Don't—or I'll whup your ass, dawg. I'll shoot you." Instead of just saying you're scared. Or really hurting. Or afraid.

COLLEGE

Sam graduated from high school and was surprised to find out that not only had his mother submitted an application to Sacramento State University on his behalf, but he had been accepted as well. "My mom's doing the paperwork. I'm doing the grades," he laughs.

He still loved to learn but could not fathom how college was going to improve his immediate situation. He saw his mother, a strong and smart woman with three college degrees who still struggled to find jobs that paid her what she was worth, who was told over and over that she was overqualified while she tried to figure out how to pay the rent every month.

Sam, always cunning, saw that college offered a unique opportunity. Sam took his monthly financial aid checks to the person he dubbed his local Weed Man, and then doubled his checks in profits by aggressively reaching out to his fellow students.

So I got to Sac State. And when I got there, it's a beautiful college campus. I'm like, "Whoa! I'm in college! Damn! I'm in college!" So . . . I got me a gun [laughter]. Well, that's the life I lived—I got my pistol. I got my marijuana. And I went to school every day. As a hoodlum. A thug.

What I did see working for me [by being in college] was I had developed a network and I started selling a lot of marijuana. I took over my whole neighborhood. I started trafficking to different states and cities within a year and a half.

Sam was the only one in the neighborhood to go to college, but he tried to convince his friends of the benefits of higher education by showing off the bevy of women he carpooled to school with every day. He brought his friends to campus one by one. "[I told them] you can do this! I'm gonna take these guys and they will come sit in the classroom with me. And I was taking it real serious even though I had a gun and I was smoking weed."

One day, Sam and some of his neighborhood friends were playing pool in the campus's student union. The police came, accusing them of not being Sacramento State students. Embarrassed and enraged, Sam complained to upper administration, and, getting nowhere, he declared, "Fuck you! Fuck your school. I'm leaving. Your school is racist." Looking back, Sam seems momentarily regretful but then perks up within seconds, laughing at a new memory. "So I went to Sacramento City College. I got thirteen people from my neighborhood enrolled in school! We used to go to school three cars deep every morning!"

Sam was, in his own words, just as "criminally minded" at Sacramento City College as he was at Sac State, if not more so. Sam surprised himself by missing the daily structure of high school: "Once that structure started to disappear, I found myself more in the streets." Always looking to further the collective wealth and status of his gang, he burglarized homes and cars. He sold guns. He continued to convert his financial aid checks into marijuana. He took on a telemarketing job as a cover for the dope sales, never cashing the paychecks.

His mother was at a loss. Sam admits there was nothing she could say that would change his mind when he was seeing such positive results.

THE CRIME

When Sam was nineteen, he made a plan to murder his neighbor. Sam had been insulted when the neighbor asked him to sell dope for him, and then alarmed when the neighbor implied there would be violence if the business deal ever went awry. Sam, filled with the same hotheaded bravado that led him to quit Sacramento State, started telling himself and all of his friends that he was going to kill this man. He created what he now ruefully calls a "bullshit web" that cornered him into believing that killing his neighbor was inevitable.

Just before his twenty-first birthday, after ruminating for almost two years, Sam smoked some weed and waited for his neighbor to step outside.

> I did plan to kill him. When he came out, I put the shotgun to the back of his head. I told you the movie *Scarface* [made a big impression on me]? And he said to always look a man in the face before you kill him. So I ascribed to that. I thought that was the respectful thing to do.

Sam says he had loaded three rounds in his shotgun. His first two shots were with intent to harm and to have the neighbor turn around and look him in the eye for the final round.

> I stood over him to kill him with the third one. But that was the one that flew out when I cocked it and it landed in the driveway. By the grace of God, we both got lucky that night. I did not kill him and the man did not lose his life.

Sam ran away.

LWOP

Sam went back to New Orleans. The police officers who had been harassing Sam in Sacramento since he was fifteen still lurked and eagerly built a case against him. California's governor, Pete Wilson, issued a warrant for his arrest, and the US Marshals escorted Sam back to California. Sam spent two years in county jail awaiting trial and sentencing.

Sam was sentenced to life without the possibility of parole for attempted murder.

Sam was stunned. He refused to believe it. He refused to believe he had been sentenced to die in prison. He spent his first years in county jail, doing everything he could to avoid being sent to Calipatria State Prison. When he finally could not avoid it any longer and he arrived at Calipatria, he said it felt just like home. It was dangerous. It was a place where he could extend his criminal reputation.

Almost immediately, he met an inmate named Jazz who gave him books about Black revolutionaries, metaphysics, and religion. He read Mumia Abu-Jamal. Malcolm X. George Lester Jackson. The books filled his mind and stoked his militancy. Sam was always resisting. He could not lie down. To lie down would be to give up. To give up would be to die. When it came time to lock up in his cell every night, he froze, the very idea of it causing him to panic. So he began to volunteer for jobs in the prison—porter, kitchen worker, yard work, recycling crew—anything to keep him out on the yard and avoid being locked up. He became a familiar face to correctional staff and they left him alone, although he observes that he was at the height of his criminality during his first ten years in prison. Sam mostly focused on building the respect and authority he had cultivated under his prison moniker, "LSD." In his cell, he stashed more than a dozen knives. Correctional officers, staff, and nurses brought in kilos of drugs, SIM cards, and cellphones for him to sell in exchange for money or sex. He saw no reason to change.

TURNING POINT

Several years into his prison sentence, Sam met the first White person who ever stood up for him. Sam fondly credits Correctional Counselor William Hobbs ("CCII Bill Hobbs") for changing the trajectory of his life. Sam had had a run-in with a correctional officer (CO) who sent him to the hole for several months.

CCII Hobbs reviewed Sam's file, thick with disciplinary actions, and invited Sam to talk about himself. CCII Hobbs put the file down and said bluntly, "You sound like a pretty nice guy. But in your file—you're a dick."

CCII Hobbs advised him to stop sparring with staff and then surprised Sam with an invitation to work with him inside the program office. Sam couldn't believe prison administration would be so naive as to allow the "fox in the henhouse," but CCII Hobbs also sparked an awareness that deep down, he was needing something different, and so Sam took him up on the offer.

Sam's inner change was gradual. He did his job, but he still believed that he worked for the people, and thought nothing of accepting money to magically arrange bed changes or make disciplinary paperwork disappear. While Sam worked, he also listened to the prison staff around him, a process of cultural immersion that helped Sam realize—much to his surprise—that a great deal of the social stigma he had internalized all his life was similar to what people from all walks of life experienced. When he overheard staff talking about cheating spouses, drug abuse, domestic violence, and money problems, some of his own ingrained shame began to chip away.

And then CCII Hobbs came up with an even more preposterous idea. He wanted Sam to work for him as his clerk, *and* Sam had to enroll in college. Sam imitates Hobbs with a deep, bass voice:

> So I want you to work for me. And aside from working for me, you are going to go to college. You should be in college because you're very smart. So you're going to Palos Verdes. I'm going to start you with a speech class. And I teach the class so I will know if you don't show up.

Sam grins. "So that's how I got back into education. Because CCII Hobbs insisted." He pauses for a moment and shakes his head slowly at the memory. "Fuckin' Hobbs, man . . . I'm so glad he did that. He changed the trajectory of my whole life. I love Hobbs."

Sam enrolled in the Palos Verdes classes, did well, and enjoyed it, later graduating with an AA degree from Lassen Community College. Sam's transformation was not a straight line, however. As Sam's "points," or security level dropped, it was time for him to leave Calipatria. CCII Hobbs stepped in on his behalf one last time to get him transferred to Solano State Prison, which he thought would be a good environment for Sam. Sam recalls CCII Hobbs's parting warning: "I had to suck a lot of dick to get you transferred there. Don't fuck this up."

Sam called Solano prison heaven. He saw green grass, men sunbathing without shirts or shoes on, and he could hear music playing in the neighborhood. Soon after he arrived, Sam was approached by a correctional officer who offered to bring in a cellphone for him. When Sam asked him how much, the officer accused him of illegal activity and turned him in. Despite CCII Hobbs's warnings and efforts, Sam lasted only eighty-eight days at Solano before being kicked out to Old Folsom State Prison.

When Sam got to Old Folsom, he was still invested in his criminality, and, according to him, he was at the top of his game. He hid his weapons and kilos in his cell, fed drugs to the entire yard, got cellphones from correctional officers, and had sex with nurses and teachers. Sam says he'd done it all, but "I was still dead inside."

Finally, somewhere around the tenth year of his incarceration, he says he "gave up the keys to the car . . . because I'd rather be broke on the streets than a millionaire in the pen." Sam was getting tired of prison politics, but most importantly, he wanted to get out and be with his mother while she was still alive. He began to fall away from the hard-core criminality and dared any of his men to challenge him. No one did.

Sam was transferred to New Folsom, where he was struck by the pall of despair and desperation. Inmates were committing suicide and overdosing on fentanyl all around him. He told a prison administrator that people had nothing to live for. She responded, "Then do something about it." Sam liked the challenge and used the time to blend his lived experience with his book knowledge to create the 10P Program, "Prisoners Parole Portfolio as Positive Programming and Prior Preparation Prevents Poor Performance," a curriculum designed to move inmates from antisocial to prosocial mindsets, which he continues to offer at Lancaster State Prison as a free man.

Sam became a literacy tutor for those preparing to pass their GEDs, a job which he enjoyed. Sam also assisted Lake Tahoe Community College with the development of their new associate of arts degree program launching at New Folsom, and he then helped to recruit students. Sam says he was denied parole during his time at New Folsom, and he knew something had to give. For him, the change happened when he stopped smoking weed. "Once I stopped smoking weed, I made the full break from my criminality. I focused on the future." In addition to marijuana, he gave up his knives, drugs, alcohol, gangs, and the criminally-minded mentality. He surprised even himself when he became the face of rehabilitation and transformation for New Folsom before he was transferred to Lancaster's A Yard.

LANCASTER—A COLLEGE MAN

Sam Brown was in the second decade of his LWOP sentence when he arrived at Lancaster. At the time, he did not think he would ever get out of prison, and his previous years of criminality were not that far behind him. When he wandered into the education building at Lancaster to find out how he could finish his associate of arts degree with Lake Tahoe Community College, he was shocked when Jimmie Gilmer, a student from Cohort 1, told him he was right on time to enroll in the second cohort of the Cal State LA Prison BA

Graduation Initiative. Sam hadn't known a bachelor's degree was possible, but he was intrigued.

"[I said to myself] Here's your opportunity. God won't let me fail. Even though I've been trying, he won't let me! He's been leading me so I'm just rolling with it now."

What convinced him more than anything to go forward was his mother's uncontained enthusiasm.

> My mama got really excited. My mama loves me getting degrees and learning. She takes it so serious! So, just because I wanted to continue to do something to make her proud—like the school stuff for sure—initially my mom was the catalyst. But I always loved learning. . . . Also one: I felt guilty that my mom went to college. My sister was in college. My brother was in college. Then I went to the pen and I derailed it. My little sister after me—she went to college and then she stopped. I felt like I did that; it was my fault, right? So getting that degree was important to me to demonstrate that while I got off the road I got back on track. Two: [I wanted to show] that you can make a terrible decision and then get right back on track. I wanted to move on.

When Sam reflects on what aspects of being in a bachelor's degree program in prison impacted him the most, he talks about becoming adept at understanding and maneuvering within all of the multiple and varied subcultures that marked prison life. He describes the unique culture of the Prison BA Graduation Initiative.

> [The Prison BA program] requires discipline. It requires determination. It also required a past level of certain accomplishment. We couldn't [just decide to] be in the BA program, we had to agree to put some type of work in. . . . That being part of a subculture that everybody just couldn't get into came with a certain level of prestige, which in turn came with our responsibility, which means that it came with a certain level of maturity and evolvement and growing.

The culture of the BA program on Lancaster's A Yard required all students to step outside of their comfort zones and to adapt and expose themselves to new and vulnerable situations. The multiracial, multiethnic, multicharacteristic nature of his cohort members and the faculty immersed Sam in a culture quite unlike what he was accustomed to in prison for many years. Sam refers fondly to Dr. Kamran Afary and the narradrama performances the professor elicited out of the students, despite their initial fears and misgivings.

> You got the Black square dude. You got the White depressed dude. You got the angry politician dude. You know, we've got the whole spectrum but we are required to be a cohesive unit. And not only that—we were proud to be a

cohesive unit, publicly! We gotta go do these corny-ass plays or something and come out here and represent. . . . But it's my classmates, my cohort. And so I became a part of that culture that was willing to step out and not be afraid to be a person or in front of people in the yard. That's a culture in and of itself, right? And when it's expected, accepted and recommended for you to do this? Well, when you do it, that builds character. So being in that group, it built character for me.

In a letter Sam wrote to Cal State LA in May 2018, he shared:

Education is a powerful transformative tool. One in which those being transformed can feel proud of and a sense of ownership as they are active participants in their own transformation. However, the quality of the transformation is directly correlated to the quality of the information being exposed and the character of the people that are making it available. . . . Here, there are a group of men being transformed throughout every aspect of their entire being. I am one of them. In addition to exposing me to top-notch professors, forwardly progressive thinking people, and brilliant agents of social change that are compelling me to evolve as a human being, you have also infused a spirit of genuine love, righteousness and respect that is conducive to optimizing performance. None of this is lost on me and I want you to know that there are no words that can adequately express my respect and gratitude. (S. Brown, pers. comm., May 14, 2018)

Figure 1.1 Aaron Benson and Sam Brown perform at Lancaster State Prison. Photo: R. Huskey, 2019. Courtesy of California State University, Los Angeles.

Sam graduated with his cohort on Lancaster's A Yard on October 6, 2021. A few months later, he was paroled and walked the graduation stage again in May 2022 on the Cal State LA main campus as a free man.

TRANSFORMATION

Sam is enthusiastic when he talks about the myriad ways he believes that earning a bachelor's degree in prison has impacted his life. He talks about how he blended his classroom readings and discussions with books that he was reading independently, heightening and strengthening his critical thinking and analytical skills. He talks about caring and compassionate faculty who pushed him to explore his theory of emotionally illiterate criminality, saying, for example, "She cut no corners and she cut no slack." He is quick to distinguish his bachelor's degree (magna cum laude, mind you) as affording him a level of credibility and confidence that he brings with him to every interaction and every meeting.

> What has the bachelor's degree done for me? It has done so much. I mean, even just socially. I may not know what it does in practice yet as far as like in the professional field because I haven't utilized it to get a job. But college degrees are not only used to get jobs. College degrees are used to open doors, right? For me, I've gotten in many doors and have had many discussions and I've been able to kick down a lot of barriers for many other people to get jobs. And when I go and I represent, I let it be known I am a graduate from Cal State LA and I'm part of the bachelor's program and I'm part of this elite group. I love letting it be known. So when I speak that way, and people see how I changed my life, talking about that college degree breaks down their stereotypes. When I tell them that I've put in this many years to get this degree, people are shocked and surprised—pleasantly surprised—and it gives a little more veracity to my statements. And then I tell them a person with a college degree doesn't recidivate—that it's like zero percent and we need to support these programs. I got their ear. I tell them we need to stop making people who are incarcerated out like they're just villains. [We got to focus on] being rehabilitated because education is a public transformative tool. And if you bring in more college degrees and self-help programs, they'll do better than forced labor. This is my conversation. And my degree allows me to have that conversation.

Sam has used his education to write the act against involuntary servitude, originally proposed as Assembly Constitutional Amendment (ACA) 3 in 2021, and reintroduced as ACA 8 in 2023 (Harvey 2023), and he has loved every opportunity he has had to testify and mention that he has a bachelor's degree from Cal State LA and to show that he is indeed an intelligent and capable human being.

Sam has seen a ripple effect with his nieces and nephews. Being incarcerated while completing his bachelor's helped him to remain relevant with the kids and to motivate them to do well in school so that he no longer feels that he has derailed their progress as a college-educated family.

Sam also described the ripple effect upon other incarcerated students, particularly those serving LWOP sentences, in his May 2018 letter to Cal State LA:

> Now take this account of my personal life and multiply it times all of the men and women whose lives are being transformed by way of the educational opportunities that you have made available to people that the world has written off as incorrigible refuse. (S. Brown, pers. comm., May 14, 2018)

In his interview, Sam does not pause when asked what the bachelor's degree has done for him. "I feel like I belong. To this school. To this family. To this culture. To this world. It's like, 'Hey, I'm doing it. I'm a part of it.' It did that for me."

THE FUTURE

At the time of preparing this book, Sam does not have a "traditional" job, nor is he looking for one. He is as industrious and active as ever, working on music, a podcast, his 10P program, and getting his bill on involuntary servitude passed. When his older sister and mother were ill, he was able to go to Texas to be with them.

Sam described his vision for his future on October 6, 2021, at the Cal State LA graduation ceremony inside Lancaster's maximum-security yard. He and his cohort members wrote their final performance; Sam's piece came at the end:

Straight up!
To be trained is to be taught to execute the task you were given,
to be educated is to be prepared to change the world you live in.
The proof of any education, is in its application
'Cause therein lies posterity,
and the potential for leaving a legacy

Figure 1.2 Sam Brown at LAC Graduation Ceremony, October 6, 2021. Photo: R. Huskey, 2021. Courtesy of California State University, Los Angeles.

As for me ...
I'm proud to be the founder of the cutting-edge program
that is changing lives, known as 10 P
and the original author of an Amendment to the California Constitution
To end involuntary servitude
that is now backed by four State Senators, three State Assembly members,
and is now known as "ACA 3, The California Abolition Act."

And a minute ago Terry Bell said 12 Cal State LA students have been released,
Well, make that 13
because about a month ago, I appeared before the Board of Parole hearings
and after 24 years, 5 appearances, and a 4½ hour long hearing,
I earned a finding of suitability, and am scheduled to be set free ...
[All Celebrating]

And when you asked me what I want my legacy to be ...
That's easy: Social change. (S. Brown, unpublished performance from
   Ubuntu, Graduation Ceremony, October 6, 2021)

NOTES

1. For all student stories, age given is at time of interview.
2. All quotes in this chapter are from this interview, unless otherwise noted.

Chapter 2

Allen Dean Burnett II

Name:	Allen Dean Burnett II
Age:	Forty-nine
Race/Ethnicity:	Black
Sentence:	Life without parole
Years Incarcerated:	Twenty-eight years, eight months
Released:	2020
Year Graduated:	2021, BA magna cum laude
	2023, MA
Interviewed:	June 16, 2023[1]

Allen Burnett has been asked to share his story more than any other student from Cal State LA's Prison BA Graduation Initiative. He is, in many ways, the poster child for successful rehabilitation and emblematic of the powerful transformation that can be wrought from higher education. He is quietly thoughtful, introspective, and able to articulate his emotional intelligence and discern that of others. He has overcome a sentence of life without the possibility of parole without forgetting that LWOP has shaped a part of his identity for almost three decades. Allen Burnett has been able to leave the sentence behind but not its aftermath. He has made it part of his personal mission to continue advocating on behalf of men and women who have been branded with death by incarceration.

Allen was still incarcerated and a year or two away from his release when he drew a Venn diagram on the prison classroom's whiteboard and explained his ideas about negative and positive ripple effects. He drew a stick figure that represented himself, and then concentric circles around the figure to illustrate the negative ripple effects on those who were harmed by his crime—certainly, of course, the innocent victim and the victim's family. But the negative ripple effects stretched well beyond the victim. Allen's family was also impacted: his mother, his younger sister, his aunts and uncles all suffered because of Allen's crime and subsequent incarceration.

According to Allen's theory, however, the same central person can have a positive ripple effect as well. While Allen and his classmates were earning their bachelor's degrees, they focused their energies on the positive ripple effects. As a Cal State LA college student, Allen was honoring the memory of his mother, having a positive influence on his extended family, and inspiring other men on the yard, and even his stepdaughter, to pursue an education. The ripple effect, as Allen describes it, means that it is not just the student who benefits from a college education, but even a college student with LWOP can change the trajectory of other people's lives for the better.

CHILDHOOD

Allen's parents met and married in southern California when his mother was seventeen and his father was eighteen. His father went to school in juvenile hall. His mother graduated from continuation school while she was pregnant with Allen. His mother used to joke that he went to school with her and that they grew up together. They were children of the '70s and '80s.

Allen was only five years old when he discovered his father dead from a drug overdose. Allen has been forever haunted by that terrible moment and its aftermath, his young mind assuming that because he was the one who found his father, it was his fault. Allen's aunt recently told him that when he was a child, he tried to show the adults what he'd seen through pictures. He otherwise kept his trauma deeply lodged within, silent and mute. His mother, young and immature, did not have the experience or capacity to help him or herself to process the grief.

When Allen started kindergarten, he carried the weight of his grief and unprocessed fears with him. He was a slow reader, grappled with math, and never felt as if he knew the right answer. The school said he was "retarded," a "slow learner," and that "something was wrong with him." Much to his shame, he was put in English as a second language (ESL) classes, as was his younger sister a few years after him. Outside of the classroom, Allen remembers enjoying recess and playing with other children. A few years later into elementary school, however, he was teased frequently for every-thing from his physical appearance, to being biracial, to the type of clothes he wore, and ultimately, because the kids recognized his weakness in the classroom.

HOME LIFE

Allen's mother remarried and secured a factory job near their home where she was surrounded by her old school friends and extended family members. His mother worked a lot of hours and was rarely home, but his unemployed stepfather was regularly in the house. His stepfather, whom Allen would later learn was battling the aftereffects of his own childhood abuse and traumas, was a tall, intimidating figure who abused drugs and cheated on Allen's mother. He was physically and erratically violent and abused Allen on a nightly basis.

> And then my stepfather—as much as I like to say, "as much as I hated him," I really did love him. He would order me these *Cat in the Hat* books. The books would come in the mail and I'd open it up and it would have my name on it. It was these books where I began to start learning how to really appreciate reading and stuff. And then I'd try to understand—like, why would he punch me and hit me? And I think [now] . . . it was out of guilt.

His mother and stepfather had loud, violent arguments where his stepfather would break things and punch walls. His mother liked to tell the story of the night Allen came to her after a particularly bad fight with his stepfather. Allen, clutching a kitchen knife, solemnly asked if she wanted him to kill his stepfather. His mother would smile fondly at the memory. "Oh, you and I grew up together. You were always trying to protect me."

As painful as the memories are, Allen recognizes that his stepfather was a central figure in his development. "I hated him *and* loved him because I needed him." Sometimes, his stepfather reminded him about the importance of books or reading the Bible, but more often than not, he offered lessons in violence. One day, his stepfather spied Allen getting bullied and teased by a group of kids in front of their own house. When Allen came inside, his stepfather sent him straight back out again with a marble ashtray in hand. "If anyone bullies you, you beat the shit out of him. And if I find out you didn't, I am going to beat the shit out of you and it is going to be worse."

The ashtray became a defining moment in Allen's young life. In that brief exchange with his stepfather, Allen learned how he was supposed to act and respond to others if threatened. "This is how I developed the attitude that if someone messes with me, I got to do something about it. It was okay because my dad was telling me I can do this."

His stepfather's training became instilled like a reflex. As a freshman in high school, Allen got into an altercation with a classmate while walking to the pencil sharpener during math class. Allen, angry and embarrassed by his peer's attempt to humiliate him, picked up a stapler and bashed him in the face.

Allen was fifteen years old, and this was his first brush with the law. He was fined $656.66, assigned anger management courses, and put on juvenile probation for assaulting the student. While on probation, he was assigned a doctor who understood that Allen's anger issues were rooted in the home. Allen was intrigued when the doctor mentioned that perhaps he could petition to become an emancipated minor. Allen would need to complete his high school credits and hold down a job to qualify.

Allen was determined to become an emancipated minor, but because of the violent stapler incident and his poor grades, there was not a high school in the district that was willing to take him on, until the principal from the local continuation high school stepped in. Allen tears up during the interview and pauses when he mentions the principal's name.

> His name was Tom Robins. He said, "You can come to my school. I'll take you. We would love to have you." So I went to school the first year and I got my credits. [Allen pauses.] He was a good person. I think about the people in my life who were shifting the direction I was going in out of their kindness. I'd never met people like that before.

Allen thrived with Principal Tom Robins and his continuation school.

> I was in a class called "Opportunities." Initially I had two teachers; one was an ex-police officer. They were helpful. Encouraging in the classrooms and smiling. We would talk and do art and then we could get to the point where we understood the information in a way that was conducive to us because there were kids there who were dealing with the same shit I was dealing with. Our teachers were like our parents in a sense. . . . I loved going to class. I loved being there in those two classrooms in between those two teachers. It was great. I learned all the cuss words in Italian—you know you got to mix it up a little bit, right? And I didn't have a problem being challenged by an ex-police officer who happened to be a teacher who rode a motorcycle. He was a Christian and he was rough, but he was kind.

Things at home were increasingly difficult. He saw very little of his mother, but his stepfather was a constant, unpleasant presence. He had been stealing Allen's money that he earned from washing cars since middle school. Aggressive and confrontational, he told Allen that he was ugly and stupid. One day when he was fifteen, his stepfather called juvenile probation because he knew Allen had a gun in the house—which he knew because he stumbled on it searching Allen's room for money. Just before the officers came to arrest him, Allen suddenly realized he was no longer afraid of his stepfather. He saw through his stepfather's shields of malevolence, vengefulness, immaturity, and hypocrisy, and much later, he would be able to see his stepfather as "a hurt individual."

Allen spent thirty days in juvenile detention, and when he emerged, he was more determined than ever to get out of his house. He renewed his efforts to become an emancipated minor and focused on earning his diploma. "I wanted out of my house. I wanted my own place. I wanted a car. And when I set my mind to something, I was going to get it." Instead of feeling as if he needed his mother and stepfather, he gravitated toward the local gang, where he sought comfort and acceptance from the group.

Allen earned his high school diploma on the cusp of his sixteenth birthday, the youngest person to ever graduate from the school. Allen remembers his mother, teachers, and friends proudly celebrating his success. Allen says it was the first time he had ever accomplished anything on his own. He was ecstatic.

AN EMANCIPATED MINOR

Shortly after earning his high school diploma and freedom from his mother and stepfather, Allen found a telemarketing job.

> My job was from 4:00 to 10:00 p.m. They had a lot of young people there and it was a bullshit job. People on parole. People doing drugs. People sleeping around inside the stairwell. That's where I started experimenting with drugs. I started selling drugs at that job. I got my first car from that job. And then I got caught under the influence of PCP. And I went back to juvenile hall.

When Allen was arrested, his mother's heart was broken.

> She said, "I don't want to see you die the same way your father did." And so she wouldn't—she wouldn't come to see me. [Allen stops, puts his fist to his mouth to stifle a groan, and moves his head back and forth as if to shake off the pain before continuing.] There was something called "Boys Receiving," and I remember standing at the window, going, "Okay, this is the day my mom's gonna come." . . . She didn't come.

His mother could not bring herself to see him during his eight months in juvenile hall, but she pushed hard behind the scenes to help him get the services she felt he needed. Unlike the other kids, Allen already had his diploma so he did not have to go to school, but he did get to meet with a psychologist. Allen's voice thickens with emotion once again while describing yet another person who tried to change the trajectory of his young life.

> His name was Dr. Grant Loomis. I would sit with him once a week and he would tell me all these amazing things like, "You're smart. You're handsome. Your

birthday is September 21. That's a special day because that's when the seasons change. You're left-handed—that's a special thing. You can go to college."

Allen had never thought of going to college before, but he did remember seeing a movie once where someone went to college to become a real estate agent. When Allen left juvenile hall, he enrolled in community college, although he knew deep down he didn't want to be a real estate agent. "I wanted to be Dr. Grant Loomis," Allen says with a smile. "I wanted to work in juvenile hall because he was such an inspiration in my life." Among Allen's treasures that he still keeps with him are two letters from 1989 that Dr. Loomis wrote to the courts on Allen's behalf.

When his eight months at juvenile hall were up, Allen was determined to avoid trouble and get himself off of probation. He stayed away from drugs, got a job, saw a counselor, and checked in with his probation officer regularly. Allen enrolled in two community college classes, one of which was in criminal justice. But the campus intimidated him. There were too many people around, and he felt conspicuously younger than everyone else. "It was . . . it was just a fucking struggle," Allen laments. He was anxious for more direction and support, and though he still managed to earn a C in each class, he did not return after his first semester.

Allen had earned his freedom, but he yearned for structure. He rented an apartment not far from the beach and drove his own car, although without a driver's license. Asked to reflect on what was important to him at this time, Allen responds:

I'm a teenage boy, really striving for acceptance from my friends. My position—because of my accomplishments—I was looked at as a little bit older. So people would look to me like, "What should we do next?" That was good for *my* insecurities—but it also allowed me to be more violent and that allowed me to have more control because I really wasn't in control of myself. I figured I would sell drugs and get another telemarketing job.

CRIME

On April 26, 1992, Allen was jumped for the second time in his life. He was kidnapped by an opposing gang and left for dead in a park. His mother sent him to his aunt's house for two weeks to recover from his wounds. While he was away from the influence of his friends, his mother begged him to join the military to keep him safe. But when Allen returned home, he felt the sting of humiliation and the pressure to commit revenge.

I just had this, you know, like, "What are you going to do now?" And I felt that if I didn't do something, then I would lose my relationship with my friends and that was always what had been the most important thing for me at that time. So we said, "We're going hunting." That's what we called it—hunting. For about a week, just driving around looking for these guys [who jumped me].

Allen and his friends planned to steal a car so they could do a drive-by and exact revenge on the rival gang members who had jumped Allen. There were three young men in particular whom they were looking for.

My intent was to murder them. At the time, that's what I felt I was capable of doing. I wasn't fueled by anger. I was fueled by humiliation. I was fueled by this sense of injustice about what was done to me. . . . It was my intention to take their life because of this explicit need for acceptance. The need to be looked at in a way that would represent this whole identity I built up about who I was as a person. They just broke it down within a matter of minutes. I needed to restore that because I didn't want to be "dumb, stupid, or ugly." I didn't realize it, but at the time, I felt that if I let this go, I will be all of those things that I didn't like about myself again.

While they were out hunting, Allen and his friends stumbled upon an innocent man. They hopped into the man's car, kidnapped him, and then drove to the house of the rival gang. After spraying the house with bullets, Allen's friend suddenly turned to look at the owner of the car, then shot and killed him. Later, Allen would learn that the man was on his way to work. He lived with his mother. He worked two jobs and was a student at the same community college Allen had attended. The man was about to be married. "And because of all of my . . . stuff. My mess. I took all of that away from him," Allen says ruefully.

Six days after the innocent man was killed, Allen was arrested and sent to jail. He was eighteen years old, and he was fighting the death penalty.

LWOP

Allen spent twenty-two months in jail awaiting trial and sentencing. His defense attorneys instructed him not to talk about his case with anyone and to focus on the violation of his constitutional rights. He was offered tips on how to fight his case, and he spent countless hours in the law library to research loopholes or a pathway out. In the process of fighting for his freedom, Allen's culpability was never discussed. Allen was never forced to confront the ripple effects of his crime or the terrible tragedy of the man's murder. That would not happen until many years later.

While he was in jail, Allen was surrounded by violence and vicious race riots. He identified as an "active gang member in a radicalized, racialized environment." He was pulled into countless brawls, for which he was praised by other gang members. Allen sought out fistfights to elevate his prison reputation, but at the same time, he was quietly trying to better himself. He hunted around for a math book to keep his mind active. He tried to read the Bible, then delved into other religions. He read books about making and having friends, pausing to ask himself if he really had any true friends.

When he received the sentence of life without the possibility of parole, Allen admits that he didn't understand the severity or what it really meant. He did not know that there were more than 5,000 people sentenced to LWOP in California and that he was one of 56,000 in the country. In fact, he did not know anyone else who had an LWOP sentence, and he was ashamed when others would ask how long he was in for.

> LWOP was something shameful. It was shameful because it was like if we were in a class of people that were separate from everybody else in the prison system. [With an LWOP sentence] I couldn't be out past a certain time of day. I was not allowed to have family visiting. I couldn't go to an institution that allowed me to drop down a level. I could work only certain jobs. I was segregated, isolated, and I felt different from everybody else. It was a scarlet letter that we walked around with.

Allen was sent to New Folsom, which he describes as "rockin' and rollin'." People who couldn't pay back their drug debts were getting butchered. People were getting raped. It seemed like there were constant riots. Because of his gang status, Allen met up with some homies right away who offered him shower shoes and safety by numbers.

> I was a Crip and we were always together. We had a strict rule that if anybody · messed with any of us, we were gonna tear this whole place up. And it was a solid structure. It was based on fear. It was based on power and it was based on the fact that we need to protect each other because there's this history about being a Crip in the California prison system that they brought in from the '70s . . . so I began to find my place in there.

TURNING POINTS

Allen was at New Folsom for two years before he finally got a job. He was assigned to vocational landscaping, which Allen remembers fondly, largely because the lead staff member, Tony Johnson, was someone who cared and who made a difference in Allen's life.

He loved his wife. He talked about his kids all the time. And he would sometimes let us come into his office on Fridays and watch movies. He and I would
talk and he seemed to really like me. I ended up becoming the supervisor, the
lead man on the crew. There were men there who didn't know how to read.
Tony said, "Look, we have to help these guys read. They're making sure now
that you guys are educated and some of you are illiterate. So I need you to sit
with the men every day for thirty minutes. And you read with them. Just listen
to them." And I loved to read because my stepfather used to send me books and
stuff as a child. And I loved to do it. I loved to help. I got a nice certificate for
my participation. I still have it. I was so proud of that stuff.

Later, when Allen was transferred to another institution, Tony Johnson
stepped in on his behalf again, proudly vouching for Allen's character and
talents. Because of him, Allen was able to finish his trade program in vocational landscaping at another prison.

The experience spurred Allen to begin thinking about building what he
called a portfolio of positivity, which later included pursuing higher education, participating in positive programming, and, eventually, developing and
facilitating training for his peers. His motivation was his desire to be transferred to a lower-level institution where he would have more access to the
prison yard and dayroom. And he wanted to get closer to home so that he
could see family more frequently.

Yet the LWOP sentence haunted him. Other men serving LWOP asked
him why he bothered with a portfolio of positivity because he was never
going to go home. They were mostly older men who had been in prison
many more years than Allen had, and they had long ago given up the dream
of going home.

Even as he strived to transfer to a lower-level prison, Allen was still violent on the yard, having been indoctrinated at Folsom to "not stop until they
shoot." Just weeks after his parole, Allen was invited to speak to a group of
high school students via Zoom, and he admitted that in prison, "I was the best
of the very worst men." His character and identity during the first half of his
incarceration were defined by violence.

Allen was twenty-seven when he was transferred to Pelican Bay. His cell-
mate was an older Crip and shot caller who embraced his LWOP sentence,
though he lamented missing the passing of both his parents and longed to be
with family. Allen and his cellie were caught with a knife in their cell, and
they spent four months in the hole together. During their confinement, Allen
was both repulsed and frightened by his cellie's complacency. He hated the
way his cellie seemed to accept his life sentence.

His stories became warnings to me. They made me reflect on the path I had
chosen for myself. I began to fear the future. I didn't want to die in prison and

more so, I didn't want to lose my family while serving life without parole. I didn't want to be alone. I realized I was only feeding the hopelessness. By choosing violence over change, I was creating a hole I would never climb out. (Burnett 2017, 26)

Desperate to do whatever it took to distinguish himself from his cellie, Allen asked for library books to feed his mind. He wanted to be different. He *believed* he was different.

After Pelican Bay, Allen was transferred to Corcoran. He recalls watching a basketball game with another man serving LWOP. They were both in their tenth year, and Allen suddenly said, "What are we supposed to be *doing?*" The other man responded: "This is it. Just get used to it."

Allen could not accept that. He began to change and encouraged others around him to change as well. He discouraged his friends from making decisions in prison which could have a cascading effect and negative impact on others. With an LWOP sentence and more years than the others, Allen knew he did not want to continually bear the burden every time a peer made a poor choice. Allen exercised his leadership skills and promoted visiting and hanging out with each other positively, joking around and playing sports as opposed to sustaining a culture of continual vigilance and the protection of one another. Allen renounced his gang life.

EDUCATION

Allen was transferred to yet another facility and soon met another advocate and someone who believed in him—his guidance counselor, Mr. Mayor.

He always ended our conversations with, "You're a very good man." I liked that. It made me feel good that he saw quality in me. No one had ever told me I was a good man before. I believed him. (Burnett 2017, 27)

Mr. Mayor worked two years behind the scenes to get Allen transferred to Lancaster because he believed Allen would thrive on the Honor Yard and benefit from the rehabilitative programming. When the opportunity to go to Lancaster finally came, Allen panicked, afraid that the facility would make him look soft and ruin his prison reputation. Mr. Mayor gave Allen a hard look, then proceeded to read a list of programming and opportunities that awaited him at Lancaster. Mr. Mayor did not back down, and he did not let Allen back out. Allen would learn that change is possible even without going into protective custody, or as they call it today, a sensitive needs yard.

As soon as Allen arrived on Lancaster's A Yard, he met other scholars, most of whom were enrolled in the correspondence program at Coastline

College. Prior to Lancaster, Allen had taken it upon himself to take a few college correspondence classes, so he was immediately intrigued by all of the college students who were eagerly sharing textbooks with each other and making plans for the future. Allen hoped he could take some Spanish classes and imagined that this would make his mother proud.

Allen enrolled in Coastline College and remembers waking in the middle of the night and fumbling through the institutional television channels so that he could catch the Spanish class recordings. And indeed, he did make his mother very proud. Allen sent her a folder of his papers and grades at the end of every semester. He says, "She was stoked and that made me feel good."

Allen's mother was a staunch United Auto Workers representative, and he learned from her about advocacy and leadership. She pushed him to submit his commutation application even though he worried the odds were not in his favor because he was LWOP. Allen's mother was unrelenting, so he took a chance and submitted his papers. He remembers her as his biggest advocate until she passed away in 2016, just before he completed his associate of arts degree.

When Allen was presented with the opportunity to enroll in the Cal State LA bachelor's degree program, he initially shrugged it off, though he knew his mother would have pushed him to do it. After earning his entire AA degree through correspondence courses, he did not think he had more education in him.

> So the BA program is another sixty units? [At first] I'm like, "Nah, I'm cool. I'm good." [Then] when we started the BA program, it was kind of a challenge because I didn't know what the hell I was doing. I don't think any of us did. [The instructors] said, "You can write! Just write!" And I was like, "Is that really true? Don't you have to say that?"

At times, Allen doubted the validity of his instructors' platitudes, worried that they were making concessions just because they wanted the bachelor's degree program to be a success. Allen recognizes now that his occasional doubts and those of his classmates were largely the result of having been defined by their prison sentences for the majority of their lives. But it was also because so many of them, like Allen, had had complicated and humiliating early experiences with education.

Allen had a few lapses in confidence in the beginning, and there was even a time when he remembers faculty and program staff gathered around him after class to prevent him from throwing his arms up and quitting altogether. Allen admits the moments when he really struggled were when old labels and taunts from his childhood would float into his head: Was he capable enough? Was he smart enough? Was he worthy?

He slowly became more self-assured. He was excited to be introduced to Black faculty members, the first Black teachers he could recall having in his entire educational life. He appreciated the feedback he received on his papers and considered it a critical part of his growth. He liked when the professors challenged the class; from his instructors, he was inspired to embrace different ways of thinking. More and more was expected of the students, and Allen was there for all of it. He loved it.

> The bachelor's degree put me in a place where I developed a voice. The voice had been there—I just had never used it before. And it allowed me to bring the ideas and stuff that I had learned from experience into this space and talk about them. And write about them in a way that was important. . . . And that gave me some other purpose. You know, it ignited something in me that had always been there.
>
> I found my purpose in pushing back. [While the BA] was taking place, then you had these laws changing in California that were [addressing] life without parole. When I began the BA, it wasn't my intention [to do this], but I began to advocate for myself and for LWOP stuff. That's what the bachelor's degree did for me.

Allen's self-image as a scholar was complicated by his identity as an LWOP prisoner. When the Second Chance Pell experiment resurrected Pell Grants for incarcerated students in 2016, the laws were originally written to exclude individuals with life sentences. Cal State LA's Cohort 1 students were more than 80 percent LWOP and thus technically ineligible for Pell Grants. Allen and his classmates were prepared for the struggle, although their internal frustration persisted.

> When the BA program came, I felt like I can do these things and still have life without parole. So when the pushback came about us getting this degree, we were ready. It wasn't just about me getting this degree. No—this is me *humanizing* myself. This is me saying, "Fuck you. I'm a human being. And there's others here like us."
>
> I always thought that if I do all this stuff, I can tell them that I'm worthy of this opportunity. I knew that at the end of the day, I was going to have a bachelor's degree *and* still have a life without parole sentence. So there was still this impostor syndrome, this depressing state that when something good happens to us, we can't even accept it. We can't even appreciate it and we'll fuck it up, you know? Because that's how we've been geared. That's how we've been trained [by the carceral institution].
>
> But then you would say, "I believe in you guys. You can do it!" And it was like, "We're gonna get this degree. Even if we might still be in prison."
>
> I knew that this was a place where I can be somebody different from what was being said about me [as LWOP].

In an unprecedented move, California's Department of Corrections and Rehabilitation (CDCR) acknowledged that LWOP students were worthy of a university education. The director of rehabilitation services, Dr. Brant Choate, wrote a memo stating that California's laws were changing, and even men and women with life and LWOP sentences had a chance to come home. They were allowed to enroll in college.

Two years into the program, while still incarcerated, Allen wrote this reflection:

> I wonder what God is doing? It has been hard for me to really grasp what has been going on in my life these last two years. I have been blessed with an opportunity to attend Cal State LA, a major university—me, a prisoner sentenced to Life without Parole? I have been blessed to have my daughter attend the same university—me, an incarcerated father? I have been blessed to have my words, my thoughts preserved and shared in books—me, the *worst of the worst*? And I have been blessed to be a part of two impactful plays *Imagine That!* and *A Fresh Start* because of Cal State LA.
>
> I feel like God is moving in the direction of telling the incredible story of how education has changed the lives of so many people. It is mind-boggling how all these events have led to this point. This is something we only see in movies. I am so thankful to be a part of this story. I wonder what God is doing. (A. Burnett, pers. comm., September 5, 2018)

Figure 2.1 Allen Burnett (center) performs with Cohort 1 and 2 students at an event for family and friends at California State Prison, Los Angeles County. Photo R. Husky, 2019. Courtesy of California State University, Los Angeles.

THE FUTURE

Allen Dean Burnett's sentence was commuted by Governor Gavin New-som, and he was released in 2020 after serving twenty-eight years and eight months. It was the height of the COVID pandemic, but he immediately continued with his classes on the Cal State LA main campus and graduated magna cum laude in May 2021.

A family member of Allen's victim wrote him a letter following his parole suitability hearing. They said they believed him when he said he was sorry. They also said they heard him promise he would "do all these things" if he were so fortunate to be freed, and they were counting on him to fulfill his promises.

Allen, who is dedicating this section of his life to making the amends he promised he would, believes that getting a higher education is an important part of his commitment. He graduated with his master's degree in communication studies from Cal State LA in the spring of 2023. His thesis, *Life Without the Possibility of Parole: The Impact of Hope in Advocacy*, was a triumphant investment of his entire being. And yet, he is still reluctant to share his thesis, worried that it isn't good enough. That it reveals some academic weakness, although at the same time, he knows this isn't true:

> [The master's degree] means that they were wrong about that sentence [LWOP]. It means that people can change and people can be successful and give back to the community. That's what it means to me. . . . It means I'm not the worst of the worst. I'm not a "super predator" anymore. I have a master's degree.

Since his graduation, Allen has been dedicated to helping others with LWOP, connecting them with resources and advocating to change policies and laws forever. He's frequently invited to speak, write, and be interviewed. He is a recognized leader in the field, made wise from experience and empathy, the natural leadership skills that have always been a part of him now focused on the greater good.

It is bittersweet, to know his mother missed this chapter of his life. She was the one who cajoled and pushed him to turn in his commutation application when he thought it was a hopeless exercise. Yet she did not get to see him as a free man.

> It sometimes makes me sad because she was the person who believed in me the most. I wish I had just a little bit of the knowledge that I have now—just to go back and talk to my younger self and say, "My mother doesn't really know what your future looks like, but she knows it's gonna be great."

Figure 2.2 Allen Burnett addresses Cal State LA graduates as a free man during their commencement on October 6, 2021. Photo: R. Huskey, 2021. Courtesy of California State University, Los Angeles.

Figure 2.3 Allen Burnett walks off the stage after receiving his diploma. Photo: J. Flores, 2021. Courtesy of California State University, Los Angeles.

NOTE

1. All quotes in this chapter are from this interview, unless otherwise noted.

Chapter 3

Billy G.

Name:	Billy G.
Age:	Forty-six
Race/Ethnicity:	Caucasian/Native American
Sentence:	Life without parole, plus eighteen years and eight months
Years Incarcerated:	Twenty-five
Released:	2019
Year Graduated:	2020
Interview Date:	April 18, 2023[1]

A day or two after Billy paroled, we made plans for him to visit campus. I walked out to meet him halfway, and I smiled as I watched him approach. He was on the main walkway by himself, looking up at the sky and savoring the trees, the birds, and the profiles of the different campus buildings. He snapped multiple pictures of everything he passed. When he saw me from a distance, he started taking video as we approached each other, huge grins on both our faces. Later in the day, we had lunch on campus with the classmates who had preceded him, and he was ecstatic when Cal State LA professors who taught his classes in prison walked into the restaurant as well.

Billy's homecoming was pre-COVID, and the campus was bustling, the total student population almost 28,000 at the time. He had only a few classes to complete, and his time on the Cal State LA main campus was busy. Billy worked with his mentor, Dr. Kamran Afary, on the editing of the *Prison BA Journal* and attended conferences, classroom presentations, and workshops as a guest speaker. Now that he's graduated, he's found meaningful work with a social justice nonprofit where he continues to advocate on behalf of incarcerated men and women, especially for those serving LWOP sentences. While Billy is extremely serious about the work and his commitment to "being the change he wishes to see in the world" (the maxim on his email signature), he also makes a conscious effort to appreciate the gifts and opportunities his unexpected freedom provides. Levelheaded and unfailingly responsible, Billy is engaged, present, and a strong support to his mother and siblings. And he takes advantage of his ability to work remotely by traveling extensively throughout the country with his longtime girlfriend and their adopted dog.

EARLY YEARS

Billy was born in Tulsa, Oklahoma, and he spent his early years in the back-woods not far from his birthplace. He has fond memories of playing in the streams among lizards, frogs, and other creepy-crawlies, but his large family was impoverished, dysfunctional, and violent. There were seven children, four boys (of which Billy was the youngest) and three girls. The siblings "found a precarious balance between beat downs and buddies," a defining dynamic that characterized Billy's relationship with his brothers until he was incarcerated (G. 2017, 87).

Billy's father was in and out of trouble during his early years, and when Billy was six and a half years old, his father was murdered. Shortly thereafter, a tornado whipped through his town, destroying their home. The family packed up what belongings they had left and moved to Pomona, California. It was a tumultuous time for the entire family, and Billy describes California as initially shocking. His exposure to crime, drugs, and poverty was suddenly magnified and very different from the woods of Oklahoma.

Billy was bright, and he picked things up quickly, but school was "tough." He thinks his mother also knew he had a lot of potential and was as support-ive of him as she could manage, but she worked too many jobs and hours to be the type of parent who regularly attended school events or paid much attention to his grades. Besides, his home life was too unstable to establish his academic reputation. Billy recalls moving twenty-five times and attending at least a dozen different schools between the ages of seven and seventeen. Sometimes, they moved so that his mother could find better work. More often, they moved because his brothers had gotten into some kind of trouble, scorching relationships and reputations in such a way that it required the entire family to uproot themselves and seek a fresh start.

Without being able to establish a meaningful foundation in any given place, Billy says he felt like an outcast and was socially stunted during his preteen years. As a result, he often felt apprehensive in the school environment, where he was regularly teased and picked on as the new kid. Still, Billy insists that school was a reprieve from his home life, where he was bullied by his brothers and sucked in by their chaos. Billy hated doing homework, but he would complete his assignments at school, if at all, because he knew that once he got home, it would be madness, rendering schoolwork impossible. In California, the six youngest siblings (his oldest sister had moved out on her own by this time) lived crammed into tiny apartments where tempers flashed and noise was constant—largely instigated by his older brothers, who Billy describes as mischievous and seemingly destined to follow in their father's footsteps as "alcoholic criminals." By comparison, Billy says, "Any chaos at school was trivial compared to my home life."

Billy developed defense mechanisms to weather the constant turmoil, including a caustic, biting wit that he employed to protect himself emotionally from his peers and brothers—a sharp and observant humor that still drifts about his edges today. He also sought ways to anesthetize himself from his constant disappointment and frustration, which he wrote about candidly in an autobiographical story titled "Butterflies."

> Developing into a hurt, angry, impulsive, violent, drug-addicted criminal, I smoked cigarettes and weed from the age of 7 to 17, selfishly stealing stuff in order to buy weed or abate the jealousy of not having things that the other kids had. I felt material things would bring me love and acceptance. The emotional numbing [from] marijuana suppressed healthy mental growth. I lived a life outside the norm and the law, choosing to stay in a cycle of negativity. (G. 2017, 88)

Despite his circumstances, Billy remembers getting straight As in elementary and middle school. He also recalls that he was industrious. He offered to wash the neighbors' cars and mow their lawns. He even helped his neighbors pick fruit, which he would then take to the farmers market to sell. There were also brief moments of positive reinforcement from empathetic adults. Billy remembers that his elementary school teacher, Mrs. Welch, noticed his love of reading and encouraged him to read aloud to younger children. He also remembers her being sweet and generous when he once made a mistake instead of publicly shaming him, and the generosity of her spirit impressed him then and now. He remembers when a physical education teacher recognized his athleticism and encouraged him to keep working at it, offering a small burst of acknowledgment and positive attention that he was unaccustomed to from home.

Mostly, however, it was his brothers who served as his role models, albeit negative ones. As a child, he aspired to be like them, while at the same time, he recognized that their trail of mayhem and havoc caused constant disruption in his family's life. Billy evolved and adapted his own behavior to survive in their volatile company. He learned he could distract his brothers with humor. He sought the upper hand by proactively calculating their needs and motivations to avoid being caught flat-footed and defensive. His brothers were not above being impressed by their younger sibling. Billy's protective armor was buttressed every time he weathered their violence without flinching or outmaneuvered their antics.

While he admired his brothers, he was conflicted, too. He grew up fantasizing about how he could be the family hero and shield his brothers from their own shenanigans. He imagined becoming a police officer so his brothers would never get arrested. Later, he envisioned himself a lawyer who would defend them in court so they would never have to go to jail. When I expressed surprise at Billy's childhood career aspirations, he shrugged at the irony. To the adult Billy who has thoroughly examined his life's experiences and traumas, it is painfully clear that his younger self's actions, dreams, and motivations stemmed from his deepest desire to put an end to the disruption and dysfunction he and his family endured.

During his ninth-grade summer, Billy got a job working with state county fairs, which took him away from home. When he returned from his summer job, he learned that his brothers were wanted by a gang for stealing marijuana. As usual, the entire family was planning to move right away to escape further trouble from the gang, but Billy had reached his limit. He could not tolerate the idea of starting at yet another new high school, and he was frustrated at the lack of control he had in his own life. On the eve of his sophomore year, Billy decided to drop out of high school. Instead, he created a savvy and industrious three-year plan for himself that included enrolling in JobCorps, a residential career and vocational program for youth. He plotted time to study for his GED, and then planned to join the military when he turned eighteen.

It took less than a year for his brothers to upend Billy's life again. Before he could complete his JobCorps program, he was being moved with his brothers to Utah. His mother and sister returned to California.

In Utah, Billy took the rap for one of his older brothers and was arrested for possession of a firearm. Billy explained to me that it was understood that the youngest person on the scene would always take the blame because the consequences for a juvenile were less than that of an adult. Billy always knew that as the youngest brother, it was his responsibility to assume culpability. Billy shouldered several weeks in juvenile hall without complaint and then made his way back to California to rejoin his family, who had moved again.

Eight months later, in June 1994, when Billy was just seventeen years old, he would commit the crime that would lead to his life without parole sentence.

Billy is introspective about the time leading up to the moment of the crime and his arrest. He knows now that he was vulnerable and in a poor mental, emotional, and spiritual space. The ongoing abuse from his brothers exacted a steep toll upon his psyche, which he was still struggling to numb through marijuana. Because he'd suffered years of feeling like he had no control or agency in his own life, he felt entitled to take whatever he wanted. He had no compunction about stealing from cars or burglarizing homes. Although he says there was still a glimmer of empathy and generosity within him, he was psychologically deadened. He had lost hope.

> I didn't really feel like I had the big dreams or aspirations to become that lawyer, judge, or millionaire anymore. I just didn't feel like I had that capability in me anymore. I felt like at some point in time, the flame had dwindled so far that it was now unrecognizable. It wasn't lighting me up anymore. So instead, I was an angry, pissed-off kid. . . . Growing up, I became really good at [fighting] because of self-defense, but I absolutely hated it. I didn't want to hurt people. And at the same time, I think the person I was hurting the most was myself. Not only emotionally and mentally, but also physically putting myself into really dangerous situations beyond my years and beyond my criminal sophistication.

CRIME

Billy was starved for adult attention and approval when he first met Jim. Billy was impressed by Jim's air of maturity and his criminal credentials as a three-striker. Jim, in turn, acted as though he genuinely liked Billy, even taking him for a ride in a borrowed Corvette. On one of the first days of summer in 1994, Billy told his brothers he was going with Jim to a party in the mountains. Billy's older brother Don initially protested, but eventually agreed to accompany them. At a restroom stop on their way up the mountain, Billy casually spied a car to burglarize. Billy and Jim had guns on them, which was their norm. Unlike their countless other car burglaries, however, this car had four people sleeping inside. There was an unexpected scuffle, and one of the occupants was shot and seriously injured; another was killed.

Billy, Jim, and Don fled the scene in shock and crashed their car in their haste to escape. Billy hid but was arrested ten days later. He wrote about his fear and self-loathing in "Butterflies."

> Nothing could have prepared me for the guilt and shame that I experienced for my evil deeds. My soul was soiled, my spirit stained, and I hated myself for causing so much suffering and pain. Knowing that I was responsible for the death of another human, I felt like the lowest creature on earth. I sat huddled in a garage when I learned definitively that the victim was dead. Regret and remorse erupted from my heart and poured from my eyes. In that moment, every bad deed and awful choice littered my face with tears as my conscience became conscious. (G. 2017, 88)

CHANGE

Billy was four months shy of his eighteenth birthday when he was arrested,
so he stayed in juvenile hall while he awaited trial. Separated from the negative influences of his brothers and family, and granted an unusual sense of
stability that he was unaccustomed to, Billy started carving out his own
identity in juvenile hall. He found a mentor in one of the counselors on site,
Mrs. Gilbert. Mrs. Gilbert played cards with him and talked to him like "a
real person." When Billy turned eighteen, he was transferred to Los Angeles
County Jail without an opportunity to say goodbye to Mrs. Gilbert, pick up
his belongings, or take the GED he had been studying for. Billy was uprooted
again.

The county jail population was older than at juvenile hall. Billy was one
of the few with no tattoos, but the proud owner of some black Nikes that
were instantly coveted by others. His survivor's instinct told him he had to
establish his place quickly and physically in jail. Soon, though, he became
immersed in books, reading voraciously. He gobbled up historical fiction
and books about war. A character in *Lonesome Dove* taught him there was
nobility in fighting back against bullies. Billy says he began to find his moral
compass by becoming introduced to the values and ethics of "prosocial" characters in the books he devoured.

Billy went to trial in 1996. During sentencing, he recalls his attorney telling him "this is an exercise in futility," because the judge would give him
the death sentence if he only could. Billy did not get a death sentence, but he
received life without parole, plus eighteen years and eight months. He was
sent to Tehachapi State Prison the day after Christmas. He was twenty years
old.

SURVIVAL

Billy employed his intelligence, quick wit, humor, and cunning to survive
his first ten years of incarceration. He sought the counsel of old-timers who
advised him to stay away from prison culture's most dangerous entrapments:
"racial politics, homosexual drama, and drugs." Billy focused on studying
for his GED test and easily passed. To preserve his safety, he sought work
that would keep him off the prison yard as much as possible. He volunteered
to type and do clerical work. Although he didn't actually know how to type
at the time, his assignments kept him indoors and safely surrounded by correctional officers. Although Billy was an avid reader, he explained that his
options as an LWOP inmate were extremely limited at the time. In the 1990s,
Pell funding was being taken away from incarcerated students because of the

1994 Violent Crimes Act, so there was no avenue toward higher education. LWOP prisoners were also prevented from pursuing vocational programs or obtaining most prison jobs because the department of corrections did not see the value of investing in inmates who were destined to die in prison.

THE TEN-YEAR WALL

Billy was forced to come to grips with his LWOP sentence at a very young age, likening his mental journey to Kübler-Ross's (1969) stages of grief that include denial, anger, bargaining, depression, and acceptance. Billy recalls the bottled-up outrage, trying to fathom how, at eighteen years old, he could reconcile spending the remaining eighty or ninety years of his life incarcerated. His reckoning came roughly ten years into his sentence.

> There comes a point where it's like, people go one way or another at the ten-year mark. The wall really sets in and it's right around the time where your [legal] appeals are exhausted. Reality starts to sink in for most people who are in for long periods of time . . . they start to personally go through their own growth and maturation to where life becomes a little bit more solid in their understanding of it. And I was no different.

At Billy's ten-year wall, he says he started to wonder what was in his future. "I was like, 'Okay, what am I going to do? Is this my life?' I'm going to die in prison, probably by one of three ways: I'm going to get stabbed, shot, or die of some type of disease. This is how my existence is going to end in here." Billy says he knew even before his ten-year mark that he never wanted to intentionally harm anyone ever again. In fact, he says, he had a huge emotional breakdown, and by the time he worked his way through it, he decided that moving forward he would funnel his energies only toward helping others rather than hurting them, a philosophy that sticks with him today. On the dry and dusty prison yards that populate California's high desert, Billy, ten years into his life sentence, sought friends who bolstered and challenged him, and pushed himself to focus on a positive mindset.

LANCASTER

After ten years in, Billy recalls that there were two important people who intercepted him on his journey. One was a captain, known fondly as "Mama D." Billy was scheduled to be transferred to Calipatria (widely known as Killa-Patria among inmates across the state) State Prison, but Mama D refused to let him get on the bus to Calipatria. Instead, she insisted that he be transferred to Lancaster. Billy had also heard about the Honor Yard at Lancaster but was worried about being green-lighted for being on a yard that was absent of racial politics. The other was an old friend he'd met many years before, who sent him a kite and convinced him to give Lancaster's A Yard a try. In 2005, Billy's life changed.

> Eleven years into my sentence, I ended up at the state prison in Lancaster. The Honor Yard and inmates on the "honor roll" replaced 11 years of witnessing institutional violence and the constant threat of riots. The comparisons between California's normal prisons and the Honor Yard should not be underscored [sic]. I was accustomed to guys wearing mean mugs and snarls, daring me to say something, but the anger and venom changed to smiles and handshakes, asking me if I needed anything. . . . [There] I tackled the unresolved traumas that were perpetuating my feelings of depression. A big help was openly talking to a group of honorable men who also made bad choices that they openly regretted. I learned, grew, and developed my inner child into a kind, caring, and helpful man. (G. 2017, 89)

On Lancaster's Honor Yard, Billy finally got to pursue higher education, and he enrolled in correspondence courses with Coastline College. He was the captain of a softball team. He also co-led a group called Men for Honor. Many of the co-leaders would become part of the Prison BA Graduation Initiative's first cohort as well. Together, they pored over the transcripts of incarcerated men who had presented themselves before the California Parole Board. Some had been successful; others less so. The Men for Honor understood that there were certain responses and evidence of personal development that the board was expecting to learn about during the hearings. Billy and the Men for Honor team began offering classes on anger management, causative factors, and finding value in others to help men prepare for their hearings. While Billy witnessed laws changing and resentencing opportunities arising, he never believed that he would personally benefit from a change to his LWOP sentence. Still, he was deeply invested in offering workshops and mock hearings for the people around him. Billy explains his attitude and motivations at the time this way:

> If they're gonna keep me in here, I'm going to get as many people out as I possibly can. And not only am I going to get them out, they're going to prove to the world they have value . . . that people are better than the worst decisions they made in their lives.

THE IMPACT OF COLLEGE IN PRISON

Billy completed his associate of arts degree with Coastline College and was one of the first students enrolled in Cal State LA's Prison BA Graduation Initiative in 2016. In 2017, the first cohort had an opportunity to meet some of the funders who had invested in the program's pilot years. Billy was selected to speak before his cohort, family members, funders, prison administrators, and other men from the Honor Yard. Billy described the beginnings of his own transformation and that of his classmates:

> During the week, when we spill from our cells, books in hand, we are not reminiscing on where we have been, but talking about where we are going.
>
> With smiles on our faces and a bounce in our step, through the battle-scarred and tattooed men, we converge at the education's intake gate.
>
> Curious minded passers-by are perplexed that we are discussing Classic Literature. Calmly debating if Carl Jung's claims are correct, "Can we write ourselves into one another's mythologies?"
>
> Because of the first-ever, professor-taught bachelor's program, in a California prison, a whole new genre of thought, experience and literature
>
> has been opened up to us. Some of us have clicked a mouse for the very first time and now are RET-OR-ITIONS [sic] in the making.
>
> No longer is it an anomaly to hear maximum-security students openly debating whether archetypes exist, using persuasive arguments that are filled with pathos, ethos, and logos to punctuate our points and beliefs. (B. G., unpublished speech, June 2018)

For Billy and his classmates, the transformational power of the bachelor's degree is not so much the theories or the literature in and of itself. More so, Billy says, the true impact of the Prison BA Graduation Initiative is rooted in the humanizing connections and relationships, not unlike the ones that had touched the trajectory of Billy's life before.

> For some of us, we are the first generation in our families to go to college. Within our families and amongst our prison peers we are cultivating this movement for the pursuit of inner and higher education. When we are in the classroom and computer lab, regardless of our past, we are all Golden Eagles spreading our educational wings, discovering beautiful Jewels of knowledge at every turn. Because of the continuous support of the people in this room, making these long trips into the desert's hot glaring sun, traversing through searches and security, we are afforded the chance to uncage our words and expand our minds. You are the ones that we celebrate, every minute of every day. Thank you for writing

yourselves into our mythologies and giving us a second chance to be the change
we wish to see in the world. (B. G., personal communication, 2018)

Billy valued all of his professors, and he still connects with many of them
regularly. While some, including Kamran Afary, Sarah Black, and Sharoni
Little, are deeply etched within his most precious Cal State LA memories, he
also recognizes that the most profound learning experiences came from being
in a prison classroom with his peers:

> I think it's just the atmosphere. Because oftentimes, being in that [prison] envi-
> ronment, you're alone with yourself, even if you're surrounded by people. . . .
> [When we're] in community with people who had shared experiences and we
> combine the experiences with education, you're combining those things inside
> of you with what you're learning. So what you're learning from the person next
> to you as they give you their POV—that's one of the things that really sticks out.

While Billy notes that the bachelor's degree program contributed to the
distinctive spring in his step when he would walk to the education building
during late afternoons on the yard, he also believes that the college program
helps to lift everyone, even those who may have never imagined earning a
college degree.

> There's always a desire for upward mobility, whether it's mentally, physically,
> emotionally. . . . I think having the ability to get your high school diploma and
> then an AA degree (or multiple AA degrees), vocational degrees—those were
> like your bar. And so here's all these folks that are making a conscious decision
> to stay away from politics, stay away from drugs: they want to be the best type
> of person they can. Bringing in the bachelor's degree is a larger bar. There's a
> higher bar now that people are able to attain and you're talking about Maslow's
> hierarchy of needs. Like, another piece of the triangle is coming up.

THE FUTURE IS NOW

In 2016, Billy presented his case before another judge, where the district
attorney said he was the "poster child of rehabilitation" and cited the need to
legally reconsider his case as a minor. Suddenly, the man who had helped so
many before him plead their case before the parole board finally had his turn.

In 2019, after serving twenty-five years, Billy emerged from Lancaster's A
Yard and promptly came to the Cal State LA campus, where he finished the
classes necessary to earn his bachelor's degree. He spent six months in transitional housing up the hill from campus and found support and camaraderie
from his professors, the students from the Prison BA Graduation Initiative

who came home before him, and the programs on campus designed to facilitate the transition of formerly incarcerated students. He is joyful when he talks about the campus:

> It was amazing. Being on campus and with others who are on their own adventures in the world is remarkable. To have the freedom on campus that was lacking before. Walking on campus . . . the birds, the trees and the grass.

He is grateful, too, for the support he received during the beginning of his transition.

> I got a sense of what the world is and what society is and what it will take to be successful. There were some tough moments, but the preparation to get to that point is what moved me through those fear barriers.

Since Billy's momentous graduation in 2020, he has found a job working for a social justice organization and giving back to the community as he had committed himself to doing years ago. He knows that a college degree was part of evening out a playing field that is mostly not in favor of someone formerly incarcerated. Having his college degree got him through the door for an interview. Some of his classes helped him think about how to present himself and look at issues with a critical eye. Now, he has a job he enjoys and has the opportunity to work remotely, and he has been able to travel and see parts of the world he had never visited before. And though he "thoroughly enjoyed it," he has had enough college for the time being.

He is doubtful that his college degree, the first and only in his family, has impacted them much. His brother was released from prison six years before him; his codefendant, Jim, is still incarcerated. Billy is quite certain, however, that his degree has impacted other people who are inside, seeking to better themselves and hoping that college will be a part of their journey. The Cal State LA video on the bachelor's degree program and the graduates has played repeatedly on institutional television, and Billy hears often from men who are both inspired and seeking guidance. In the meantime, he will continue to advocate for LWOPs to have access to education:

> I think having goals and opportunities for people, no matter their circumstances in life, having things that they can accomplish and strive for is literally the secret sauce to them holding on to hope and dream and a feeling of worth and value within this really precious life that we're given. They know the value of that [education] and know that it gives them something else to accomplish and strive for, when probably throughout their lives, they've been told the opposite. That they were never going to amount to anything.

Behind the numbers are parts of people's lives and experiences. And underneath those people's lives and experiences are really just beings that want to fit in and want to be loved and want to love. They want to experience the gift of life, and education affords the opportunity or at least another pathway for them to be able to engage not only with themselves, but their community and peers. And I think that's where the magic is.

NOTE

1. All quotes in this chapter are from this interview, unless otherwise noted.

Chapter 4

J. H.

Name:	J. H.
Age:	Thirty-six
Race/Ethnicity:	Korean American
Sentence:	Twenty-five years to life
Years Incarcerated:	Fourteen
Released:	2020
Year Graduated:	2021
Interview Date:	July 14, 2023[1]

J. H. is the youngest of our Prison BA Graduation Initiative students to be released, and he looks perpetually youthful. Still, the stress of the past year shows on his face; a dull exhaustion has replaced the usual twinkle in his eyes and his customary grin. He admits he's been anxious and hasn't been sleeping well. His nights are fitful—he has dreams about his mother, who passed away just two months ago, her young life taken too soon by a painful cancer.

When J. H. was released two years ago in the middle of the COVID pandemic, he shared a photo of his mother fêting him with a delicious, multidish meal to welcome him home. A few weeks later, she ventured fearlessly into the bowels of a rough Los Angeles neighborhood and left him home-cooked meals at the door of his transitional home, where he was quarantined with COVID. During the past year, J. H. reversed roles with his mother and shared in her caregiving responsibilities with his sister and stepfather. He moved his mother and stepfather into his apartment building, where they rented a unit directly above him so that he could trot upstairs and be with her every morning and between tattoo appointments in his own apartment.

Despite her protracted pain, his mom was a fighter, a quality she passed on to her son. For the time being, J. H. tucks away some of the current angst and anxiety by focusing on a new wine bar he has invested in with a friend. There, he becomes fully absorbed in supporting both the front and back of the house operations, whether it is working with a new chef to come up with a tasty dinner menu or washing endless dishes after closing time. He celebrated the grand opening of the bar with friends, family, and many of his former classmates and other men he once knew in prison. Many more men whom J. H. knew from Lancaster State Prison had also attended his mother's memorial service a few months before—an odd place for a reunion, of sorts, but all of them took the opportunity to share warm embraces with each other and to tell each other "I love you"; such is the community that the men from Lancaster's A Yard have built together.

EARLY CHILDHOOD

J. H. does not remember his earliest school years, but family lore has it that he was exceptionally smart and bright enough to skip a grade at the magnet school he attended. His reputation as an outstanding student began to decline in the third grade when J. H.'s parents divorced and he and his younger sister went to live with their father. After the divorce, the family unit moved frequently, and the instability dampened J. H.'s interest in academics while he navigated being the new kid and constantly trying to fit in at each new school.

Before the divorce, J. H.'s mother had been the target of his father's anger and abuse. When J. H. moved in with his father, the violence was directed toward him and, later, his sister. J. H. recalls the time he pierced his little sister's ears when she was eight years old and their united fear when their father found out:

> My dad saw the earrings and abruptly ended the meal. He yelled and asked who did it for her. The answer was obvious as I sat there in silence, terrified of the beating I would get. . . . He took us into our room and gave us one more chance to come clean. We both faked ignorance. I was ordered to look towards the wall. He started with my sister, spanking her as he demanded that she tell him who pierced her ears. . . . My turn came next and he ordered me to put out my hands. The yardstick let out a furious shriek as it crashed across my palms. My persistent silence continued to warrant more swings, but this time, I felt I deserved it for what I put my sister through. As tears rolled down my face, I looked to my sister's heaving body as she sobbed in the corner, facing the wall. *I'm so sorry.* My heart broke. (J. H. 2018, 81)

During his childhood, there were subtle messages that pursuing higher education was expected, but the expectations were never emphasized, despite the fact that J. H.'s father had taken some college classes years ago. Instead, J. H. viewed school only as a momentary reprieve from the tensions at home. J. H. was no longer invested in doing well, nor did he feel capable of excelling. Still, he was nervous to show his father his report card, even though his father had long since stopped asking if he had completed his homework every night. When his father stopped paying attention, J. H. figured school was no longer important.

The abuse J. H. experienced at home soon translated into angst and rebellion at school. J. H. was instigating schoolyard fights as early as the third grade, becoming increasingly defiant and uncontrollable as the years progressed. The beginning of his freshman year in high school was especially tumultuous. J. H. wrote me a letter in 2018:

> In my freshman year, I went to three different high schools. For various reasons like fighting and selling drugs. I finally dropped out of high school in the 10th grade. Wait, let me rephrase. It was more like I was kicked out. I see now even in the way I wrote the previous sentences that I didn't mention my trouble with education. It was something that I was ashamed of, embarrassed about, not being able to follow along with my peers. Looking at a test and not knowing a single answer. Of course, since I'm Asian, stereotypically, everyone expected me to be good at math. This was another embarrassing pressure since I failed pre-algebra three years in a row. It wasn't because I wasn't capable, but a culmination of things. Bad decisions on my part, uninspiring teachers, laziness, and the lack of interest of a 14-year-old boy. I recently looked at my old high school transcript and I failed almost every class. The only "A" I had was in tennis which only required that I show up. (J. H., pers. comm., 2018)

When J. H. was in the tenth grade, he was arrested for selling marijuana at school, an offense that got him expelled from the entire school district. Kicked out of school and, consequently, his father's home, J. H. went to live with his mother in south Los Angeles. J. H.'s mother, who worked full-time, was at a loss for how to keep her troubled son occupied and out of mischief during the weekdays. Together, they found a drop-in computer lab for teens in the neighborhood, and the plan was for him to stay there while she was at work. On his first day at the computer lab, J. H. met the kids who would soon include him as a part of their gang.

A high school dropout at the age of fourteen, J. H. had no vision for his future other than being a career gangster. He admired the older gang members in his group, and he observed how they were making money by selling drugs. He was enthralled by how respected they were by the neighborhood youth. J. H. imagined himself becoming a highly regarded "Big Homie" someday, too, but beyond that, he was unclear about what lay ahead. He was reckless and impulsive, often putting himself in dangerous situations well beyond his experience, such as driving drunk and fighting. He knows now that he was in over his head, but he squashed his empathy and sensitivity to everyone but his sister. J. H.'s sister recalls the year their father canceled Thanksgiving out of spite, but J. H. snuck out on his bicycle and brought home Kentucky Fried Chicken to ensure his sister and grandmother would have a Thanksgiving meal, risking even more harsh punishment from his father (J. H. 2018, 86). Her big brother was her hero.

When J. H. was seventeen, he was arrested for stabbing someone during a fight at a local club. He spent more than a month at Central Juvenile Hall awaiting trial. J. H. recounts his interaction with his mother on visiting day:

> My mother's appearance is gaunt and fatigued. The stress of her son in Juvenile Hall is obviously taking a toll. As she approaches me, my heart pounds in my chest and ears. I can no longer hold back my tears. . . . She tries to hide her shock when I tell her what I have done as shame and regret compel my profuse apologies. . . . My mom grips my hands tightly and looks intently into my eyes. "J. H., promise me you will stop living the way you have been, promise me that you will be good." Her eyes gloss on the verge of tears as she begs me to obey her.
> "I promise, Mom, I promise." (J. H. 2018, 58)

The juvenile court recommended a sentence of two to four years for assault with a deadly weapon. After his mother's visit, J. H. learned that she had hired an attorney who whittled his case down to the forty days served and two months of house arrest. J. H. was ecstatic with relief, but the night before he was released, he admits, "Promises to God and my mom become brittle recollections I consciously try to avoid" (J. H. 2018, 59).

In fact, J. H.'s behavior became much worse. Juvenile hall was a battleground for kids trying to overcome situations similar to or worse than his own. When he emerged from juvenile hall forty days later, he had adopted a dangerous mix of newfound bravado and confidence, combined with a growing chip on his shoulder. He would commit his life crime just a few months later.

CRIME

At 18 years old, I punched my own ticket to this prison-bound convoy. Living my life in the revolving doors of bars and nightclubs, I basked in the glow of strobe lights and glory of street fights. Gang affiliated, mixed with alcohol, drugs, topped with an umbrella of low self-esteem, made for quite the nasty cocktail. Impulsive with the propensity of always trying to prove myself, my goals usually consisted of looking up from the bottom of a tilted bottle and selling enough drugs to support my criminal lifestyle. While celebrating my 18th birthday, my gang and I got into a bar fight with another group of guys. . . . It was senseless, without reason, and secured my window seat to prison. (J. H. 2017, 11)

J. H. and one friend were charged with aiding and abetting murder and received sentences of twenty-five years to life. The friend who actually stabbed and killed the victim fled the country and only recently began serving his sentence.

J. H. was sent to the infamous Pelican Bay State Prison, an institution he had heard about well before he started serving the first seven years of his sentence there. In his essay, "The Longest Ride," he shares:

I was embarking on an 18-hour drive, with a life sentence, to one of California's most violent prisons, Pelican Bay. The stories told about my destination could be the sequels to Stephen King. (J. H. 2017, 10)

J. H. did his best to blend into the rough prison environment to survive, but inside, he was terrified. Under the cover of darkness, he cried every night in his cell. During the day, he worked on submitting appeals for his case during the first three years of his sentence, refusing to accept any accountability or responsibility for his role in the crime. Each appeal was quickly denied, however, forcing him to more closely examine the circumstances and choices that led him to prison, while also having to reconcile that it would be many years before he would be released.

Moving forward, I have spent many nights, wallowing in regret and remorse, wishing I could turn back the hands of time. However, the hands of time do not tick that way. [My victim] will never be able to spend time with his family, his newborn child, meanwhile, the world ticks on without his contributions. (J. H. 2017, 11)

J. H.'s criminal lifestyle pretty much ended when he got to prison. In fact, his incarceration became a wake-up call for most of his old friends, who began to eschew their youthful rebellion to pursue jobs or higher education.

Unexpectedly, higher education found J. H. in prison, too. He was focusing a lot of his time on drawing, which would later progress to tattooing other inmates, but he managed to earn his GED early on at Pelican Bay and then became a tutor and a teacher's aide. J. H.'s boss liked him and allowed him to hang out in the education room, which kept J. H. safe and removed from the larger prison environment. Suddenly, the young man who had dropped out of high school in the tenth grade not only became a regular fixture in the education room, but he was effectively tutoring other students as he discovered a good portion of the inmates only had third-grade reading levels. J. H. enjoyed helping them, and the proximity to the education room positioned him well when college became available.

In a group interview with KQED reporter Vanessa Rancaño, J. H. shared how he found education midway through his incarceration:

> I've been incarcerated for 12 years now. Education in prison—I didn't even think it was going to be an option. And so for a long time, for like at least the first seven years of my incarceration, I was just roaming around. Just lost, not really knowing or having any kind of purpose or any kind of goals. (J. H., pers. comm., 2019)

COLLEGE

Many of California's laws around criminality, sentencing, and charges against youth began to evolve after 2010. In 2014, a California law passed that said a murder charge must include a specific intent to commit a crime. It also said that a murder charge requires analysis of the perpetrator's mental state and proof of premeditation and malice. J. H. benefited from the change of laws, and in 2015, he was resentenced from first-degree murder to a lesser charge of second-degree murder.

J. H.'s lawyer told him that rather than continuing to face down a life sentence, there was a real possibility he could go home within another six or seven years. The lawyer encouraged J. H. to do whatever he could to show evidence of change. Pelican Bay did not have an abundance of rehabilitative programming on the premises, but the lawyer strongly encouraged him to start taking college classes. J. H., feeling a twinge of hope about going home for the first time in many years, took the lawyer's advice to heart and immediately enrolled in Coastline College's correspondence program, the only higher education available at Pelican Bay at the time.

J. H. admits, with some embarrassment, that his primary motivation for college in that moment was getting out. He was singularly focused on going home and being with his family again. Despite his poor childhood history with schooling, in prison he was a confident, capable, and successful student. He enrolled in a correspondence psychology class with Coastline, and although there was no classroom interaction or guidance from the instructor, J. H. loved it.

> The psychology class opened my eyes to a lot of things. Like, education really did help me see things from a different way. I learned about conditioning, and I realized how a lot of these theories and stuff applied to my own life. And I was

like, "Okay, I can see that happening in my life and I get it—it makes sense. No wonder I was so angry. No wonder why I didn't have a lot of self-esteem." It put a lot of things in my life into perspective for me. It gave me the grace to forgive myself for the situation I was in. I didn't blame myself as much.

J. H. enrolled in more psychology courses and was mildly surprised to find that he did well in all of his classes. Unlike the days of his youth, he says he was eager to put in the effort, and he was pleased to see the payoff. His self-confidence grew, and he thrived.

Looking back now, I think I've always been smart. I was just young. I didn't care, you know, because there was no validation. There was no reward and no incentive to do good. So now I had the biggest incentive to go to school: to get out. And then it was also building my self-esteem. When I did good, I didn't necessarily need somebody else to tell me that I was doing good. I felt good about myself, right?

J. H. lobbied to get himself out of Pelican Bay and transferred to Lancaster State Prison. He had heard rumors that men from Lancaster's A Yard had a successful track record with earning sentence reductions and commutations, and he hoped that Lancaster would get him on a similar fast track toward home.

J. H. made it to Lancaster's Honor Yard after spending seven years at Pelican Bay. Lancaster's focus on rehabilitation and peer support was in stark contrast to Pelican Bay's supermax environment, but J. H. forced himself to embrace A Yard's prosocial activities and opportunities. He made a commitment to be the person who would always say yes instead of the person who typically said no. Whereas he had largely isolated himself at Pelican Bay, J. H. sought out opportunities to be involved at Lancaster. He hung out in the art room, gifting me a beautiful painting of a horse that has hung in my office ever since. He enrolled in self-help classes and eventually facilitated them. He joined the Paws for Life program as a dog trainer and coached men preparing for their parole board meetings.

As soon as J. H. arrived on Lancaster's A Yard, he began networking and consulting with other inmates about his goal of getting home. "As soon as I landed, I just started asking random people who I needed to talk to [about] trying to get home." Men he'd never met before sat down and counseled him for hours; some of them are his closest friends to this day.

And then, of course, he stumbled upon the Cal State LA Prison BA Graduation Initiative.

J. H. was super-motivated to participate in the BA program's second cohort, largely because he knew how rare a bachelor's degree in prison was at the time. Nor had he forgotten his lawyer's advice that college degrees help elevate opportunities to be considered for parole. Although he was new on Lancaster's renowned A Yard, he was well-liked and had networked and become friends with many of the students in Cohort 1. J. H. took advantage of every opportunity he could to get in front of Cal State LA administrators to advocate for a space in the next cohort, and he asked other students to lobby on his behalf as well. His persistence was rewarded and suddenly the tenth-grade high school dropout was enrolled in a bachelor's degree program in prison. As he would tell Cal State LA faculty and staff in a heartfelt letter, "To be a part of Cal State Los Angeles is a dream that I never even dreamed of" (J. H., pers. comm, 2018).

Still, J. H. experienced several setbacks and disappointments on his journey to get home. In 2018, as part of a Communication Studies assignment, he recorded a two-minute segment on his overwhelming disappointment at a failed resentencing hearing.

When he read that he believed that I still pose an unreasonable risk to society, it felt like my whole world was crashing around me. Everything I had hoped to do with my family—finally being free after 12 years—had suddenly come to a heart-wrenching halt. I remember the first few nights after the denial, I would wake up in the middle of the night crying. It was like my body was grieving before my mind. The day after my denial, I also felt shame and embarrassment. I felt like I'd let down a lot of people. I felt like a failure. There were also moments of frustration and anger. I knew in my heart the decision was not fair—that I am not the person I once was. However, I understand their concerns and despite their decision, I have decided that their denial was a judgment of who I was and not who I am today. The most encouraging part of this whole experience was the support and the role that people in my life played during this hardship. My mentors, friends, and family were very affirming and helped me find peace and strengthen my circumstances. While I still think about the sadness from time to time, there are many more moments of happiness and love that I experience in the moment and share with the people around me. (J. H. and Lalanne 2018)

During his resentencing trial in 2018, J. H. was moved to Men's Central Jail in downtown Los Angeles. The jail is notorious for its overcrowded facility, the colorful mix of people, and dangerous conditions. While J. H. awaited trial, he desperately sent messages to Cal State LA, begging for someone to send his homework assignments and forward his handouts and books, so that he would not fall behind. Cal State LA advocated on his behalf, and I implored jail administrators to move him to the educational section of the jail so he could focus on his studies, but also because we knew he would be safer there. Jail officials agreed to move him, outwardly praising him for his doggedness and commitment to college, but secretly wondering if he was some kind of celebrity with powerful connections.

After the unsuccessful retrial, J. H. still had two more years of prison time in front of him, so he resolutely reimmersed himself in the bachelor's degree program. He was still focused on the ultimate goal of going home, but he was able to appreciate the bachelor's degree for its own experience as well.

> I loved it because it was so different from Coastline. With Coastline, there's no interaction. Everything feels very individualistic. But with a cohort, there is a collective of students all learning the same things and the interactions with the professors was a game-changer, too. You actually get feedback and a lot of the affirmations that I never had growing up. It helped my self-esteem. At Cal State LA, every assignment I did, every paper I wrote, or every research assignment I did, I put my all into it because I knew that it actually mattered. . . . The entire educational process was about how these things apply to your life. It was much more personal and very centered around my own experience.

J. H. was a standout in the narradrama performances, and his central participation in the plays ignited an interest in acting that he pursues today. Unlike many of his cohort members, who panicked and side-eyed Dr. Afary at the first mention of class performances, J. H. embraced the opportunities from the get-go.

> I am currently taking Dr. Kamran Afary's and Professor Amad Jackson's class. It has been so exciting! We are acting out plays and dissecting characters in our thesis-driven papers. I may have been bitten by the acting bug and I am fully invested in my characters. (J. H., pers. comm., 2018)

At one performance held for family and friends, his mother and sister were in the audience. They clutched each other, tears pouring down their faces, every time J. H. recited a line. They had been unwilling witnesses to the most painful twists and turns of his journey for so long that his full transformation had not become real to them until that moment. He radiated self-confidence, hope, and a fresh exuberance.

Even J. H. seemed to be surprised by the ways that earning a college degree was shaping him for the better.

> Our professors are engaging and passionate and I thank each and every single one of them. Thank you for investing in us when no one else would. Thank you for seeing more than the crime we have committed and the blues that we wear. But seeing the human being that we are and the potential for positive change that we possess. Being a part of this Cal State LA program has not only helped me become a better person, but it has brought great pride to my family. And for

that I am especially grateful. I am excited to see where this journey takes us, as we soar above the fray of hopelessness and despair and into the vast world of education and knowledge. (J. H., pers. comm., 2018)

HOME

In 2020, during the height of the COVID pandemic, J. H. was resentenced and found suitable for release; the goal that he had focused on for so long had become a reality. In some ways, J. H. believes that being released during the pandemic was to his benefit, that the relative inactivity in the outside world gave him time to ease into and adjust to his new life.

Barely home a week, he contracted COVID at his transitional home and was quarantined for two weeks. He had three more classes to complete to graduate, and, with little else to focus on, he was eager to finish. He took his classes virtually, like all Cal State LA students on the main campus, and he was largely anonymous and unknown to all of his new professors. He participated in the commencement ceremony with three other released cohort members, but he regrets that his mother was unable to join in the celebration that day. She had just been diagnosed with cancer and had her first radiation treatment the day of his graduation.

Perhaps more than anything, he believes that the Prison BA Graduation Initiative gave him the confidence to articulate and pursue his dreams. Despite the challenges of being an unsigned actor, J. H. put his package together and has gotten some parts in a few television series. With the support of good friends, he opened his tattoo business right away and built a steady stream of clients, whom he serves according to his schedule. And with the resources he had carefully saved since the day he came home, he co-invested in the wine bar in a lively section of Koreatown. Life is, he admits, stressful. But at the same time, he has matured and grown so that he feels confident and secure in making bold moves and venturing into the unknown.

At the end of August 2023, a few months after his mother had passed, J. H. had a court date for a final resentencing. The resentencing hearing was on his mother's birthday. His charges were reduced to felony assault. He had a bittersweet celebration with his sister and his stepdad, where they toasted his victory and his mother's birthday. J. H. knew his mother had been watching out for him, again.

NOTE

1. All quotes in this chapter are from this interview, unless otherwise noted.

Chapter 5

Jason Keaton

Name:	Jason Keaton
Age:	Thirty-five
Race/Ethnicity:	Black
Sentence:	Twenty-one years
Years Incarcerated:	Fourteen years, one month
Released:	March 2022
Year Graduated:	2021
Interview:	April 22, 2023[1]

Just two years before he was released from prison, Jason had a very clear vision of what he wanted his post-incarceration life to be like:

> I want to be able to give back to the community that I took so much from. I want to be able to share my experience with children out there who I know are going through the things that I experienced growing up. And I know that they're at that vital point in their lives to where either they're going to go left or they're going right. And I hope to share my narrative and my experiences with them to help them make the right decision. That's what I plan to do with my education. (J. Keaton, pers. comm., 2019)

Jason Keaton is one of only two students from the Prison BA Graduation Initiative who participated in a Cal State LA graduation ceremony both *inside* the prison yard as an incarcerated student and then again just a few months later on the Cal State LA main campus as a free man. His family was there, madly cheering him on, at both ceremonies.

Jason was eager to put his newly acquired bachelor's degree to use as soon as he came home. Soft-spoken and serious, his gentle demeanor masked the ambition and determination within him to harness his communication degree and achieve the vision he had set for himself just three years before. Shortly after paroling, Jason was accepted into a paid internship program that pipe-lined him directly into a case manager position, where he helps vulnerable families and youth whose challenges remind him of his own early years and struggles.

Not long after paroling, Jason started living the dream. While incarcerated, he wrote and self-published his autobiography, *Rough Around the Edges: My Journey*, and he is currently working on the sequel. He's been featured in radio and print news stories that highlighted his education and successful transformation. He travels the world with some of his oldest and most loyal friends. And he's expanding his family. He's a new father to a precious baby girl, who, Jason reports, is doing all of the things babies are supposed to do at this early stage, which include keeping her parents up all night and costing a near fortune in diapers. Jason has a demanding work schedule, but he desig-nated some of his weekend downtime (when he might otherwise be detailing his car or taking a leisurely trek on his motorcycle) to meet with me on a bright and warm Saturday to share and reflect upon his story.

EARLY YEARS

Jason grew up in Compton, California, the second oldest of four children, each of whom had a different father. Jason's earliest memories of his mother are that she was loving, generous, and attentive. As he reveals in his auto-biography, *Rough Around the Edges: My Journey* (Keaton 2020), at some point in time in his young life, he came to understand that his mother was a gang member, drug dealer, and drug addict. Because Jason and his three siblings each had a different father, each had different life experiences and role models while growing up. Jason's older brother by ten years had a strong relationship with his father and received a lot of guidance; Jason never knew his father and did not have a lot of discipline.

When Jason was eight years old, his mother's drug addiction consumed her, and she stopped caring for the children. His grandmother took in all four of the siblings—and, occasionally, his mother—to live with her. The years between third and fifth grade were so turbulent that Jason's demeanor began to change and he felt himself shutting down mentally and emotionally. School was already challenging for young Jason ("School wasn't my strong suit. Recess was probably my favorite subject," he wryly admits), and even though he was in the classroom daily, he was mentally absent and constantly preoccupied with worry about his mother. He worried about experiencing a repeat of something that had hurt him at least once before: that she would forget to pick him up from school or that she had overdosed. He worried she would be arrested, go missing again, or be physically abused again by any of the random men in her life.

Jason was regularly teased in elementary school, either for having a "crack-head" for a mother or for being overweight. In the fifth grade, Jason started fighting back, and the act of physical violence provided him such relief from his bottled-up anger and frustrations that soon, instead of being the kid who was teased and beaten up, *Jason* became the school bully whom everyone was afraid of.

When he was twelve years old, Jason's fragile world collapsed when he discovered his mother dead from an overdose in the bedroom he shared with her.

As a kid, watching all of the domestic violence, [I had] all of these feelings of powerlessness. Feeling afraid. Feeling angry. But always seeing my mom get up after all that. . . . Finding her overdosed in the bed that we shared together—I felt powerless again, but there was nothing I could do. And this time, she didn't get up off the ground. And that shattered what was left of my heart.

In the aftermath of his mother's death, Jason, who had for years kept his emotions and feelings quietly controlled within him, suddenly turned his rage and frustration outward. While his grandmother's house had once been a sanctuary of caring and protection, Jason could no longer stomach being inside her home because he could not stop replaying the images of finding his mother dead in the bedroom there. Jason took to the streets, where he connected with other kids in his Compton neighborhood. Today, Jason recognizes that part of the attraction he shared with many of his friends was that they were all trying to escape similar or even worse difficult life experiences, a social phenomenon he refers to as "trauma bonding." At age fourteen, he was feeling the allure of gang life.

I didn't care about anything but being accepted amongst these other individuals who were also hurt themselves and just didn't know better. We all adopted a certain style of living that was antisocial. For me, just seeing these individuals and seeing how they didn't have a care in the world, I knew I wanted to be a part of that. I wanted to be accepted. Once I became accepted, I was willing to do whatever it took to maintain and grow it. That's all I cared about.

When I got to middle school, I became immersed into the gang lifestyle because I didn't feel I was receiving the love I wanted at home. So I started to gravitate towards the streets for that love and for that acceptance. And in high school—fortunately I was able to graduate—but I was distracted as well because it was more of a fashion show.

The high school fashion show Jason focused on primarily was girls, cars, shoes, and socializing. At first, Jason attended school regularly, if only to appease his grandmother, who emphasized the importance of education. Jason was kicked out of many high schools for fighting and bad grades, but he managed to earn his high school diploma at eighteen through continuation school.

Five months after graduating from high school, Jason was arrested for a string of residential burglaries. He was ordered to spend nine months in juvenile fire camp. When he got home, he found jobs with T-Mobile and Fry's Electronics, but he also returned to the streets. His older brother, Guy, who had a strong relationship with his own father and had managed to escape trouble in the neighborhood by joining the military, tried imparting his own blueprint for success on Jason, pleading with him to change his ways. Jason was not inclined to listen to anyone at the time.

> The truth was, I was too afraid to do something different with my life. Too afraid of the unknown. I placed myself in a box and because I became very acquainted with its four corners, I became content, I became comfortable, and I became complacent. (Keaton 2020, 64)

Jason's "box" limited the things he cared about and his vision for himself. Jason regretfully admits: "I didn't have the capacity to see the future. My future was the next day. I was operating with an underdeveloped brain, so I had no dreams about my future, other than thinking about a new pair of Jordans or just waiting for what tomorrow would bring." As a teenager, he cared only about his gang status among the group he had trauma-bonded with and adopting their antisocial style of living. Jason, always deeply sensitive, admired the way the other gang members acted as if they didn't have a care in the world. He tried to emulate their hardened demeanor, emanating a cold shield and an attitude that conveyed an aura of "retaliation and damage."

CRIME

Less than a year after returning home from the juvenile detention camp, Jason participated in a drive-by shooting during an intense time of gang wars and violence in his Compton neighborhood. He felt justified for choosing retaliation as a way to solve problems, and he does not recall feeling remorseful. Jason went on the run after the shooting and was arrested a month later. Just nineteen years old at the time of the shooting, Jason was tried as an adult and sentenced to twenty-one years in prison for manslaughter with gang enhancements. He was sent to High Desert State Prison, known to be one of the most violent prisons in the state of California.

PRISON

In the beginning, Jason was very much the same person inside prison as he had been on the outside. His first four and a half years at High Desert reflected the same gang mentality he brought with him when he arrived. He says: "I still had the same character defects, acceptance issues, and insecurities. I was unable to believe in myself. I was unable to tap in to my natural-born leadership skills." Instead, he focused on survival and self-preservation.

Rather than be a leader or someone who stood out, Jason preferred a low profile, yet he was always the first to accept ugly assignments or danger-ous tasks. "Need someone beat up? I'll beat them up. Someone needs to be worked out as a form of discipline? Then I volunteered to do that exercise." Jason's willingness to take these risks afforded him greater protection from the group.

In survival mode, Jason could not pause to think about what it would take to improve himself or what he needed to do if he wanted to try to come home early. In the initial years, he could not even imagine a life outside of prison. Still, he called his grandmother regularly, which grounded him emotionally and spiritually. When he talked to her, Jason stepped out of his carceral real-ity, and for a brief few minutes, he felt human again. Without her strong, unfaltering rudder, Jason cannot imagine surviving prison.

He did his best to stay connected to his younger brother, Chad, as well. Jason was worried about Chad because he had heard he was running the streets, and Jason feared that he was—and continued to be—a negative influ-ence on his younger brother. Jason enlisted his longtime friend, Kendrick Lamar, to help him keep an eye on Chad, which Lamar wrote about in a song entitled "Uncle Bobby & Jason Keaton":

Your brother's getting older, and the streets is getting colder

And you're hoping that he's focused to stay on the right road (Lamar, 2009)

In 2012, Jason was transferred out of High Desert to Corcoran State Prison, which brought him closer to his family. However, he was still hardened and far from rehabilitating. At the time, Jason was still "in the lifestyle. I'm still selfish. I'm not accepting responsibility or accountability for any of my past actions or choices. It's still all about survival."

TURNING POINT

Something began to change inside Jason when his younger brother, Chad, was murdered in 2013. Soon after, he enrolled in community college. The metamorphosis was slow and gradual, but Jason recognized that he was getting tired of the person he was, and he looked toward education to help him make the change. In a group interview with KQED reporter Vanessa Rancaño, Jason reflected:

> For me, education has been a lifesaver. When I decided to turn my life around, education was a thing that I gravitated towards. And I was reluctant because I remembered I barely graduated from high school, but when I looked around at my peers who had also changed their life around, [I realized it took] real courage. [I remember seeing other students] that I looked up to because they were out in the dayroom with these books and they had a crowd around them. Everybody was wondering what were they doing. You know, it didn't seem like it was something cool. But just seeing them and seeing other people kind of be the pioneers of higher education while I was incarcerated, it motivated me to want to do that. I stopped hanging around negative individuals and I stopped participating in negative things. I needed something else to do to occupy my time and education was that. (J. Keaton, pers. comm., 2019)

Before his brother's death, Jason had made a new friend at Corcoran, Carlos, who was also taking small steps toward change. One day, Jason and Carlos spied a bright yellow sign-up sheet for Feather River College. The paper was dangling precariously from a single piece of tape, but both men recognized the opportunity as a rare gift. Jason, who had been a poor student throughout school, surprised himself when he made the unlikely decision to enroll in college classes. Feather River College offers associate of arts degrees and certificates to incarcerated students through correspondence courses, and the program had a strong presence at Corcoran. Throughout their time in college classes together, Jason and Carlos encouraged, challenged, and cajoled each other to persist. When Jason felt discouraged or overwhelmed, his older brother, Guy, was rooting him on, too.

Jason's mindset began to open and evolve at this time. He wondered why he and his friends wholeheartedly embraced the gang lifestyle and its consequences but were so terrified of positive change: "How am I not afraid to do all this crazy foolishness in order to survive, but I'm afraid of school? I'm afraid to take a test for math or write an essay." Jason challenged his personal and academic insecurities. "I told myself over and over, I know how to do this [school]. I'm going to challenge myself."

Just before the Feather River program officially started, his younger brother was shot in a drive-by shooting. Chad survived for a month and had multiple surgeries. He died unexpectedly during the fourth procedure. Chad's untimely death came at a vulnerable time for Jason, just when he was pushing himself through education and forcing himself to stay on the better path. Despite the temptation to succumb to his old ways of handling anger and grief, Jason chose to persevere with school.

> The part of my heart that grew back [after my mother died], that had started to heal, shattered again. I wanted to be destructive and go crazy, but I knew that I had hurt my family so much already that I couldn't just operate out of selfishness or do what I was conditioned to do. I needed to process my decisions. I needed to grow up.

He distracted himself with his college classes and found himself in a community of twenty other scholars. After the introductory courses, the classes became a little harder, so the students formed study groups and supported each other. As he started to do better in school, Jason's self-esteem improved; he matured and healed some more. He was starting to believe in himself for the first time in his life, and his confidence was expanding beyond the classroom. Jason was drawn to the safe haven of the classrooms and spent less time on the prison yard, which helped him to separate from negative influences to break in a new identity.

While he was enrolled with Feather River, Jason grieved his younger brother, processed his guilt and regrets, and sought ways to evolve his destructive mindset to one of rehabilitation.

Other inmates noticed the change and gravitated toward him, sheepishly admitting: "I wish I was smart enough to go to college," or "I wish I had my GED so I could start college, too." Jason became their role model, and their admiration helped him to feel positive about his future for the first time.

> I was thinking, "Damn! These are the same individuals I was looking up to, but now they're looking up to me because of the decisions I'm making and because I was brave enough to go and sit in class and retain it." It was extra motivating when those I once aspired to be like now aspired to be more like me.

As the relationships with his old homies morphed and developed, Jason maintained an empathetic spirit, recognizing common patterns of trauma, missteps, and failures. He refrained from judgment and blame, and focused more on accountability and generosity. Jason smiled at me broadly. "I had begun to find my healing."

TRANSFORMATION

In 2016, with just two more semesters of community college to go before earning an associate of arts degree, Jason was up for transfer. He lobbied hard to go to Lancaster because it was closer to home and he hoped he would see his family more regularly. But he also knew he wanted to go to Lancaster because he had heard rumors about the emphasis on education and a face-to-face community college program. He had no idea that a bachelor's degree was possible for incarcerated students or that Cal State LA had a program there.

Jason made his way to Lancaster's A Yard, and shortly after his arrival, he saw a sign-up sheet for the second cohort of Cal State LA's Prison BA Graduation Initiative. The sign-up sheet was reminiscent of the one he and Carlos had stumbled upon for Feather River years ago, only this time, the sheet of paper was neatly taped to the wall. Jason found a new friend at Lancaster who played the same bolstering role that Carlos had played for him at Corcoran. Like Carlos before him, now Deon cajoled Jason with an enthusiastic "If you do it, I'll do it!" Together, Deon and Jason agreed to make education their priority and singular focus. Jason explains their agreement: "We said we're not here to play. We're not here to befriend people. We're here to take classes, obtain this degree, and go home."

Lancaster's A Yard was drastically different from the violent yards he had become accustomed to at High Desert and Corcoran. During his seven years on A Yard, Jason earned more than thirty certificates and became a program facilitator in some key rehabilitative programs such as Personal Development, Alternatives to Violence, and Gang Awareness and Recovery.

BACHELOR'S DEGREE

"It was amazing," Jason sighs happily when asked what the BA program experience was like for him. Jason, who had been slowly working on his own healing and development prior to the bachelor's degree program, felt the Cal State LA program lent him a higher sense of purpose. He walked differently. He felt different. He relishes the memory of him and his classmates striding toward the education building, books tucked in arms, stunning the other men on the yard with their collective sense of purpose. "We were the rock stars of the yard!"

The positive ripple effect extended across the prison yard, even reaching some prison staff and correctional officers. His friends were shyly curious about what the Cal State LA students were reading. Some said they couldn't wait to go to college, too. Jason and his cohort knew they were inspiring others to pursue an education.

> I am able to not only be a positive role model but also set an example that change is possible. I no longer let my past define me, I look forward to writing my future. My grandmother is proud of me and it makes me happy. My life now has a purpose and continuing on this journey is my focus. (Keaton 2018, 4–5)

Jason reflects further:

> It all goes back to the grassroot essential of our lives, of the need for acceptance and wanting to look like something for our parents. We all had voids we were missing and they once showed up as negativity. But now, people aspire to be like us.

Jason concedes that certainly not all of the prison officials supported the idea of a free bachelor's degree program in prison, but there were a dependable few who were cheering him on and encouraging him to keep at it.

The biggest cultural shift, though, was what was happening inside Jason. Being in college not only gave him something to look forward to every day, but he knew that his college classes were forcing him to access new parts of his brain and different ways of thinking. Jason observes that so much of prison is prescribed—what time to eat, wake up, shower, and turn out the lights—while college allowed the students into the world of "adulting," where they were invited to think critically and formulate their own ideas.

In 2018, a little less than a year into the program, Jason wrote the following note to the Prison BA Graduation Initiative:

> I would like to begin by expressing my gratitude for who you are and for what you do. You guys are truly heaven sent. My name is Jason Keaton. I have been a student at Cal State LA for two semesters now and thus far, my experience has been life changing. Prior to, I wasn't aware of how higher education possessed the power and capability for one to change their perspective of self and of the world, coupled with having the opportunity to know you all has done so for me. If I had to describe my experience at Cal State LA the first words that come to mind are: remarkable, once in a lifetime, challenging (in a good way), and a blessing. Once more, thank you. You all have enabled me to enable myself to have a brighter mind, a brighter today, and a brighter tomorrow. I have been incarcerated since the age of 19. Today I am 30 years old. I am ashamed of being a prisoner, including the horrible decisions I made causing my incarceration. However, I am proud to be a college graduate. In addition, I am grateful for this amazing opportunity to be able to continue my education at Cal State LA.
> Humble and Grateful,
> Jason Keaton (pers. comm., 2018)

PLANNING FOR THE FUTURE

On October 6, 2021, Jason and his classmates donned black robes and tas-seled hats to walk across the graduation stage that had been temporarily erected on the hard, dry dirt of A Yard.

News reporters jostled to interview the graduates, and for days afterward, Jason's broad smile and heartfelt quote were shared across multiple media platforms.

> Prison inmate and graduate Jason Keaton said he can't believe it really hap-pened. He said he has plans for the future.
> "It's upon me to get myself together and then go back to the community that I helped tear down, and help build that community up," Keaton said. (Stallworth 2021)

As a troubled teenager, Jason lived day to day without a vision for what would come next. Earning a college degree opened up possibilities Jason had not been able to previously imagine. "I knew school would help me get through my time, but also accomplish something I would never have been able to accomplish before. [I've started] to think about my future. . . . Now, I can start planning!"

The bachelor's degree gave Jason hope for his future, which he was able to articulate by developing distinct goals and aspirations, in addition to express-ing a strong sense of agency and confidence that he could achieve these goals. Jason's newfound hope not only transformed him, but it had a positive ripple effect on his family as well.

> It's just been boosting my self-esteem, my value and my worth even more. I used to call home and share all of my negative decisions. I ended up break-ing their hearts. But due to my positive decisions now, I started to mend those pieces. Now I'm calling home and speaking about the future and speaking about the steps that I'm taking to make the future brighter. It's just been a beautiful thing. When I return back to society, I hope to continue my education with Cal State LA. I want to be a social worker. (J. Keaton, pers. comm., 2019)

Jason's capacity to heal and repair his connections with his family and others was a benefit that he did not fully anticipate. He did not realize that a face-to-face bachelor's degree program would help him repair some of the deepest wounds inside of him.

> It's not just the BA itself—school is school. School was there. But when someone treats you like a human . . . when someone goes out of their way to show you that you are cared about and to help you, it made us feel better about

ourselves. Reminding us that we were human helped everyone tap in to a different mindset. To reset. Because you [Cal State LA] didn't see us as just the sum of the bad decisions we had made. You see us as individuals who are striving to be better. You see us as individuals who should have mercy and an opportunity for a second chance.

For Jason, being a part of a university program and graduating with a bachelor's degree while incarcerated created a profound paradigm shift. He says, "Instead of looking for the light at the end of the tunnel, I started realizing that I *was* the light in the end of the tunnel."

Figure 5.1 Jason Keaton at the Prison BA Graduation Initiative commencement ceremony on October 6, 2021. Photo: R. Huskey, 2021. Courtesy of California State University, Los Angeles.

A COLLEGE GRADUATE

At the time of his graduation, Jason was one of just thirty-seven men in the state of California who had graduated with a bachelor's degree while still incarcerated. It was October 6, 2021, and it was a warm and dry day in the high desert of LAC's prison yard. There were news crews and cameras everywhere. Jason and his classmates beamed in their caps and gowns. Despite it being during the height of COVID, Jason's grandmother and siblings made the trek to the high desert to attend. Asked how he felt on that day, Jason said, "It was a total confidence booster." He had grown from the insecure and angry gang member who was sent to prison at nineteen years old to the beaming college graduate who claims he felt like he embodied Kanye West's song lyrics, "You can't tell me *nothin'*" (West 2007).

Jason was released in March 2022, and he wasted no time setting up what he needed to do. At that time, of the sixteen students from the Prison BA Graduation Initiative released since its inception, Jason was the first student to return home as a college graduate. Unlike his classmates, he had completed all of his requirements, had no more classes to take, and was returning to society after fourteen years and eight months with a degree under his belt. Jason was unfazed about the changes that had taken place in the world during his incarceration, saying he felt confident and both physically and emotionally ready to reacclimate.

> When I rehabilitated myself, I was able to realize that coming home wasn't just about me. It was just as much about my family, my loved ones who have made those sacrifices—emotionally, mentally, physically, financially—to do this time with me. (Barajas 2022)

Jason was levelheaded, ambitious, and quietly resolute when he returned to Los Angeles a very different person than he was when he committed his crime at nineteen. He is focused on helping others and serving a community which he once helped undermine.

> For myself, this is a personal mission. I could have come home and honored my little brother and my mom in the same way I had conditioned myself to do so for so long. But now, I'm just putting one foot in front of the other and trying to do things that are great. I'm standing obedient, with purpose, and trying to do for more than just myself.

Jason loves the community of Compton and is proud to have moved back to his hometown, where he also volunteers with the local nonprofit, Children

Striving Together, as guest speaker to motivate kids and teens who remind him very much of himself (Outhyse 2022).

Jason began writing his autobiography and self-published it in 2020 while still in prison. His brother Guy had sent Jason journals throughout his sentence and encouraged him to write as a therapeutic release, which Jason had incredulously dismissed ("You want me to what?!? I ain't going to be writing in no journal."). Although not much of a reader before college (Jason says he was more of a "magazine guy—just flippin' through the pictures"), the more books and autobiographies he read in prison, the more he realized he had an important story to tell. Jason is thoughtful about how having a college education helped him to be comfortable in sharing his story as a vehicle to help others. He reflects on what one of his earliest mentors and faculty members told the students about the power of writing, not only as a way of empowering themselves, but also by serving as a voice for others. The book, he says, has been the only book many of his friends in Compton have ever read.

Within weeks of getting out of prison, Jason signed up for an eight-week paid apprenticeship with Careers for a Cause, which offered him career assessment, job shadowing, and connections to potential employment opportunities. He was then immediately picked up by a homeless outreach organization, and most recently, he has become an outreach navigator with Los Angeles Centers for Alcohol and Drug Abuse (L.A. CADA), where he blends empathy and his own lived experiences to help others who are experiencing unnamed traumas.

Jason says his employers can't believe that he was incarcerated for almost two decades, and credits the humanizing aspect of getting a college education for helping him to succeed. "The four-year degree process challenges your beliefs, the way you think, the way you talk. . . . It was a major part of my self-help. I think we come out and we're different; we're different as a result of the academic journey."

Jason also notes that college provided him with the "skeleton" for adulting, which includes time management, critical thinking, and excellent communication skills. He prides himself not only on his ability to churn out a twenty-five-page paper and be able to talk about it in a knowledgeable way, but also his ability to prioritize tasks and execute.

He has adult responsibilities now, so he expresses that having a well-paying job is critical. He has a young daughter and wryly notes that diapers are expensive. He wants to own a home. He wants to make sure he has good credit and pays the bills on time. And he notes that there is an inner child in him that he wants to take care of as well. The inner child that couldn't afford more than one scoop of ice cream now gets two. The inner child who once didn't have new shoes will get his choice or maybe even an extra pair.

Figure 5.2 Jason Keaton at his on-campus graduation ceremony in 2022. Photo: R. Huskey, 2022. Courtesy of California State University, Los Angeles.

At the same time, Jason is not particularly focused on getting rich and making lots of money, as much as he just wants to help people and make a difference. Every morning, he says, he is motivated to get up and start the day because he knows there are homeless families and children who need him. He attributes the desire to give back in part to his college experience. "I realize how much you all gave to us. It was only right to turn around to do the same for others."

In his future, he sees himself earning a master's degree so he can "see those initials at the end of my name," he jokes. Despite those who once bet against him, he does not see himself ever going back to prison, except to return as a free person and to inspire his brothers with hope. He wants them to know that it is possible, that one day they, too, will be able to show everyone who believed in them that it wasn't all for nothing.

NOTE

1. All quotes in this chapter are from this interview, unless otherwise noted.

Chapter 6

Thaisan Nguon

Name:	Thaisan Nguon
Age:	Forty-two
Race/Ethnicity:	Cambodian
Sentence:	Life without parole
Years Incarcerated:	Twenty
Released:	March 30, 2021
Year Graduated:	2022
Interview:	April 14, 2023[1]

Thaisan is tightly wound energy and good humor when he bounds into my office a good half hour before our scheduled interview. His thin frame is hungry, and with easy familiarity, having spent years wandering around our offices while a student at Cal State LA, he explores cupboards and drawers, seeking chips and granola bars before finally landing on some instant noodles that he heats up in the microwave. Unlike many of his formerly incarcerated brothers who ate more than their fair share of instant ramen, Thaisan can still stomach an old-fashioned cup of noodles.

He takes a phone call from his boss, a financial planner, whom he addresses with affectionate annoyance. He is talking about things like whole life insurance and other transactions that I do not understand, but he radiates confidence and self-assurance. He is in control and is no longer an uncertain trainee in her company, but a seasoned professional.

Before we start the interview officially, Thaisan has an Asian Mom story he is eager to share—knowingly suggesting that this is a topic with which I am familiar. Thaisan tells me that he was recently at a big family dinner, and, like my own Chinese father or grandfather would have done, he snuck away before the meal concluded to pay the bill. This act of generosity and adulting caused the uncles to offer warm platitudes to Thaisan, during which time his mother beamed with pride for honoring her and the family. For Thaisan to even be home and able to dine with his family after serving an LWOP sentence for twenty years is reason enough to celebrate. For Thaisan to afford treating his entire family to dinner in the presence of his mother was more than they had ever wished for.

EARLY YEARS

Thaisan was less than a year old when his family escaped from the Cambodian genocide and came to the United States. To this day, he knows little about the difficult paths of his mother and father. In a report from Human Rights Watch, Thaisan shared just a snippet of their troubled past:

> "It was . . . traumatizing for them to speak on it," he said. That trauma deeply impacted his family life; his mother was physically and emotionally abusive to Thaisan. "[T]hat's how the war had affected her," he said. "In a sense, violence had become normalized to her." (Human Rights Watch 2023, 25)

Thaisan, his parents, his older sister, and his younger brother settled in California. English was Thaisan's first language. His memories of preschool are nonspecific as far as academics, but he does remember enjoying socializing and playing with other kids.

Home life, however, was difficult for Thaisan and his family. Thaisan prefaces a brief animated video he wrote while in prison with these words:

> My family and I came to America to escape the Cambodian genocide and although we arrived here with nothing but our names, we carried a lot of baggage. I myself did not experience the horrors of the genocide the same way my parents and older sister did; nonetheless I experienced it in ways that their trauma has manifested through them into me. As the years passed by and they learned how to mask/suppress/deal with their trauma, I was left alone to negotiate a new iteration of the genocide's trauma. The most vivid impression I have felt from this phenomenon was . . . not being wanted. This feeling had haunted me my whole life as I trekked down many wrong roads in pursuit of changing the narrative. I wanted to be accepted. . . . I wanted to be valued . . . . I wanted to be embraced. . . . *I wanted to be loved.* (Nguon and Trias 2018)

By the time kindergarten rolled around, Thaisan felt unsafe at both home and school. Cambodians were the most recent immigrant group to arrive in Long Beach, California, which made them vulnerable to racist bullying attacks. The school grounds were so contentious and felt so unsafe that it was difficult to focus on learning. When Thaisan tried to solicit help from his teachers, he was told to "stop tattle-telling" or to solve the problems himself. Discouraged by the lack of support and empathy, Thaisan began to shut down in the classroom.

When Thaisan was eight years old, he moved to Massachusetts with his father. In preparation for third-grade enrollment, Thaisan was assessed by the school. Thaisan summarized the assessor's findings as, "This kid don't know nothin'," and the school wanted Thaisan to redo the second grade. His father protested, arguing that Thaisan would be able to catch up, and the school relented.

Despite his father's high hopes and promises, Thaisan struggled throughout the third grade. Most of the curriculum went over his head, and he told his father he wasn't learning anything. "I felt legit dumb in the third grade," Thaisan says. He felt as if there was some kind of block that prevented him from learning and absorbing information, and there was no one to help him figure out how to unblock it. As a result, he ended up repeating the second grade.

Thaisan was vaguely aware that he was not meeting family standards with regard to academic success. His parents and other adults in the extended family regularly compared him to his cousins or siblings, which made him feel angry and even more inferior. Rather than being motivated by the comparisons, he shut down even more.

After the second grade in Massachusetts, Thaisan returned to Long Beach and was introduced to a gang. They were a group of similarly marginalized and beaten-up Cambodian boys who banded together for their own protection. Thaisan embraced the gang culture, which disparaged the value of education and school. He felt a gravitational pull toward the gang that drew him away from school. Focusing on the gang gave him an excuse to turn away from the classroom. "I felt like a stupid kid anyway," Thaisan says.

When he started middle school at thirteen, Thaisan was officially in the gang. Ironically, the timing conflated with a moment in his life when he was beginning to "get" school a little more. Although he started to realize that he could, in fact, learn, he leaned harder toward the credo of the gang and "dumbed himself down" in the group.

Education was the last thing on my mind. I didn't feel like it was going to help me survive the mean streets of Long Beach, if you will. I didn't see the benefit of learning world history or algebra or earth science because when I step out of the classroom, this kid is going to mean-mug me and shove me against the wall and embarrass me in front of these other guys and girls. I didn't want to be seen as someone weak. I was more concerned about not being seen as a pushover.

At fifteen, Thaisan returned to Massachusetts. This time, he did not have enough units to qualify as a sophomore in high school, so he repeated the ninth grade. Although it was initially demoralizing, Thaisan admits that being held back turned into a great blessing.

> You know, the educational system in Massachusetts was way different than the educational system in California. I felt like I wasn't being nurtured or catered to in California in terms of helping me learn things. But in Massachusetts, all of my teachers in all of my classes had that *passion*. It brought back so much positivity and gave me so much belief in myself. . . . The way they would approach the conversation [with me] wasn't pointing out my deficiencies. They would try to get to know me.

Thaisan loved being in school in Massachusetts. He found teachers who cared, who pulled him aside to offer support or guidance, who helped him demystify math in such a way that he truly understood algebra as a concept. His mentor and math teacher, Ms. Hickey, taught him "There is always an answer," a philosophy which he adopted and found useful in other aspects of his life.

His ninth-grade English teacher, Mrs. Rosa, was similarly impactful, and she continues to be a force in his life today. Although writing is still difficult for Thaisan, she coupled a mixture of unorthodox writing exercises with unflagging encouragement to strengthen his skills. She told him to write in a journal every day and not worry about punctuation or grammar. She encouraged him to apply himself. She pushed him to read. She planted seeds of confidence.

In fact, she would refer to Thaisan as her "second son," and she was unfailingly generous. When Thaisan was first arrested, she paid for his lawyer. During his entire twenty years in prison, she stayed in touch with him. When he was released and had a chance to go to the East Coast to visit her, Thaisan apologized to her for all the things he'd put her through, much in the same way that he apologized to his own mother. He told her how grateful he was to have her in his life.

GANG LIFE

There were gangs in Massachusetts, but nothing like what Thaisan was used to in California. There wasn't a need for him to present as "hard-core, gang-banged out" in Massachusetts, so he allowed defense mechanisms to ease while he was on the East Coast. Instead, Thaisan focused on being an everyday teenager and student, so much so that when he returned to Long Beach as a junior, he viewed school as a priority.

> I was like, "Man, I've completed two successful years. I got good grades." I felt like I needed to see this through. I could see college on the horizon.

But he was still a gang member. For a while, he tried to balance the two identities. He was enrolled in trigonometry and chemistry ("I was learning all these cool things!" Thaisan exclaims). Monday through Friday, he did his homework. On the weekends, he hung out with friends from the gang. At first, they tried to tease him for not cutting classes or ditching school with them. But he was older and more worldly from his experiences as a bicoastal student, and they respected him for it.

Thaisan's future aspirations at this time were murky. Someone recommended that he get an MBA, and although he didn't know what that meant, the idea of being paid to travel for work appealed to him. He imagined that he would be able to continue bridging a scholarly life in college with his gang activities.

But at the age of seventeen, Thaisan was caught robbing a liquor store. "Classic gang member shit I saw in a movie." He was sent to the California Youth Authority (CYA) for three years. He was released at twenty years old with his GED, high school diploma, and an uncertain direction in his life. He thought about being an actor. He thought about becoming an accountant (a profession that his younger brother would ultimately pursue). What he did know is that he wanted to disassociate himself from the gang. "I see myself going to college still. I see myself leaving that life alone," he says. "Sometimes, the world doesn't work out the way we planned," Thaisan reflects.

While locked up in the CYA, Thaisan learned that his younger brother had joined his gang. Thaisan was crushed and felt deeply responsible for his younger brother's choices. Thaisan had hoped to retire from the front lines and to take on the status of an "OG" gang member. Instead, with his brother as a fledgling gang member, Thaisan knew he would be compelled to serve as a protector, mentor, and guide. He would not be able to step away as he had planned.

Thaisan came home after three years in the CYA, got a part-time job, and enrolled in classes at the local community college. Shortly thereafter, his younger brother was jumped by three rival gang members at a nearby liquor store. In a rush of adrenaline, all of Thaisan's educational and life dreams fell to the wayside and the familiar expectations and credos of gang life leapt forward. All he could think about was avenging his brother. Thaisan made sure that he and his brother were always armed.

CRIME

Thaisan, his brother, and their friends were obsessed with exacting revenge on the rival gang. Thaisan rallied his brother and other gang members, hyping them up and sounding the battle cry. They searched relentlessly for the young men who had jumped his brother, until finally, they spied their enemies sitting in a car in a local parking lot. Their own car held Thaisan, his brother, and two friends, but they all knew it was Thaisan's younger brother who would have to take the shot. One rival member was shot and killed instantly. The other passenger survived a gunshot wound to the head.

In the moment, they celebrated. They had done what gang members do. Only later would Thaisan realize that he had led his brother astray.

> The thing I tried to wean [my brother] away from—I ended up pushing him deeper into the lifestyle. That's the sad part about this. In my mind, I think I'm helping him. But I'm actually making his life even more horrible. Imposing my warped understanding of the world onto him when he's just a kid.

For a very long time, it was difficult for Thaisan to talk about his crime or to assume responsibility. While awaiting sentencing in Los Angeles County Jail, Thaisan's primary concern was that they were facing the death penalty.

> Mentally, I was so sad for my brother. I know that I should have said that I cared about the people we harmed, but I didn't. That's how callous I was. I just cared about my family. [My brother] was fighting the death penalty because of me. I was so disappointed in myself. I had to shut myself off from that feeling. [And] I wasn't thinking about the harm I caused the person who died or his family. Or the passenger. I didn't want to take responsibility for any of those things. I was separated from my humanity. It made it easier for me to have relationships in a transactional way but not an emotional way. That's not a good way to live. That's not a wholesome way to go about my life.

PRISON

Thaisan and his codefendants did not receive the death penalty. Instead, they were sentenced to life without parole. During the first several years of his incarceration, Thaisan's identity as a gang member defined his choices, behaviors, and activities—most of which were negative.

> I was not a productive or positive person before pursuing my college degree. I wanted to build on the reputation I had as a gang member because I believed that kind of reputation would shield me from being harmed. I got into fights if I

felt challenged and assaulted people when they broke any prison rules. I always had a knife/shank at my disposal because I was in a constant state of paranoia and survival mode.

Thaisan and his brother were at the same prison for a while, and one day, approximately ten years into his sentence, his younger brother walked into the cell they shared with a sheaf of papers and instructed Thaisan to fill them out. It was an application for Feather River College, a correspondence associate of arts program.

Thaisan remembers his initial response vividly. "Man, why the fuck would I sign up for college? What am I going to do with a degree in prison?" Then, he remembers his younger brother—the brother that he had so anxiously tried to nurture, protect, and guide—paused and turned to give him a hard look. "What? You're going to say no to a free education?" (Human Rights Watch 2023, 25).

For Thaisan, it was a turning point.

For him to stop and address me like that—it made an impact on me. I was like, "Damn, if my little brother is going to tell me to get an education, I'm gonna get an education." I thought about all the things I'd done in my life to misdirect him. And then here he is, putting an opportunity in front of me to direct me to the right path. So I took the application. I filled it out and he did the same, too.

The two of them enrolled in Feather River College, a community college with a correspondence program that was just starting on their yard at the California State Prison, Corcoran. Although Thaisan confesses that he was nervous because more than a decade had passed since he'd done anything academic, his excitement and that of his classmates on the yard was palpable. "We were just like, 'Oh my god—this is amazing.'"

Education didn't change things immediately for Thaisan, however:

I'm introduced to this new world outside of prison. But I'm still in prison. So I still do prison activity things. I just felt like this is how I'm going to be able to navigate the prison waters. Not that I'm identifying myself as Gang Member Thaisan, but there are all these kinds of politics going on in the yard where I had to duck and dodge and weave and use my old reputation to keep myself out of harm's way.

For the most part, Thaisan was able to skirt prison violence, but he was involved in buying and selling cellphones for profit, activities that he felt were justifiable because he did not want to burden his family further by asking them for money. Thaisan and his brother had been split up and were now living in different prisons. After getting caught with a cellphone for the second time, his counselor offered him a deal. The counselor knew how badly Thaisan missed his brother.

> He said, "Man, I know you want to see your brother again. But if you keep catching these points, you may never see him again. Look, you're going to college like you do. You're making all the right moves. But you got to stay away from that cellphone. Give me three years of clean time and I'll send you to whichever prison you want so you can be with your brother."

Thaisan rose to the challenge. He stopped messing with cellphones and focused on his schooling. When the three years of clean time were up, Thaisan was just a few classes away from graduating with his associate of arts degree, and the counselor was ready to make good on his promise. But Thaisan and his brother had matured during the past few years. His brother had been thriving on his own: taking college classes, leading study groups and other rehabilitative classes, paving his own path of transformation. He no longer needed his older brother to be his savior. Thaisan had also changed, and although he did not see a way out of his LWOP sentence at the time, he was committed to his personal growth. He had heard about the diverse programming opportunities on Lancaster's A Yard and going somewhere that was without gang politics appealed to him. Rather than asking his counselor to reunite him with his brother, Thaisan petitioned to transfer to Lancaster.

HONOR YARD

Thaisan was transferred to Lancaster's A Yard without knowing there was a bachelor's degree program on the yard. It didn't take long for him to find out, however, because he was soon meeting enthusiastic students from Cohort 1 who, after learning that he was just finishing up his AA degree, immediately directed him to the Cal State LA bachelor's degree program. Thaisan was pleasantly surprised to have students from different racial and cultural backgrounds strongly encourage him to pursue college. Terry Don Evans (who was Black) and Darren Robinson (who is White) also had LWOP sentences, yet they never failed to tell him that he was capable and would be successful. With his LWOP sentence, Thaisan still thought he was going to die in prison, but he says the idea of being there with a college education made LWOP an easier pill to swallow. With the support and camaraderie of the other Cal State LA students on the yard, Thaisan pushed his anxieties aside, applied, and was accepted.

> I was, in a sense, turning the tide and trying to be a more positive and better version of myself. I thought about how proud my parents would be if I got a college degree in an environment where I was told I wasn't worth shit. . . . I already

knew what education was doing for me and it was going to make me a better person because I already felt that within me. I wanted to show the people who have encouraged me my whole life that I could be a good student, continue to pursue higher learning and that their words were not in vain. That it didn't fall on deaf ears. That even though I didn't cultivate those seeds they planted earlier in my life, those seeds remained and I eventually watered them and tended to them and it grew to this.

Despite Thaisan's initial insecurities and concerns, he thrived in the bachelor's degree program. He strongly believes that it helped him on his journey of transformation and rehabilitation by its very nature as an in-person program. The readings they were doing in the classrooms and the discussions they held as part of their study groups were interpreted through their life experiences, lending depth and meaning they may not have understood before. Thaisan shared his experience in a focus group with KQED reporter Vanessa Rancaño:

> I started to see myself in the books I was reading, like Shakespeare. And I'm like, wow, this is complex, you know? Whoa, that's me too! You know, I'm kinda complex in that way. The hero in the book is really not a polished hero. He has all this baggage behind him. And I start to see myself in that person as well. But then I see these redeeming qualities in that character, now I can see those same redeeming qualities in myself. I started to get in touch with the things that I've abandoned since I've joined a gang. (T. Nguon, pers. comm., 2019)

He appreciated the ability to communicate with his Cal State LA professors when he didn't understand something or was frustrated. He benefited from the deep relationships and the community that came from being a part of a cohort that supported and challenged each other at the same time. A year into the program, he wrote a letter, reflecting on the connections and relationships that were being built:

> Being a part of the Cal State LA program is such a blessing and it has enriched my life tremendously. The fact that I am able to interact with my professors in a classroom setting makes a big difference in my learning process. The feedback and real time response I am able to receive is priceless because it gives me the opportunity to adjust and make corrections to any academic approach I might be considering. More importantly is how the Cal State LA program is helping me heal from my childhood traumas and confront the shame I bear for all the horrible decisions I made that led to the loss of a beautiful life. Whether it is by design of the curriculum or just the natural progression of human interaction, I often see our class time being very therapeutic for me because of the transformative value our discussions possess. I love listening to my classmates when they voice their thoughts and ideas because it gives me the chance to broaden my

perspective on certain subject matters. And as if developing bonds with professors and each person in my cohort was not enough; I truly feel a connection to
the Cal State LA student body as a whole. (T. Nguon, pers. comm., December
27, 2018)

Thaisan says that the most powerful part of being in the Prison BA Graduation Initiative was the many different humanizing aspects.

[The BA Program] really allowed us to get to know each other more. And it
allowed somebody that wasn't wearing blue to see us as human beings. And
when we see ourselves the way other people see us—if somebody that is in front
of us is acknowledging our agency as human beings first and foremost and not
even as a prisoner, but as a *student*—then you embrace that identity even more
so. If a person feels dehumanized, they're going to behave in the world as such.
But if a person feels like they are appreciated for their humanity—there can be
aspects of negativity that may cross their paths, but it is not going to deter them.

The bachelor's degree pushed Thaisan to reflect inwardly on a personal level.
"It allowed me to be . . . more intentional in my reflection, challenging myself
to ask, why did I think like that? You know, like what made me behave this
way?" With the support of his brothers on A Yard behind him, he turned to
therapy to deal with depression and unpack his family's history of trauma.

Thaisan experienced powerful moments of redemption and healing
throughout the program. Under the careful guidance of Dr. Kamran Afary
and Elizabeth Malone, the cohorts practiced the art of narradrama by writing
about their pasts and performing in front of Cal State LA guests and family
members. Thaisan reflected on a 2018 performance in a letter:

It was such an honor to perform the two plays for you, our faculty, our families,
peers, and correctional staff. My mom and sister have never seen me in a setting such as the one we experienced on the 27th. Being able to perform those
two plays in front of the women who raised me was an extraordinary way to
communicate to them how sorry I am for what I did when I decided to commit a
senseless crime and how much I have changed since that awful day. (T. Nguon,
pers. comm., 2018)

HOME

After serving twenty years in prison, Thaisan's sentence was commuted,
and he came home on March 30, 2021, during the waning days of COVID
restrictions. In a 2019 focus group with KQED reporter Vanessa Rancaño,
Thaisan credited Cal State LA's Prison BA Graduation Initiative as a factor
in his commutation:

I started to feel compassion and empathy and, you know, I started to, like, become a human being again. Education has that transformative power where it can just make a person really take a deep reflection on themselves and get back to the root of who they really want to be. I can sit here right now and say because of education, I don't have a life without sentence anymore. The governor gave mercy upon me and commuted my sentence. So, you know, education has been a very powerful thing in my life for sure. Most definitely. I love my Cal State LA family. I love them to death. The experience that I've had since being a Cal State LA student is the most enriching experience I've ever experienced in my life. (T. Nguon, pers. comm., 2019)

Thaisan says it was amazing to come home and finish his remaining classes on campus. He even took a filmmaking class, which he enjoyed, and is a hobby he continues to pursue. He also immediately immersed himself into the Cal State LA community by volunteering to assist at the campus COVID vaccination clinics every day. He easily made friends with other students from different disciplines and was open and proud about his trajectory from prison.

The opportunity to graduate with his bachelor's degree on campus as a free person, in front of his mother, siblings, and extended family members, was a highlight of his life. He remembers his sister piling leis around his neck and his mother glowing with pride, cupping his cheeks and giving him an affectionate kiss along with the biggest hug he has ever received from her.

I'm so glad I was able to experience this [graduation] out here. I thought about our guys inside who were able to graduate at the prison and I wish they could also graduate on campus. That would be so amazing. I just want them to feel what I felt on campus with my mom and my sisters and brothers hugging me. I want that for them. Because it was such a soul-enriching event. I'll carry that memory forever.

Today, Thaisan says that the bachelor's degree helps him to feel more confident, maneuvering and code-switching between diverse spaces both as a formerly incarcerated gang member who once had LWOP and as a college graduate who now advises educators about planting seeds much like the ones his mentors did with him. He tells them, "It might not grow in that moment. You might not even be able to watch it grow. But once that light bulb turns on, it's going to take root and it's going to grow."

Although it is not a link he consciously thinks about all the time, he believes that reduced recidivism is a natural by-product of a college degree. This, he says, is a result of knowing oneself better, less rigid thinking and being open to new perspectives, and better decision-making. He credits the faculty, his cohort members, and other Cal State LA students who didn't even know him but told him he could do it. "I hold on to those positive moments of encouragement that I have had with all of the people who have crossed my life. I use that to fuel me because they're still in prison and I'm out here and have the privilege to speak on their behalf."

Figure 6.1 Dara Yin (left) and Thaisan Nguon. Thaisan Nguon attended the Prison BA Graduation Initiative commencement ceremony as a free man on October 6, 2021. Photo: R. Huskey, 2021. Courtesy of California State University, Los Angeles. Center for Engagement, Service, and the Public Good.

Figure 6.2 Thaisan Nguon celebrates his bachelor's degree graduation on the Cal State LA campus with his family in May 2022. Photo: S. Kellis, 2022.

THE FUTURE

Thaisan has been working a full-time job since shortly after he was released. He also works part-time for Human Rights Watch as a member of the National LWOP Leadership Council and is a cofounder of Street Cred Education Consultants, Inc. He often volunteers with The Prism Way, Cambodia Town, Inc., and Neutral Ground. Now that he is out, as are his brother and codefendant, he is focused on maintaining a positive mindset and doing things that he always dreamed about, including skydiving, rock climbing, parasailing, and visiting Disneyland. Thaisan's new dreams include becoming a film documentarian.

NOTE

1. All quotes in this chapter are from this interview, unless otherwise noted.

Chapter 7

Tin Tri Nguyen

Name:	Tin Tri Nguyen
Age:	Fifty
Race/Ethnicity:	Vietnamese
Sentence:	Life without parole
Years Incarcerated:	Twenty-two
Released:	2020
Year Graduated:	BA, communication, summa cum laude, 2021
	Master of Business Administration, 2023
Interview:	April 8, 2023[1]

I first met Tin in May 2016, when I was introduced to all of the men who would make up Cohort 1 of the Prison BA Graduation Initiative at California State Prison, Los Angeles County (LAC). Hair neatly clipped and a tentative but broad smile across his face, Tin approached me as he still does today—by calling me "ma'am."

"Ma'am," he said enthusiastically. "I called my mom yesterday and I told her that I was going to be in a BA program and she was so happy, she started crying! You know how Asians are about their education!" We shared a knowing nod of agreement—I do, in fact, know how Asians are about their education. "She said she can't wait until I graduate. She will do whatever it takes to be here for that—even if she has to take the bus."

Now it is a bright and warm Saturday afternoon in April 2023 when Tin breezes into my office for his interview. He has just finished class, one of his last four before he graduates with his MBA degree in just a few weeks. He is neat and casual, dressed in a light gray polo and gray slacks, his black baseball hat pulled down low on his forehead.

He wears his characteristic grin, but he is agitated and frustrated. He is just coming out of class where he and a partner were required to make a presentation. The instructor told him that he had stumbled during his portion and did not seem as prepared as his partner. Tin is convinced he will be receiving a low grade. Tin is notorious among his cohort for wanting the highest grade possible. Often, his instructors at Lancaster teased him for his constant requests for "extra credit," anything that could help keep his grades at the top.

He started and ended our interview obsessively mulling over the conversation he had with his instructor about his performance. But during our two hours together, he is focused, thoughtful, introspective, and, at times, deeply emotional.

EARLY YEARS

Tin's early memories begin with the fear and confusion of escaping Vietnam in a rickety boat during the late 1970s. He has some snippets of happy childhood memories while playing with his brothers and swimming during their time at a refugee camp (T. Nguyen in Roy 2018). Tin's formative years were in Pomona, California, after his family's permanent relocation. It was the early 1980s, and Tin's life was fraught with hardships, tension, and physical violence.

Tin recalls the difficulties of starting elementary school as a new refugee who did not know English and who was also functionally illiterate in Vietnamese. Unable to communicate with his teachers, Tin felt inadequate, not smart enough, and alone in school. He remembers the shame of struggling through ESL classes as the only Vietnamese speaker. He has no recollection of any of his teachers. He does not remember engaging with any of them.

Tin's academic frustrations were exacerbated by being the only Vietnamese kid at his school, which made him the frequent target of bullying. Although Tin acknowledges that "kids will be kids" and that "kids can be mean," it is also true that the school-age years of being bullied were a defining factor of Tin's development.

The constant taunts of "ching-chong," "jap," and "dirty gook" were the least of my miseries. Because they wanted to test my kung fu, I was punched in the throat and smacked on the back of my head during long walks home from school. To this day, I still have a vivid memory of being run over by a bike—my books were everywhere, I was facedown, and a BMX wheel was on my back, pinning me to the ground, while the guy snickered, "You should've gotten out my way," and spit on me. He then rode over me. I cried as I picked my stuff up off the ground, while other kids walked by and laughed, but no one helped. (T. Nguyen in Roy 2018)

The schoolyard bullying created a churning anger within him that was amplified at home. Now, as an adult, Tin recognizes the immense pressure his parents were under as immigrants in America and especially how challenging these circumstances were for his father. As a child, however, Tin was mentally and physically wounded by his father's anger and frustration.

> My father was a very good man who loved his children and always sacrificed for his family. Yet, there were a number of factors that enabled his violent behavior. First, he was raised in a traditional culture where the father's words are absolute and indisputable, and corporal punishment was the norm. Back in Vietnam, my father was a person of some importance and social standing, so for him, it was a letdown being in America—after losing everything and making all the sacrifices that he did—to become a nobody who had to rely on his wife and whose children wouldn't even listen to him. I can only imagine how this ate away at his pride, driving him to the edge. (T. Nguyen in Roy 2018)

While Tin says toxic masculinity and corporal punishment were the norms of the time, he ruefully acknowledges that today, Western society would define his father's actions as abuse. Tin recognizes the factors that caused his father to lash out, yet it didn't change the fact that among his eight siblings, he suffered the brunt of his father's violence. The older brothers were big enough to run out of the way or resist. The youngest were babies and left alone. In the middle were daughters who were not touched because of their gender. And that left Tin feeling unsafe both at home and at school.

Still, there were unspoken expectations that all of the children in Tin's family would succeed in school—expectations that Tin never felt he could meet. His father would often say that he was "dumb as a cow" or "dumber than a cow." A memory of overhearing his father complaining about him to his uncle still stings. "He said I didn't have much brains, so we better hope I would be good with my hands. To this day, 40 years later, I still remember that conversation. And the message that I was never going to be smart enough. I thought I was dumb." The desire to prove his father—and himself—wrong still drives his ambition today.

ADOLESCENCE AND THE TEEN YEARS

By fifth grade, Tin hated school and declared it was "terrible." He began cutting classes and ditching entire school days, preferring "to hang out in a tree and smoke stolen cigarettes." At thirteen years old, he was stealing cars on a weekly basis and getting pulled over by officers who teased him for not being able to reach the gas pedal. Soon thereafter, the authorities convinced his mother to send him to a juvenile detention camp, the first of two times in his young life. Tin recalls that when his mother noticed that the juvenile camp was located just next door to an ICE Detention Center (adjacent to what is now Lancaster State Prison), she made him promise that he would never go to prison.

But being sent to Lancaster seemed an inevitability. He was filled with rage and anger from the constant bullying at home and school, and he felt disconnected and alone. Tin's only role models were his older brother and cousin. He marveled at how they commanded so much respect by threatening violence, even among the dominant White majority in their neighborhood. He observed how violence and fearlessness afforded self-protection. Tin recalls a defining moment of his youth when he lashed out viciously at a child who had taunted him relentlessly for an entire day.

> What I remember most was all the kids around me cheering. It was a turning point because then I realized that violence is how you get respect. It is how you could be part of the group and be included. So that's when I saw that violence could be power.
>
> When I let my anger out. When I let my rage out. When I used violence—I don't get bullied. I'm in control. No one called me dumb. And, of course, no one can make fun of me or my "ching chong" anymore.

When Tin was around fourteen or fifteen years old, he and his best friend were messing around in a café on a school day. They traded insults with the waitress before her boyfriend became involved and shot Tin's best friend in the heart. Tin's voice drops to just above a whisper as he recounts the fear in his friend's eyes as he held his head in his arms. Tin remembers the labored breathing (he mimics the painful, short gasps during our interview) and the frightened look that crossed his friend's face when he realized he wasn't going to make it.

Tin and his friends eschewed the sadness and grief of the funeral and focused instead on revenge. Rather than deal with the trauma of watching their friend die from a gunshot wound to the heart, they formed a gang, declaring that they would never leave the house without carrying a weapon. They promised themselves and each other that if they ever found the guy who shot their friend, they would kill him. They masked their individual pain by abusing drugs. Tin quickly progressed from marijuana to cocaine to crystal meth, "unleashing a demon" from deep within himself. His deepest addiction at the time and the habit that would be the hardest one for him to break, however, was his unwavering loyalty to the gang.

When asked what the most important thing was to him at this stage in his life, Tin is unequivocal. "Gangs," he says simply. "Gangs were the biggest part of my addiction. Drugs I could let go, but gangs I couldn't." For Tin, being a part of and leading a gang provided a substitute for everything else that was missing from his life. "Gangs offered family, loyalty, brotherhood, camaraderie. Vietnamese pride. Power. Power that helped to mask my own insecurities."

CRIME

At the age of twenty-five, Tin made a decision that would forever change the course of his future.

> In 1996, during a robbery in San Jose, I killed Mr. Stanko Vuckovic. Throughout the years, I have replayed that moment repeatedly. I asked myself, "Did I pull the trigger?" or "Did the gun go off during the struggle?" After years of contemplating, I realized there were other factors just as significant. The point is that I cocked the gun, that I chose to use the gun in the robbery, and above all my decision to rob this man and take what was not mine were all what caused his death. Yet, these were not the only factors. Other elements, such as abusing drugs, joining a gang and choosing a life of crime, were all the bad choices I made that led me to that very moment. (T. Nguyen in Roy 2018)

The murder of Mr. Stanko Vuckovic led to Tin Nguyen's sentence of life without possibility of parole. He spent a number of years at Pelican Bay before eventually making his way to Lancaster in 2004. Tin remained at Lancaster until his sentence was commuted by Governor Jerry Brown, and he was released in 2020.

THE JOURNEY TO A BA DEGREE

Tin confesses that while in prison, gang life was the most important thing he focused on until the start of the Cal State LA bachelor's degree program. Even though the Honor Yard was a "vacation" from what he was used to because of the absence of prison racial politics, Tin was convinced that his time on Lancaster's A Yard was only a temporary reprieve, and soon enough he would incur an infraction that would send him back to the general population yard that was more like the war zone he was accustomed to.

Tin is characteristically unflinching and candid when he reflects upon his past, largely because it elucidates his dramatic transformation. During an unsuccessful parole hearing, the commissioners asked Tin about a "kite" that was "dropped" on him in 2012. He answered bluntly: "I was a drug dealer. I brought in phones and contraband. Someone owed me money." A commissioner then queried, "What would happen if someone owed you money?" Tin responded, "I was going to give him blood." The commissioner: "You were going to put a hit on him?" Tin: "No, I was going to do it myself."

Tin Nguyen, an active gang leader on Lancaster's A Yard whose priorities at the time were fighting for the right to use certain tables and showers and smuggling in contraband and drugs, stumbled upon college in 2006. He recalls seeing a fellow inmate studying a textbook. Intrigued, Tin asked him what he was doing. "This is not for you," the man replied.

Tin was affronted and motivated at the same time. He accepted the insult as a challenge and found someone else on the yard who helped him enroll in two classes from a community college correspondence program. One of these classes was in astronomy. Tin had to read the textbook three times, but he aced both classes and was motivated to do more. School stirred up a different side of Tin's competitive streak. A friend on the yard took four correspondence classes. So did Tin. Tin pushed himself and made the President's List. He thought to himself, "I'm not a dumb cow," and his confidence grew.

In the beginning, Tin's ulterior motives to pursue higher education were "negative and trauma-based." Although he always had a strong desire to better himself, he had an equally strong desire to prove his detractors wrong. He wanted his mother to be proud of him, and he also wanted affirmation that he wasn't stupid. Tin wanted to prove to himself that his father was wrong when he said he was dumber than a cow.

The gang members on the prison yard thought he was wasting time, but because he didn't completely walk away from criminal activity during community college, they left him alone. He was still selling drugs in prison when he received his associate of arts degree from Coastline Community College. He set his sights on a bachelor's degree.

Before the Cal State LA Prison BA Graduation Initiative started in 2016, the only way an inmate in California could pursue a bachelor's degree was through correspondence institutions such as Adams State University, which is based in Colorado and costs an average of $660 per three-unit course. Tin convinced his sister to foot the bill, claiming he had no money, even though he was still selling drugs. He expresses guilt and embarrassment for the lies he used to get his sister to pay for his education. "I was very manipulative," he admits wryly.

Tin becomes animated when talking about the unexpected juxtaposition of an active gang member who is pursuing higher education.

Think about this as a researcher! We know a lot of research says that higher education changes a person, right? That education is supposed to help them improve their rehabilitation and transformation. But think about this—I got my AA degree and I was going to Adams State and yet I was still very active [with gangs].

In other words, Tin was *not* transformed by higher education during his early years in community college. He began "filing down the chains" in earnest in 2012, when his mother came to visit him at Lancaster and he was out of his mind on drugs. He was embarrassed and ashamed that his mother saw him that way, but the process of change was slow. He still couldn't bring himself to completely walk away from gang life so he "kept one hand in the cookie jar." Tin explains, for example, that he may not have been the one to order a hit himself, but he may have served as a respected advisor at the table who helped make the final decision. In 2014–2015, during the first Cal State LA class he attended, Tin was investigated for possession of contraband and sent to the hole. Ironically, school was still important to him—to this day, he is irritated that he earned only a B+ in the class. His instructor reminded him that if he hadn't been sent to the hole, he would have done better.

TRANSFORMATION

The transformation was gradual over the years, but Tin can identify when and why the chains to his destructive past were finally severed. "I stopped everything when I knew the BA program was real. That's when I took my hand out of the cookie jar."

I think [it was different] with Adams State and Coastline. In my opinion, it is very impersonal. You turn in the work and they give you a grade. . . . But the experience of being in an in-person BA program and talking to all of the professors. . . . You're no longer looked at as a number. A monster. A prisoner. But as a student. A human being. It kinda holds you accountable for your actions. That's when I truly, truly started moving towards the (transformational) direction and I started saying "No. No. No."

Tin felt beholden to the founders of the Prison BA Graduation Initiative because he knew what a unique and rare opportunity it was to have access to an in-person college degree program that was free.

Now, I'm accountable for this. I'm accountable for being a role model, you know what I mean? A model student. A model inmate. Because to be honest, if I wasn't, I don't know how I could ever face you.

Figure 7.1 Tin Nguyen prepares to present his painting to the president of Cal State LA.
The painting features people who have made a positive difference in the world. Photo: J.
Flores, 2017. Courtesy of California State University, Los Angeles.

The transformation eased forward. "Only a few more links to file. Drugs were
gone. Gangs were gone. Prison politics—gone. All of this was filed down
to a point, but there was still a link holding on. I think the program—which
includes all of the staff, faculty, students, and the former educational coordinator—had the weight to snap the final chain." When Tin broke the final
chain, he decided to move his focus from one of negativity to being someone
who would make a positive difference in the world.

Tin often referred to his LWOP sentence as being a part of the "walking
dead"—a pitiful group of individuals with no future, no dreams, and the
only expectation was to die in prison. Pursuing a bachelor's degree created
an internal shift within him, even if he did not expect to ever come home.
He wrote about himself and his educational journey in the journal *Words
Uncaged: Human.*

> Tin has become alive. No longer walking among the living dead (serving life
> without parole), aimlessly roaming the prison yard and desperately searching for
> what he craved: hope, love, and purpose. He has dreams and aspirations . . . he
> knows that he is going places. . . . No matter if he is sitting in a prison cell, he is
> no longer at a standstill, at the mercy of his circumstances. He will grow along
> with the world and move along with his life. (Nguyen 2017, 65)

Figure 7.2 Tin Nguyen's bachelor's degree graduation portrait. Photo: R. Huskey, 2021. Courtesy of California State University, Los Angeles.

CHALLENGES

Tin was widely known for his outstanding work ethic and academic diligence, but that did not mean school was easy for him. Since English was his second language, he was a slow reader, and he lacked confidence in his public speaking and writing skills.

Prison culture also made him reluctant to ask for help.

> You see, when you live in an environment (maximum-security prison) where the strong prey on the weak, you will learn quickly not to show any weakness. Asking for help is considered a weakness. . . . Because of Dr. Roy, that wall came crumbling down. The mask of a hardened convict slowly came off. I no longer had to put on that tiring façade of "I don't care, stone cold or I'm doing life, try me?" My perspective on asking for help was slowly changing. I began to view asking for help as a sign of maturity and strength, and not weakness. This built confidence and strength within me, and I developed the insight and courage to leave my comfort zone of fortified walls that I have built in the last 18 years. I now could engage myself in an academic discussion with my peers, which has helped me to improve both academically and personally. (Nguyen 2017, 64)

There are structural barriers within the prison that make college attendance challenging as well. Although the public often assumes that incarcerated students will do well in school because they do not have the same obligations and distractions as college students on the outside, the Prison BA Graduation Initiative students regularly encountered roadblocks, passive resistance, belittlement, and chiding from the correctional officers, the majority of whom are resistant to the idea of prisoners earning college degrees. Tin recalls the common jeers the students would hear on any given day: "Why are you getting a BA? It's not like you're going to use it. You have life without." Or "Maybe I should send my kids to prison so that they can go to college for free, too."

After Tin made the decision to walk away from the gangs that he once led, the gang made a concerted effort to drag him back down. One day, he walked to class holding his books, and one of his old homies tried to tempt him back into his old ways. He asked Tin to bring in a cellphone. "No, bro—I don't do that anymore," Tin responded. "Pffft," the homie hissed as he walked back toward his friends. "I told you all he's a wuss." A Vietnamese friend stepped in. "Leave him alone. Tin has put his sword down."

COMING HOME

Governor Jerry Brown commuted Tin's sentence, citing, among other things, his involvement in the Prison BA program, as well as his leadership in the Paws for Life program. A sentence commutation is a dream come true, but his transition from prison to college campus was far from smooth. After serving twenty-two years, he was released from prison in December 2019, but he was immediately detained by ICE and forced to live in a cramped detention center for ten months while pro bono lawyers from O'Melveny and Meyers battled to stop the threat of deportation back to Vietnam. He won the battle against ICE and was released to Los Angeles and the Cal State LA campus during the height of COVID in October 2020. Tin resumed his studies immediately, but was forced to learn Zoom and Canvas (an online learning management program) quickly. As a student without legal status, he is not eligible for financial aid, and he has worked menial jobs, won scholarships, and received individual donations to help pay his education expenses. He battled depression during his first semester of the MBA program but has sought counseling to help him work through the childhood traumas and experiences that continue to impact him today.

He says, however, that coming to the Cal State LA campus has been his dream come true. He loves being on the main walkway that cuts through the middle of campus, his backpack slung over his shoulder. "I still pinch myself when I come out of class sometimes at night."

He feels welcome on campus and ironically—considering how much he hated being in school as a child—notes that education is now his "safe place." The structure and regular demands of school provide support, purpose, and stimulation. When Tin was first sent to prison, he said that gangs were the most important thing to him. Now that he has weathered California's first bachelor's degree program in a carceral setting, and obtained his bachelor's degree, Tin unabashedly acknowledges that education is what he thinks about the most. Getting an education, he says, is the most important thing in his life.

THE RIPPLE EFFECT

Two or three years after the start of the Prison BA Graduation Initiative, the same person who taunted Tin as a "wuss" when he walked across the yard on his way to class started pursuing college classes at Lancaster. The man who stepped in on Tin's behalf and said that he'd put his sword down wrote Tin a letter after he was released. The man said he will always fondly remember Tin with his books in one hand and a cup of coffee in the other. Younger men at Lancaster whom he has never met call him to thank him for leading the way and not forgetting about them.

Now that he is home, some of the old homies have expressed great pride in him. "Do you fucking believe it? I can't believe it! Anybody but Tin! And now he's about to get his MBA!?"

After Tin earned his bachelor's degree, there was a positive ripple effect within his family as well. Incarceration in the Vietnamese community is deeply shameful, and for a long time, he was made invisible, even after his sentence was commuted and he returned home. Recently, however, he felt

a shift. His sister invited him up to her office, where he was proudly introduced to her coworkers as the brother who has gone to college and is about
to earn his MBA. Tin's college success has inspired his older and younger
brothers to return to school. His niece, a new mother with a young child,
went back to college and is about to earn a bachelor's degree in computer
science.

Tin also believes that having a bachelor's degree has contributed to a significant ripple effect within himself as well. For example, the critical thinking
and emotional skills he developed in the bachelor's program made him more
open to pursuing individual therapy and exploring the impact his childhood
traumas have had upon his life, even though the process has been extremely
difficult and painful. Tin says, "There will always be a part of Tin who is
insecure, but has tremendous confidence."

This was even true with the encounter he had with his professor just before
our interview. Tin acknowledges that no one likes to be criticized, but with
more education and perspective, it has changed his ability to handle the
setbacks. "I was calm and respectful," he explains. "I was upset, but able to
control it."

THE FUTURE

Now, with the bachelor's and master's degrees under his belt, Tin is pas-
sionate about helping his community and giving voice to those who have
been marginalized and disenfranchised, such as immigrants, the homeless,
and seniors. We pause our interview for a moment to reflect on the groups of
people he wants so much to help, noting that before he had a college education, helping people in this way would have never crossed his mind. Currently, he is working with VietRise, a nonprofit that advances social justice
and builds power in the working-class Vietnamese immigrant community.
Tin is the Immigrant Justice Coordinator, advocating and providing services
for immigrants who are adversely affected by the system. In this position, he
is constantly exercising his communication and leadership skills to help find
common ground with others. "Even though I don't have economic power, I
can still help others," Tin says. Whereas he may have once felt differently,
having a lot of money at this point is not as important to him as leaving a
positive impact on the community. He has also combined his management
and dog training experience to help a nonprofit rescue organization train and
rehabilitate dogs saved from high-kill shelters.

Tin half-jokingly wonders if his addiction to gang life has been replaced
by an addiction to education. He becomes extra-animated when he talks

Figure 7.3 Tin Nguyen celebrates his MBA with family in May 2023. Photo: S. Kellis, 2023.

about his educational future. Immediately after receiving his MBA in May 2023, he is planning to start studying for the LSAT and apply to law school in the following year. After law school, he envisions a PhD—maybe in law. Or physics. Or astronomy. "I love it!" he exclaims. "I will never stop going to school!"

NOTE

1. All quotes in this chapter are from this interview, unless otherwise noted.

Chapter 8

Charlie Praphatananda

Name:	Charlie Praphatananda
Age:	Forty-six
Race/Ethnicity:	Thai-Japanese American
Sentence:	Life without parole
Years Incarcerated:	Twenty-two
Released:	June 28, 2019
Year Graduated:	2020
Interview:	April 13 and April 20, 2023[1]

Charlie was quiet and unassuming in the prison classroom. He was usually tucked in a corner, hidden behind a computer monitor, but always polite and friendly. After he was paroled, I was surprised to discover that he was a loquacious storyteller, often punctuating his own stories with an infectious chuckle or lengthy sidebar. I was also surprised to learn—largely through these interviews—that so many of the Prison BA Graduation Initiative students said it was Charlie who encouraged and motivated them to pursue higher education. Charlie had been part of a small group of respected leaders who connected men to college classes, helped them obtain the necessary textbooks, and cajoled and prodded them when they felt like giving up. Because Charlie and other men on the Honor Yard encouraged men to obtain their associate of arts degrees, Cal State LA had a paved path to come to Lancaster to offer a bachelor's degree completion program.

Charlie came home in June 2019, the third student from the Cal State LA Prison BA Graduation Initiative to have his sentence commuted. He was released pre-COVID and finished his degree on the Cal State LA main campus, graduating in 2020. He worked for the Project Rebound program during school and would frequently drop by my office between classes to regale me with stories about his classroom experiences (how welcoming and supportive all of the students were to him and how unaffected they were by his carceral history) or funny stories about his nieces, especially the littlest one, who is deeply attached to him.

He thought for a short while that he would continue with his master's degree after earning his bachelor's in 2020, but decided to pause on his studies. He moved ninety minutes away from campus to live with his family, which allows him to help his parents and carpool his niece while saving money on rent, but it also limits meaningful job prospects in social justice, the field he is most interested in pursuing. He's recently started working part-time with a new reentry organization in Los Angeles, guiding other LWOP men and women who have recently come home and helping them navigate their new lives.

EARLY YEARS

Charlie describes his initial years in school as "okay" and "fun." Charlie remembers that he did what kids are supposed to do in kindergarten through the second grade: he practiced his social skills and played. Somewhere around the fourth grade, however, he was diagnosed with dyslexia and was deemed a "slow learner." To his shame and frustration, Charlie was put in special education classes where he was branded as stupid and dumb, forever altering his life path. "School was just a constant reminder of my shortcomings and failures" (C. Praphatananda, pers. comm., 2019). This was especially difficult because Charlie's twin sister was an excellent student who got straight As, was always on the honor roll, participated in the mentally gifted school programs, and took community-college-level classes while still in middle school.

Charlie and his family lived in southeast Los Angeles during his elementary school years. His father, who immigrated from Thailand as a foreign exchange student in the 1960s, worked long hours to support the family, and Charlie rarely saw him. Charlie's most influential male role models at the time were his mother's brothers, whom he saw frequently. Charlie's uncles declared that showing emotions other than rage or anger was a weakness. The uncles modeled a brand of toxic masculinity that Charlie tried to embrace behind a tough facade, although inside, he was a cauldron of bottled-up emotions and insecurities. Charlie was often bullied during his younger years, but at the age of eight, he remembers how powerful and proud he felt when he finally fought back. Although being picked on throughout his childhood years was definitely traumatic, Charlie's early experiences helped shape his adulthood desire to protect the vulnerable and his refusal to cater to bullies.

After the fourth grade, Charlie was convinced that education was "not in my wheelhouse" and viewed all school-related activities with loathing. Charlie tried to keep up in the classroom, but he was always struggling. His father tried to be supportive and encouraging, but so deep were Charlie's insecurities, everything he heard was interpreted as "criticism, judgment, or ridicule." Charlie felt defeated by the negative labels and low expectations as a special education student, investing minimal effort into school because he "didn't see the point."

Charlie's father worried about the kids growing up in an urban environment, so he decided to move the family ninety minutes inland from the heart of Los Angeles. Charlie's father and uncle had come to the United States as young men to make better lives for themselves and their future families. He had hoped that Charlie would embrace higher education or pursue a trade, envisioning Charlie with a steady job that would lead to a comfortable retirement. Instead of talking about college choices and future plans, however, Charlie's father was sounding the alarm about his young friends, warning Charlie that they were going to get him in trouble. He counseled Charlie to make better choices.

Despite his father's best intentions, Charlie sought trouble wherever he was. Charlie's self-described delinquency included skipping school, driving around town without a license, stealing, and spending weekday afternoons at ditch parties and kickbacks. Charlie's high school tried several tactics to keep him in line, to no avail. He was finally expelled in the eleventh grade.

Academic challenges aside, Charlie's confidence and teenage arrogance were high. He chuckled: "I felt sure about pretty much every decision I made—even the bad ones." He was blindly loyal to the friends his father so strongly disapproved of, calling them his "ride-or-dies." Charlie believed he was rich with street smarts even though the book smarts were a struggle. He took risks and, for a long time, was able to evade arrest. He stole cars and broke into homes in broad daylight. He got into fights. He used fake IDs and started venturing into check and credit card fraud. He sold and used drugs. Methamphetamine would lead to Charlie's ultimate downfall.

> Weed would just give me the munchies and made me want to stay home and watch TV. But when I was on speed it really just sparked my whole criminal career. I would just do crazy things. I'm not proud of them, but the stuff that I'd do on drugs . . . like one of the craziest things I did was I actually went to a gun store and stole two guns when I was tweaking. I was just sixteen or seventeen at the time.

Charlie had a girlfriend whom he ruefully believes he corrupted. She came from a good and stable family, but Charlie says: "She became infatuated with the lifestyle and so I kind of indoctrinated her into all that. I helped her find that attitude to affront people." Together, just before his eighteenth birthday, Charlie's girlfriend physically attacked a young woman, and they stole her backpack. Charlie was arrested and spent thirty days in juvenile detention.

Charlie's family and friends consistently encouraged him to go back to school. Naive and rudderless, he remembers smoking weed one night with a friend who was about to leave for college. She asked him what he was planning to do with his life, and Charlie responded that he was going to be a drug dealer, then retire. When she laughed at him and told him that he would need to have a job to earn a retirement one day, he was crushed.

At eighteen, Charlie was a high school dropout and a meth addict with a criminal record. He had no visions for his future and could not imagine what he was supposed to do with his life. He assumed he would die young.

> If you really don't care if you live or die, it kind of gives this swagger because you just don't give a fuck. Like if someone pulls a gun on you, most people would be afraid. But I would take it to the next level. I'd laugh in their face which messes people up because that's not the response you expect from somebody when they pull a gun on you.
>
> Whenever I had a gun, I seriously had a God complex. I thought I was God because I thought I could choose who lived and who died.

Much of Charlie's early training taught him to be dispassionate and callous. In fact, Charlie was sensitive and empathetic, but lacked the emotional maturity to handle difficult situations. Charlie imploded internally during a brief stint in county jail when his pregnant girlfriend experienced complications and their baby died within the first hour of his birth.

> And that kind of like just really sent me into this downward spiral. [I just felt] straight hate and rage at the world because the only things I knew about being a man was you don't feel feelings. You work. You meet someone. You have a family and you protect them. And here it is: I'm locked up. My son passes away. I can't protect him. I felt that was just like highlighting my failures in life and again, I'm not knowing how to process those feelings or deal with loss and stuff. I just started doing the only thing I knew to not feel the pain, the shame or anything, which was more drugs to the point where I didn't feel anything.

Shortly after Charlie turned twenty years old, he committed two unrelated robberies in one night between the hours of 1:00 and 4:00 a.m. In a drug-induced haze, he was fearless, impulsive, and arrogant.

> I told him, "Step the fuck back or I'll shoot you." And he didn't—not in that moment. And then—my rage. You know, it's just like, I have a gun and you're

supposed to respect me. . . . You need to act accordingly. . . . And I felt that it was like another slight at my pride. That he was trying to make me look like a fool and stuff. And it really wasn't that. I think he was just trying not to be robbed. . . . When I told him the second time, he didn't [step back].

It was kind of that out-of-body experience. . . . I was just there in slow motion. I just saw myself raise the gun and shoot him. . . . I felt like, "You made me do this. This is your fault," because again, like back in that time before I got locked up, like nothing—and when I say nothing, I mean *nothing*—was ever my fault. I didn't know how to take responsibility for anything or take accountability for anything. So nothing was ever my fault. There was always a reason why something happened. That's just how I kind of proceeded throughout life until that night.

LWOP

Charlie's parents' house was raided, and shortly thereafter, he was arrested. While awaiting trial, in jail, Charlie believed he could fight the case, negotiate a plea deal, or win on appeal.

Well, I was still delusional, in the sense that I had that pride and ego and cockiness about me. So I was like, "Oh, they can give me whatever. 'Cause I'm gonna beat this and get out on an appeal, you know?"

Despite his confidence, Charlie was sentenced to life without parole.

After all of the negotiations, court trials, appeals, and blind hope, Charlie hit a wall. He was transferred to Centinela State Prison with a life-without-parole sentence at the age of twenty-two. Charlie began to realize that rather than shrouding himself behind lies and delusions, he wanted something more out of life.

Well, not all of it changed at one time, but after receiving a sentence of life without possibility of parole—that reality came crashing down on me. Like, what did you do to your life?! It was a lot of bad moments, but you know, one thing about getting arrested is that it really just opened my eyes to everything. When you don't have drugs to numb any feelings, you can't really escape it. You have to face [those feelings].

As Charlie began to settle into prison life, he observed patterns among the older LWOPs in prison to help him decipher his own path.

They either become like the monsters that society has labeled them as— meaning they continue to be violent and do stupid things. Then you have the path of self-delusions: you get drugs, run up drug debts until you can't pay them and you either have to go to protective custody or somebody stabs you and you die. And then there's a third one: you try to make the best of what you have left with your life and that's kind of what I did.

Charlie served six years at Centinela. He took the necessary precautions to survive prison politics but was not active and violent in the way he had been on the outside as a young man. He stopped using drugs and began to figure out what "making the best of what you have left with your life" would look like for him.

I just kept thinking I ruined my life. I was definitely expecting my family would be like, "We're done." But they weren't. They stuck by me and that made a difference. They were supportive. In those moments, I felt like my family does a lot for me, what's something that I can do for them? And I was like, I'll get the GED [since] I didn't finish high school.

Although perhaps getting his GED was a logical next step for someone who was kicked out of high school in the eleventh grade, it wasn't an easy ride for Charlie. He forced himself to overcome his childhood insecurities and persist through the challenges.

So, it took me a minute. It took me three tries to complete it. Mainly the writing part was—I'm dyslexic. So a lot of times I would either misspell words or I would just mess up a whole sentence. That happens when I get real nervous and have a writing assignment or something. Once I finally did it and actually got my GED, I sent it to my family. They were happy—it just kind of showed me something about myself that I didn't realize, which is I *can* do education. I *can* go to school and maybe it's not as bad as I believed it to be.

After Charlie earned his GED, he heard rumors that Coastline Community College was piloting correspondence courses in prisons. Charlie and a handful of other men on the yard were interested in pursuing the program, but they weren't sure how they would pay for books. In any case, Charlie was up for transfer, and his cellie was pushing him to go to Lancaster.

He was trying to go to Lancaster and I was like, "Why??" He says they got this yard there called the "Honor Yard." He says I can get there. He's like, "Go there and don't fuck up. I don't care what BS goes on. There's older people on the yard. Less prison bullshit. If you go there, that's a really good spot." So—all right! Now I have to get transferred to Lancaster.

Charlie got himself to the Honor Yard. One of his first requirements was to present a plan for his rehabilitation. Charlie included higher education as a central feature to his plan.

After his success obtaining his GED, Charlie looked to community college as the next logical step. He renewed his pursuit for the Coastline Community College correspondence program and learned that there was an inmate named Robert Chan at Lancaster who was coordinating the registration. There were only eighteen spots available, but Robert helped Charlie secure his registration, then asked him curiously if he had ever done college before. Charlie admitted he hadn't.

Robert not only helped Charlie navigate through his college studies, but the two became each other's mentors and cheerleaders for the remainder of their time together in prison. Although Robert was coordinating the higher-ed programs on the yard, until he met Charlie, he himself had no intention of enrolling. Ironically, Robert would go on not only to complete his associate's degree through Coastline, but he earned his bachelor's degree through Adams State's correspondence program well before any of the men completed their Cal State LA degrees.

TRANSFORMATION

In addition to Robert, who eventually became his cellie, Charlie encountered many others who motivated and inspired him. He began dating a woman (whom he would later marry) while in prison, and though she did not know the full extent of his crime, she said she not only forgave him for his past, but believed he was a changed person.

> [I'd] never met someone who had that perspective before. It took me a long time to understand it. I've learned that if you surround yourself with negativity, you'll breed negativity.

Charlie began to move away from the self-inflicted negativity that had been such a facet of his life and strove toward positivity. He immersed himself in the self-help programming on the yard. He began to ascribe to the belief that "Every day you live is toward the memory of the victim of your crime," a value that continues to guide his life with the purpose and intentionality to make amends.

Charlie will forever recognize the memory of his victim and make amends for his role in his death. Part of making amends is living a purposeful life, even with LWOP, and Charlie realized that earning a college degree could help him achieve a meaningful life.

I came to the realization that I was going to die in prison. When that happened, I had to ask myself, "What am I going to do with my life? I totally ruined my life." All these fantasies of getting out on appeals and random thoughts of doing something that gets you out of prison, all kind of disappeared. It just came down to "What am I going to do with my life now? This is where I'm probably going to die. I'm going to die and it's gonna be shitty."

So what do you do to make the best of what you have? Once I started on the educational cocktail at Lancaster—it was like, let's see how far I can go. I took those classes and the whole education thing just opened my eyes to a lot of different realities.

Charlie enrolled in Coastline Community College, sharing books with other students as part of a self-organized book exchange on the Honor Yard. Charlie kept chipping away at his Coastline assignments, and well before the Cal State LA Prison BA Graduation Initiative was even an acorn of an idea, he was trying to figure out how he could work his way up to a bachelor's degree.

When Cal State LA finally arrived, Charlie admits he was mildly terrified. He worried that the pilot cohort at Lancaster would be unsuccessful. Charlie and his classmates knew that a face-to-face bachelor's degree program was very different from their experiences with correspondence courses, where there was little to no interaction with professors and no engagement among students.

Charlie and his fellow cohort members were also concerned that Cal State LA was going to "dumb down the program for prisoners," thus invalidating their college degree. Many correctional officers at Lancaster openly sneered about college in prison and sometimes made getting to class a challenging and humiliating ordeal, creating shadows of doubt in the students' minds.

[We wondered] are we really doing good or are they just trying to appease us? Are you guys grading us like a regular person? You're not sugarcoating us? [It's important because] I felt that there are stigmas attached to prison education, like, "You're not really learning anything. You're not really earning these grades. They're just doing that so they can get paid. You know, these fools are doing it so that they can have a piece of paper to say they earned something, but they really don't know anything."

However, Charlie really *was* earning his college degree. He was also evolving into a respected leader on the yard who was actively promoting higher education and mentoring prospective students. He reflected on his work in a paper he submitted in 2018:

Approximately 2006, there were only five of us attending Coastline Community College, pursuing our AA on this facility. During my journey, most Asian inmates, who walked a similar lifestyle that I had—gangs and drugs—lacked the enthusiasm to pursue their higher education due to their insecurity. After all, we were the Asians who didn't make the cut of your typical stereotype of being intelligent. My friend Robert and I began to persuade others by encouraging them, and of course, demonstrating to the other Asians that if we can do it, so can they. I walked their walks, no excuse. Now, the majority of the Asian inmates on this facility are pursuing higher education, through either Coastline Community College, Antelope Valley College or Feather River. (C. Praphatananda, pers. comm., 2018)

In fact, Asian and non-Asian students alike report that Charlie Praphatananda was instrumental in their decision to go to college. Charlie was persistent and encouraging, especially for other students with LWOP sentences like his own, by inspiring them to think about the legacy they wanted to leave behind regardless of their sentence.

I think a lot is human nature. Like, "Okay, we messed our lives up but what are we going to leave behind? What is our legacy going to be? Just that we were these dirtbags that created these heinous crimes and, and died in prison?" I don't want that to be my legacy. I don't want that to be what I'm known for. I'd prefer that they'd be like, "Well, you know, this person died in prison, but he accomplished all these things while he was here."

THE BA AND TRANSFORMATION

For Charlie, like so many of the students, the transformative aspects of the bachelor's degree in prison wasn't about a specific reading or writing assignment or group activity. According to Charlie, the most powerful aspect of the program was in the human connections that were formed between the students with their professors and with each other.

I can't tell you what it's like to be oppressed for years and then to be able to walk into a classroom and have this stranger just see you as a human being. They're not judging you. They don't know what your crime is. They don't know what you're here for. They don't ask those questions. They treat you like a human being, like a regular student. And that was very profound to be able to be a part of that. I think that's one thing that people really, really craved was that human connection. I think our souls craved it.

Charlie describes the impact these connections through the bachelor's degree have had on his life as "mind-blowing," both when he was still inside prison and after his sentence was commuted and he was paroled in June 2019. Although prison education research tends to focus on reduced recidivism as the primary benefit of higher education in prison (Lim 2020), the literature does not articulate *how* a college education reduces recidivism risks nearly as well as the students do themselves.

> I think that, first and foremost, being at a bachelor's level and being able to take courses [in person] changes your perspective. It changes how you view things. How you approach things. I feel it makes you a little more efficient than when you're just stumbling around. That really led to a different dynamic. . . . It doesn't seem like it's important to most people, but when you're inside and you can have a conversation with someone that you don't know, who doesn't look at you like you're just in prison, but more of like, "How are you doing?"

COMMUTATION

Twenty-two and a half years into his LWOP sentence, Charlie Praphatananda had his sentence commuted by California's Governor Jerry Brown. Charlie, who for more than two decades was convinced he was going to die in prison, was released in June 2019.

Charlie transitioned from prison to the main campus to finish his degree. On the day of his release, after struggling with motion sickness during his first car ride in more than twenty-two years, he asked his family to bring him

Figure 8.1 Charlie Praphatananda, third from left, receives his official commutation notice at California State Prison, Los Angeles County. Photo: R. Huskey, 2018. Courtesy of California State University, Los Angeles.

straight to the Cal State LA campus. There, he was immediately enfolded into a wedding shower for one of his classmates, the first student released from prison, Bradley "Woody" Arrowood. He connected with fellow students, faculty, and staff that he had known for the last three years of his program while he was inside, nibbled on a few crackers, and got his Cal State LA identification card before reporting to the transitional home just up the hill from campus.

Although he had constantly worried that incarcerated students were being academically coddled and spoiled in the Prison BA Graduation Initiative, Charlie soon found out that he was more than prepared to keep up with the classes and students on the outside. His connection to the campus deepened.

> I was absolutely loving it. I used to leave the house as early as possible. I would get to campus about 6:30 in the morning. One of the things that I did for self-care was just sit there, listen to music and just enjoy the quietness of the campus. As you sit there and chill, you just start to see it come alive. And being able to go to classes was like super exciting because I'd never had that experience. It was also a little scary at first because when you first get out, you swear that you have some kind of sign on you that everybody else can see except you that says, "I just got out of prison." But then, there was just the general acceptance of people in my classes.

He continued his education exactly where he'd left off inside and earned his bachelor's degree on the Cal State LA main campus in 2020. After the COVID pandemic waned, he and seven other classmates from his cohort walked the commencement stage, officially celebrating their graduation.

Charlie says he believes that the entire bachelor's degree program has been transformational for him. He is confident that he uses his college degree every day, benefiting from having been trained to exercise critical thinking, form opinions, and research and defend ideas and concepts. He also tries to listen for the true purpose and intention of a person's questions, skills that he uses every day, whether it is interacting with his family or dealing with his supervisors at his part-time Home Depot job. In fact, Charlie is still triggered by bullies, and he is quick to confront his supervisors with straightforward insight and respectful reasoning when he sees a coworker being treated badly or an unfair policy being enforced.

While he was in prison, Charlie would frequently talk about his education with his nieces and nephews. Now these same young people are carving out their own path, some in college, and others not. Still, they seek his blunt, thoughtful advice as they explore their college options or potential new business endeavors. Although he doesn't plan to live with his family for much longer, Charlie appreciates that he has had an opportunity to play a large role in taking care of his youngest niece, but his presence can also be a source of tension. His family initially worried that he would turn to drugs again and repeat his past mistakes. Charlie reassures them that he is a different person who has worked on understanding and bettering himself so that he won't need to make the same mistakes again. He's also invested too much of himself to go backward at this juncture.

THE FUTURE

Charlie recognizes that the long-awaited commutation and freedom that he once thought would never happen to him is not the end of the fairy tale, but the start of a new story. The process of working on oneself is an ongoing journey and one that he examines regularly from time to time. He wonders what hobbies and activities are important to him now that he is untethered. He asks himself what he loves to do. He's had to pause and think about himself in relation to others.

> Most of the time, I didn't even know why I was here. Like, what am I supposed to do? And the few little things that I did know were laced with toxic masculinity from my uncles and stuff. You know, trying to live up to that standard of what a real man is—it's an illusion. There's no way a person can be a "real man" according to what toxic masculinity teaches you because we're all human beings. We have emotions that we have to process and that is a big struggle for me. I feel stuff that I'm not used to. It's a learning journey, but it's also frustrating sometimes because there's been a couple times that I've just been floored with how intense my emotions can be.

The future is not exactly what he thought it would be, but as he says, he is a hopeful person and he is optimistic about what lies ahead. Perhaps he'll go back and get a master's degree. Someday, he sees himself working a virtual job that allows him the flexibility and income to travel. Whatever it is, he envisions work that makes a difference and honors the memory of his victim.

> It is the craziest thing. Society claims we are these dangerous people because at one point in our lives we were. We aren't, though, you know, I mean, we did unspeakable things that we can't take back. . . . I found [one thing I need to do] is living amends. . . . You're never going to bring the person back. . . . But, you have to learn that in order to honor the person whose life you took—you have to be successful.

Figure 8.2 Charlie Praphatananda walks the commencement stage to receive his diploma. Photo: R. Huskey, 2021. Courtesy of California State University, Los Angeles.

NOTE

1. All quotes in this chapter are from this two-part interview, unless otherwise noted.

Chapter 9

Risala Rose-Aminifu

Name:	Risala Rose-Aminifu
Age:	Fifty
Race/Ethnicity:	Africanoid
Sentence:	Life without parole
Years Incarcerated:	Twenty-nine years, twelve days
Released:	May 2021
Year Graduated:	2022
Interview:	April 16, 2023[1]

Risala, always punctual, arrived for his interview well before me. He uses the time to stroll around the Wellness Garden in front of the building while chatting animatedly on his cellphone with his mother. They are happily reminiscing about the time she used to take art classes at Cal State LA in the late 1970s with a young Risala in tow. They would take the bus from Pasadena, and he would sit quietly in the back of the classroom, sipping a soda and nibbling on a bag of chips. Both of his parents studied pan-African studies on this campus and were just shy of earning bachelor's degrees.

Cal State LA has changed a lot in the past thirty-five years, but the campus stirs up fond nostalgia in mother and son alike. It is clear that they are both very proud of Risala's renewed connection to Cal State LA, that it is a kind of homecoming in a way. "I love this campus," Risala exclaims before our interview officially begins.

Today, Risala exudes the energy of someone who is eager to make up for lost time—for thirty long years in fact. He talks rapidly and enthusiastically, infusing almost every sentence with good-natured humor and the wry comic timing of a practiced class clown. His schedule is busy, but he was eager to do the interview. He has worked forty hours a week as a unionized public works employee since a month of being home. And now, freshly off parole, he's beginning to travel and enjoy vacations in different states. He was thrilled to attend his family reunion over the summer and to celebrate milestones with friends and family. "The sky is the limit!" he rejoices.

EARLY YEARS

Risala, whose name is Swahili for "messenger" or "prophet," was home-schooled for a number of years and then attended a small private school in Altadena, California. Risala's parents were Black Nationalists in the 1960s, and it was important to them that he had exposure to African history and culture. Risala's early education included rich explorations into African royalty and the legacy of Sojourner Truth. He learned about important Black inventors, such as Garrett August Morgan, the inventor of the stoplight, and world leaders. He remembers enjoying school at this time, especially because his mother would go over his lessons with him, and this made homework feel engaging and special to him.

Although both of his parents were just shy of earning college degrees themselves, Risala believes there was an unspoken expectation that he and his siblings would be college graduates. Risala notes that there was a great emphasis on going to school and getting good grades or risk a "whuppin'." Risala is affectionate and matter-of-fact when he talks about his parents' disciplinary tactics when he was a child. "Parents in the late '70s and '80s, they were different. They ruled with a heavy hand. It wasn't like it is today. They said it was 'my way or the highway.'"

Risala was bright and excelled in school when he applied himself. He craved attention, however, and resorted to becoming a class clown, which ultimately took precedence over academics. Risala laughs, "If someone was going to give me attention for it, I was going to do it!"

When Risala was ten years old, his parents separated, and though they moved a mere five minutes apart, the separation impacted family dynamics. Risala's father to this day blames himself for breaking up the nuclear family. Risala lived primarily with his mother, who was notably more lenient than his father. Risala's older brother left home at fourteen, and his younger sister was only a toddler at the time of the divorce, which made Risala feel that he needed to be the man of the house, while at the same time, he had a lot of freedom to find trouble.

Risala was introduced to drugs when he was fourteen years old as a dealer, but not a user. Risala's interest was piqued by the relative wealth of some of the guys in the neighborhood. He found out how easy it was to sell a rock of crack and make a quick thirty or forty dollars. Although Risala was from a solidly middle-class household, and he knew that "I didn't *need* to be selling no drugs," he was smitten by the allure of easy money. He started selling drugs at his middle school when he was in the seventh grade, and by the eighth grade, he was averaging $60 a week from drug sales. He pocketed the other $20 a week his mother gave him for lunch money. Risala kept the money hidden, but when his mother inevitably found out, she kicked him out of the house and he went to live with his father. Under his father's "iron fist," Risala says his grades went back up and he stayed out of trouble.

When he returned to his mother's house, she struggled to "keep the reins on me" and Risala returned to the streets. At fifteen years old, Risala got his then-girlfriend pregnant with their son, Miles. Risala was a teenage father, and his "foray into criminal activity" began in earnest, although he managed to complete high school. "When you're dealing drugs, you're courting the criminal lifestyle. I graduated from high school at 18 by this here little chin hair," he says, rubbing his chin ruefully.

Risala is remorseful and saddened by his contributions to the decline of northwest Pasadena in the 1990s, when gang and drug activity were at an all-time high.

> I had a moral compass but it was skewed. I was poisoning my own people. My uncle was a drug addict and I was furnishing his drugs myself! I was creating cancer in my own family. My own neighborhood.

At the time, being his uncle's drug dealer did not give him much pause, as his ultimate goal during this period was "probably just trying to make money." Drug dealers and gang members could afford a glamorous lifestyle and were considered respectable and aspirational role models in the neighborhood, second only to athletes, especially football and basketball stars.

> When you introduce these things to a young African American boy in the hood, education takes a backburner. I didn't care about education. I wanted to be rich. I wanted to be the guy with all the money and all the girls. We looked up to football players. Basketball players. Even the track guy. If you don't make it at that, then drugs are next. You don't have too many [people saying] "Hey, who's this real estate guy? Or who is that guy who owns a successful franchise?" It's funny and it's sad that it was like this, but we didn't have too many positive idols to look up to in the hood. Athletes? Rappers? Other than that, it was the drug dealers.

Risala's mother encouraged him to attend Pasadena City College after graduating high school, but his response was, "Nah, I'm good." He was making $100 to $200 a day selling drugs and because he was a "hustler," he was always working other jobs as well. He worked at the local hardware store before getting caught pilfering from the cash register. He parked cars at the Rose Bowl, sold flowers on the side of the road, and even had a prestigious internship with the Jet Propulsion Lab. "But—I was in the mix," Risala says. "Ten months after graduating high school, my life crime happened."

THE CRIME

In his young street life, Risala obtained a firearm. And then, he started thinking that he could rob people. At this point in the interview, Risala shakes his head and leans forward across the table agitated. "I didn't *need* to be robbing anyone!" he shouts. Risala's younger self causes an adult Risala a lot of frustration and consternation.

The night of the crime was like one big party. In the flush of excitement, Risala suggested going to North Hollywood to commit a robbery against someone he knew. They picked up a friend in Highland Park, and someone Risala didn't even know hopped into the car, too. They all drove to North Hollywood, music blaring and firearms in the trunk. When they arrived in North Hollywood, Risala was still in the car when a scuffle ensued and his friend shot and killed the man they had intended to rob.

Risala was only eighteen at the time. His son, Miles, was two.

PRISON

Risala had never been to jail before he was sent to prison with an LWOP sentence. Although he used marijuana daily and drank alcohol, he did not use the drugs he sold. He carried a firearm, but he had never shot anyone. In the face of a life-without-parole sentence, Risala's parents hired a high-powered defense team, who argued with him to identify the actual shooter and take a deal for fifteen years to life. Risala refused.

> I didn't know nuthin' about nuthin'. One thing I don't do is tell. I went through this big whole emotional thing, but in my mind—snitches get stitches. They were trying to pressure me to tell. They said, "Mr. Rose, we know you didn't do it. You don't even have a record." And then they were like, "Okay, you don't want to tell? You want to be thug about it?" So I went to trial. I got murder robbery. Life without possibility of parole.

Risala was stunned. He had regrets about the man who was murdered and his family, but he didn't feel he deserved the sentence he received. In the beginning, Risala could not fathom that he had an LWOP sentence, and he spent his early days "just living the existence, knowing something had to change." For years, he hoped he could file an appeal or receive a sentence commutation, but at some point, it felt like he was wasting time. "Life without," Risala says, "is a slow death sentence."

Risala denied culpability for a very long time. After all, he was not the one who pulled the trigger. In fact, he never got out of the car. Sometime several years into his prison sentence, however, Risala recognized how his actions and choices that fateful night contributed to the untimely death of an innocent victim. Today, his voice goes quiet with regret and sorrow.

> I think about him [the victim] sometimes. He was thirty-something years old. I think he'd be somewhere in his sixties now. He had a two-year-old son, too. So somewhere out there is a thirty-something-year-old kid who is missing his father.

HOPE

Without a doubt, Risala knows what sustained him during his thirty years of incarceration. "I always had hope," he says.

> I never lost hope. Know why? Because I had *family*! I had regular visits. My parents would drive up from Pasadena. They would pick up my daughter to come and visit me. They came to Calipatria. Tehachapi. Lancaster. My mother came. My father. My cousins from New York came. I didn't need nothing for thirty years. We're not rich, but I always got packages.

His two children sustained him, too, and helped him focus on the future. His son was two years old when Risala began his life sentence, and he had a new baby girl who was seven months old. Although she only knew her dad as an incarcerated person, Risala felt fortunate to have established a strong relationship with her over the years. "My daughter would always ask when I was getting out. Or why I couldn't come to the father–daughter dance [at school]." She told him things he wasn't always totally prepared for, either, like when she started menstruating and when she lost her virginity at sixteen.

Risala had hope, but sometimes he felt like he was looking down an "opaque tunnel." About twenty years into his life sentence, and six months before he was transferred to Lancaster, Risala's daughter was killed in a tragic hit-and-run; a few years later, his son was killed in a robbery. With raw vulnerability, Risala shared the story of his loss as part of a class performance, *Imagine That!*, which was performed several times between 2017 and 2018.

Tragically, I lost both of my children within the last seven years. I envisioned my own daughter. Maccaia was killed by a hit-and-run driver here in Lancaster in 2011. She was only 18 years old, and attended Antelope Valley Junior College. Miles was gunned down in Tarzana in 2016 in a robbery. He was 26 years old. At times, I found myself lost in emotions, due to the physical loss of both of my kids. It is imperative that higher education be stressed to our youth, especially our inner-city youth. (Rose-Aminifu, unpublished performances, 2017–2018)

THE ROAD TO COLLEGE

When Risala arrived at Lancaster's Honor Yard, he ran into a student who would later be part of Cal State LA's Cohort 1, Jimmie Gilmer. He had first met Jimmie at another prison many years prior and was impressed by the change he saw in him. Jimmie was a serious student and spent a lot of time on the yard proselytizing about education. When Risala and Jimmie reconnected in 2012, Risala had his high school diploma but no community college credits under his belt. With Jimmie's encouragement, Risala enrolled in correspondence courses with Coastline Community College.

Coastline courses were not particularly difficult for him, but Risala recognized that a student could really learn something if he was willing to apply himself. Risala applied himself because he liked the challenge and he enjoyed learning. He felt that Coastline helped him to be a more proficient writer, and it offered him a positive distraction instead of just an existence on the prison yard.

Risala's blunt assessment of his early days on the Honor Yard differed from every other student I spoke with. "I didn't like it," Risala says flatly. "A Yard was *weird* to me. Guys laying on the grass with no shoes! Everyone talking about what their crime was and all that! And yet it was still prison, there were still drugs, cellphones, and stuff going on. I was like, 'I can't *stand* this! Let me go back to D Yard (a general population yard).'"

Despite his initial reservations, Risala spent his last nine years of incarceration on Lancaster's A Yard. It took him nearly two years to get used to the dynamics. Jimmie advised him to "just chill," so he tried to do just that. He worked out every day and got a job in the kitchen, soon rising to become the lead cook. He stayed out of trouble by focusing on his reading and classroom assignments.

Deep down, Risala always knew he wanted to better his education. He was inspired, in part, by his siblings. His older brother graduated from USC, and his sister was on the honor roll at a Midwestern university. Both of them went on to become teachers, and Risala was energized by their success.

While Risala worked on his associate of arts degree from Coastline, he kept an eye on Cal State LA's first cohort of the Prison BA Graduation Initiative. He was astounded when he heard the program was free, especially knowing that his brother still owed close to $100,000 for his USC degree. He was impressed when he saw Cal State LA faculty coming to the yard every week. "I was like, 'Professors coming up here teaching us?!' I watched Cohort 1, and damn, it was like getting a visit every time. But an educational visit!" He watched the success and transformation of the Cohort 1 students and heard rumors that a second cohort was starting. With some encouragement from Jimmie and others, Risala decided he wanted to be a part of it and managed to wrangle the last spot in Cohort 2.

THE CHANGE

Risala is high energy and a fast talker, but he is *extra*-animated when he talks about how gaining a college education has impacted him. He is especially enthusiastic when he talks about how being a college student helped him to open his mind and change his "warped" mentality. "Once I got ushered into the BA program, my mindset changed," he gushes. Before he was a part of the Prison BA Graduation Initiative, Risala adhered to the deeply ingrained prison culture of self-segregating racial and ethnic groups. The Cal State LA cohorts, however, were extremely diverse. Small-group exercises and activities required students to work collaboratively with other men from different racial backgrounds, ages, and sexual identities. The students worked so closely together that they quickly began to refer to each other as "brothers" and "family."

> I learned about different people and their upbringing and experiences. I learned about the Cambodian [refugee] experience. I learned about Tin's experience with Immigration [Services]. Learned about different people and their upbringings. [I started realizing] that we are just human beings. I learned that race is a fake construct. I'd never thought about these things before. But, I was like, "Damn! You're right!"

Risala pauses and looks at the huge photo propped against my office wall. It is a candid photo of Cohort 1 students embracing each other in a spontaneous group hug, huge smiles on every face. "I'm looking at all of these guys. This picture says a lot. All those guys—to see the interaction, even if they didn't like each other sometimes—they teamed up to get it *done*. I may have never met or talked to [these guys] outside of this program."

Figure 9.1 L-R: Larry Torres, Risala Rose-Aminifu, and Ninh Nguyen celebrate after a performance before friends and family. Photo: R. Husky, 2019. Courtesy of California State University, Los Angeles.

Although this level of racial mixing was new and initially uncomfortable for Risala, in the end, he exclaims, "I loved it! That helped me to come around, too. [Cal State LA] helped me unpack that and be more accepting. People can be who they want to be. I started being more accepting." Soon after Risala came home, he counseled a family member who was worried about the gender identity of his son, using the lessons he had learned from his Cal State LA classmates and professors. "I told him, 'Just be accepting. Just love him.'"

He loved all of his professors, too, and especially appreciated the exposure to their distinct teaching styles and different ways of thinking. He remembers a profound moment when lecturer Sara Black intertwined a life lesson within a teaching lesson, and he was deeply moved. Risala is fully appreciative of every faculty member who came to the yard. "It took a lot of courage for you all to come and teach us all in the blue suits."

The Cal State LA professors pushed him in a way that he was unaccustomed to in correspondence community college. When the BA program started, he considered himself a good student, but getting constructive feedback on his assignments turned out to be an unexpected yet meaningful experience. "To get checked—that was humbling," Risala says, referring to the comments he would get on his written assignments. "But that way, we knew you guys were interested in us. You guys don't know, but you treated us like human beings and that helped with our morale."

And then there were the performances. When he heard about narrative and drama therapy, he says his first reaction was, "Dammnnnn, this is some deep shit!" He was still processing the death of his daughter when he was asked to read aloud a piece that he had written about her. He found himself choking up as he read, and then heard the applause and cheers from his classmates when he finished reading. He realized that he had not told them what was going on with him and did not know the amount of support he had from his cohort. He says he did not know how much he had needed the release.

The performances were therapeutic. These people had me talk about deep-rooted trauma that I never would have talked about if I wasn't in education. There are so many people who say, "What did education *do* for you?" And I say, "Well, education made me open up about people's losses and past traumas, it made me open up. We had straight talk about racism in prison, sexuality, and political issues. Basically, [the writing and performances] helps you see yourself through other people's lives. This was all in our education. Those plays made me feel a sense of family and community. I still have them on my phone.

Risala also credits the bachelor's degree program and the drama therapy with helping him remove the mask that he had been unknowingly wearing for nearly thirty years.

I started shedding my mask on A Yard. You know, at prison, we're all wearing masks. People say, "Be who you want to be." You can be whoever you want to be. But then I started realizing, damn! I could just be myself. I don't need to be a tough guy. I don't need to say I'm active in the Black Party—whatever mask I wanted to put on that day. I don't need to put on a mask. And I'm a damn good actor. I just don't need to wear a mask anymore, because after 30 years, I realized I was acting the whole prison experience. College helped me understand that.

As the BA program went on, men on Lancaster's Honors Yard started seeing sentences get overturned, and LWOPs were getting out through commutations signed by then-governor Jerry Brown. The Honors Yard benefited not only from Cal State LA's Prison BA Graduation Initiative but also a wide range of programs, including Paws for Life, Insight Garden, and GOGI (Getting Out by Going In), in addition to a myriad of self-help groups started and facilitated by the inmates themselves. Risala says that he believes that Cal

State LA was "instrumental" in the evolution of Lancaster's Honors Yard. To Risala and others with LWOP sentences, the tunnel seemed a little less opaque.

> My state of mind is changing. Guys are getting degrees! Guys are going home! I'm hopeful, but I still don't entirely see the horizon. But I know that sometimes, if you do good, good stuff happens.

THE SKY'S THE LIMIT

Risala was released in May 2021 after serving thirty years in prison. He came home during the tail end of the COVID quarantine, when Cal State LA classes on the main campus were still largely virtual. Almost immediately, he started volunteering daily for the university, enthusiastically staffing a Cal State LA swag booth at the campus's COVID vaccination site, where he gleefully engaged students and community members. He quickly found a full-time job working the graveyard shift driving trucks, sometimes for more than sixty hours per week. He finished his required communication degree classes without fuss and enrolled in a pan-African studies class to fulfill an elective requirement and perhaps to pay homage to his parents, who once focused on pan-African studies on this very campus many years ago.

He graduated with his bachelor's degree in communication in June 2022. His family was ecstatic and enjoyed bragging about him. He reports that they crowed, "Look at him, he's fresh out and he's already got a bachelor's degree!" A news article featured his story, and his picture is all over social media. He loves to tell people that he started his college education in prison and that the cost of the program was free to him. There is still good-natured ribbing among his parents and siblings, feigned jealousy over the discrepancy in tuition between the Cal State LA BA program and what his brother still owes to USC. His outlook on life was changing. "I can do whatever I want!"

From the start, Risala has felt a tinge of guilt that he has a well-paying union job but doesn't feel that he is "using" his degree in any meaningful way. Many have assured him that when management opportunities open up, his communication degree and combined work experience will make him a very viable candidate. He worries about his decision to pause on pursuing a master's degree right away but also recognizes that he wanted to take a step back and get some perspective on what he really wants to do in the future.

In October 2021, Risala and nine men from Cohorts 1 and 2 who had been released returned to Lancaster State Prison to watch their fellow cohort members receive their bachelor's degrees behind bars. It was a hot and dusty day, but there was nothing that could quell the excitement of the graduating students and their families. For Risala, however, the day offered a painful reminder of where he once was and a guilt-ridden desire to pack up his friends and classmates and take them home. "I felt like crying walking out. I almost felt sick."

Although he worries that he will lose momentum if he takes too long of a break before starting a graduate degree, he also knows that he has some catching up to do. "Right now, I've got a relationship. Work. Bills. I'm just trying to juggle life. And everything is new to me! First car! First apartment!" Risala says. He's cooking meals. Freshly off parole in 2023, he's started traveling to faraway places.

He also can't help himself from comparing where he is to friends who never went to prison, and he senses a need to catch up and capture the American Dream. His dreams include starting his own business. Perhaps a truck driving company where he's hiring formerly incarcerated drivers. Or maybe a catering truck where he's cooking again. He wants to own a home, but he emphasizes he has no desire to be rich, only comfortable. He imagines retiring by the time he's sixty-five years old, fifteen years from now.

Risala sighs happily at the end of the interview, reviewing all of the topics we've touched upon in roughly two hours. "I just want to say that education helped me to find my humanity. And now—the sky is the limit."

Figure 9.2 Risala Rose-Aminifu walks the commencement stage to receive his diploma in 2022. Photo: E. Flores, 2022. Courtesy of California State University, Los Angeles.

Figure 9.3 Risala Rose-Aminifu celebrates his graduation with his family. Photo: S. Kellis, 2022.

NOTE

1. All quotes in this chapter are from this interview, unless otherwise noted.

Chapter 10

Jeff Stein

Name:	Jeff Stein
Age:	Fifty-two
Race/Ethnicity:	White
Sentence:	Seven to life, plus three years
Years Incarcerated:	Ten and a half
Released:	January 2019
Year Graduated:	2020, BA
	2022, MA
Interview:	July 7, 2023[1]

On a warm spring Saturday in early 2017, a troupe of Cal State LA music students hopped into a rusty van to ride to Lancaster and perform an original pop opera for the incarcerated students there. The show touched on issues of bisexuality, transgenderedness, family conflict, and the challenges of being human. The performers were nervous and often off-key, and one singer in particular, a middle-aged woman with a heavy accent, struggled throughout the show.

At the end of the pop opera, the music students sat in a row across the stage and opened themselves up to questions. There was a long silence, and I worried the men could not find anything polite to say. My heart was pounding when Jeff finally stood up and addressed the middle-aged woman directly. With a warm smile, Jeff told her that her performance had stood out to him for its poignancy and raw emotion. In that moment, he did what I have seen him do time and time again—he led with empathy and kindness.

Jeff usually has a perpetual grin plastered across his face, and he exudes buoyant enthusiasm. He is loyal to a fault, consistently seeks the good in all people, and is generous and kind at the expense of himself. Jeff is clearly a child of Orange County from the '70s and '80s because he still peppers his everyday conversation with relics of bygone days, such as "That's so rad!" or "Gnarly, dude!"

As the second student to parole midway during the bachelor's degree program, Jeff's positive attitude and patient disposition worked in his favor when he was released in 2019. Cal State LA always had the best intentions of ensuring a seamless reentry and transition experience for all of our students, but in the early days, I confess I had no idea what I was doing nor any sense of the challenges that lay ahead. Jeff was the canary in the coal mine.

I was the first person Jeff reached out to outside of family after he walked off the prison premises, and I still remember feeling my neck prickling with sweat when Jeff called me from his sister's cellphone to say that he had not been assigned to Cavanagh House, the transition home within walking distance from the Cal State LA campus, as planned. Instead, he'd been sent to a bustling dormitory of parolees located in the San Fernando Valley. "It's worse than *prison*, Taffany!" he groaned. "It's like 'Lord of the Flies' in there." I became nauseous with the imagery.

Fortunately, we had J. D. Hughes on our team. A former correctional officer with CDCR and a onetime parole agent, J. D. had been helping us navigate the intricacies of establishing a bachelor's degree program on a maximum-security prison yard since 2016, and now he was using his same charming drawl and unwavering doggedness to figure out how to bring our students home as painlessly as possible. J. D. got Jeff switched to Cavanagh House within twenty-four hours. Yet there were so many other things for me to learn, and Jeff has cheerfully led the way ever since. After graduating, he was hired as the Cal State LA Project Rebound outreach coordinator, and the fact that the program now successfully serves approximately 150 formerly incarcerated students per semester is due in large part to our learning firsthand from Jeff's earliest challenges and experiences.

Jeff was in constant motion while earning his bachelor's and master's degrees from Cal State LA. He juggled three jobs at a time while he was in graduate school (not until after he graduated did we learn about state programs that would pay grad school tuition for formerly incarcerated students). Sometimes, he would meander into my office, his eyes hollow and his face bloated from exhaustion, yet still ready to serve. He maintains a strong work ethic and gratitude for all of the second chances and help he has had in his own life, which prevents him from ever saying no.

Jeff's commitment to personal inner growth and his ongoing emotional development means that he feels deeply and tears up often, which he did several times throughout the interview, especially when he reflected on some of the people who had made a difference in his life, fueling his commitment to all of the students who are gratefully following in his footsteps.

EARLY SCHOOL YEARS

Jeff's parents met as teenagers in juvenile hall. His father was there for ditching school, his mother for running away from an abusive stepfather. Both of them became troubled drug addicts; neither of them would graduate high school. Jeff recalls moving a lot as a child, often falling asleep in one place and waking up in another. "My dad would take me from my mom or vice versa. The other would just be popping too many pills and not be taking care of business. And the other one would be a little more sober than the other, I guess, so they'd come to get me."

Jeff says there was often havoc no matter where he was. "I remember having to step over a passed-out biker. He was face-first in the gravel driveway, holding a Budweiser bottle. He had a long ponytail and cutoffs—that was all he was wearing—and I just had to step over him to get out to the street to go to school."

Despite the chaotic living conditions, Jeff maintains that his parents gave him an important bedrock in his foundation: he knew that he was loved.

> I experienced dysfunctional but unconditional love from my family and whoever was taking care of me at the time when my parents couldn't. I knew I was loved, even though things were fucked up. I never felt *not* loved by my parents, you know? And, you know, to the best of their ability, they told me good things about myself. They never told me "You're stupid!" or "You're a piece of shit" or "You'll never amount to anything." They never told me anything like that. They were teenagers when I was born; they did the best they friggin' could and I understood all that later in life. So I was able to make peace with having a less than ideal origin.

Jeff describes his school-age years as "really cool." He had nice, caring teachers who told him that he was smart, a soundtrack that played repeatedly in his head, which gave him academic confidence. Jeff also enjoyed the social aspects of school because it was a "safe" place that gave him reprieve from the "chaos and dysfunction" of his home life.

> Looking back, I realize all I ever wanted was to be safe and happy. So I liked school because no one ever ODed there. Nobody got raided there. Nobody got into ugly arguments.

School could not completely shield him from the turmoil and mayhem that characterized his parents' lives. When Jeff was thirteen, his father failed to wake up from a fatal combination of drugs and alcohol. From then on, his mother's addictions escalated so much that Jeff estimates she was in jail for nine of the next ten years. Jeff, who is the oldest of four siblings, bounced around between friends and family until he was finally emancipated at eighteen.

HIGH SCHOOL

Jeff was a talented athlete who excelled in track, wrestling, and football. A coach scouted him out and told him that he could possibly earn a track scholarship at a University of California (UC) school. To meet the UC entrance requirements, Jeff started taking prerequisite classes such as geometry and trigonometry. The classes, which required daily attention to homework, were a struggle for Jeff because he says he "just wasn't that type of student." Jeff was not an irresponsible student, however, saying he rarely ditched classes (unless, of course, "the sun was shining and the beach was calling") because he didn't want to jeopardize school or sports. "High school was really awesome. None of the street life stuff was there. And I could pass as someone with a normal background because I was good at sports and I was sociable."

Jeff was careful to hide his true-life circumstances from everyone but his closest friends and instead adopted strategies that would help him "pass" among his peers and their parents. Jeff says he often had "normal" girlfriends in high school—young women who came from nuclear families and grew up in the same home their entire lives. Rather than attempt to explain the details of his situation, Jeff said it was easier to say his mother and father had died in a car crash.

While he still managed to do well in school, he admits with some chagrin that he was arrested at least once every summer between the ages of thirteen and seventeen, usually for fighting. Jeff was very tall as a teenager and had a penchant for protecting others from bullies or older kids with a mean streak. Although he claims he was never the one to start a fight, he also realized he never lost one, either.

> I think around thirteen, I sprouted up to where I was almost as tall as I am today. Some of the older kids that were bullies probably didn't know I was only thirteen when they were probably seventeen. And then I was fighting adults and winning. And I remember saying to myself around that time, "From this point on, no one's adding to my grief."

For the most part, the grief in Jeff's young life remained unprocessed and suppressed. The loss of his father and his mother's drug addiction compounded the instability of his living situation throughout high school. During the summer between his sophomore and junior year, Jeff and his younger brother lived with their aunt and uncle, who, Jeff surmises, "just couldn't handle it."

Soon after their arrival, the aunt and uncle sent Jeff's younger brother to an orphanage and Jeff to an emancipation program that would free him of his mother's custody. Perhaps he would have benefited if he had chosen to stick with the program, but he found it too restrictive and stifling. Jeff soon quit the emancipation program and walked out.

Jeff started smoking marijuana regularly, which caused a notable academic and personal decline during his senior year. At the time, he thought he was just "having fun," not recognizing that it had become a tool to help him cope with a lifetime of challenges and traumas. While weed dulled some of his pain and anxiety, it also contributed to a series of bad choices. During the middle of senior year, Jeff left his foster parents to move in with his girlfriend. He got into scores of "gnarly" street fights, and one was violent enough that he was accused of assault and battery. His motivation dropped and his grades slid as he spent half his senior year going to court for the incident. All the dreams and aspirations he had for himself as an athlete disappeared.

Jeff did not graduate from high school his senior year.

ADULTHOOD

Four or five years after he was supposed to have graduated from high school, Jeff enrolled in continuation school and knocked out the remaining sixteen units he needed to earn his diploma. His dreams for the future had warped, and his biggest was "just to be normal."

> I always felt disenfranchised. I didn't realize that maybe half of society is made up of people who don't have storybook lives. I thought I was the anomaly, or that I was in a very small number of people who had a difficult life. But I was just like, "Fuck! I just want to be normal and fit in here!" I just could never ask for help. I internalized that whole "rugged individualist" thing. Now I know that whatever happened to me can happen across all socioeconomic statuses.

Jeff started growing and selling weed for a short while, but when he became a parent at the age of twenty-two, he decided he needed a stable income and a regular schedule. He had just broken up with his girlfriend when they found out that she was pregnant. She wanted an abortion, but Jeff asked her to reconsider. "I don't want to tell you what to do. But I'm the oldest of four and I have a nurturing nature. So, if you don't want to have an abortion, I can handle this."

And he handled it well, indeed. Jeff was a single father until his son turned nine. He would drop his son off at daycare in the morning, and his mother would watch his son later in the afternoon. Jeff worked in construction and in restaurants, often pulling double shifts. He enrolled in community college, thinking that he would become a physician's assistant. He was on the dean's list the first few semesters.

Jeff traded "weed for speed" in an attempt to help manage his hectic schedule as a father, student, and construction worker, but he didn't realize that his productivity bottomed out. He did his best to minimize his son's exposure to his drug use and the shady characters of the "speed scene." Jeff, worried about his son and recognizing that he was physically and mentally depleted, managed to stop the downward spiral and quit using speed for five years. Even after quitting, though, Jeff knew that he was not leading a productive life.

> I was totally underachieving. I was working under the table. I had a construction job that was paying good cash, but no benefits. Nothing towards Social Security. No 401(k). Looking back now, it was an extremely bad deal for me. But I could do construction without having to deal with a lot of other things. So I was definitely underachieving—not even coming close to my potential. I was just getting by.

Jeff tried to prod himself into action. He told himself that he needed to go back to school, but "life kept happening." Then, in a series of calamitous events, Jeff's safety net collapsed. His car broke down, and he couldn't afford to fix it. Without a car, he was unable to get to work. Without work, he couldn't make the rent on his apartment. Without a stable place to live, Jeff was forced to send his son to live with his former girlfriend. Jeff was heartbroken.

THE CRIME

Jeff says the three years after he gave up his son were a self-destructive spiral fueled by drug abuse and despair.

> I was self-medicating like crazy because I felt I had failed in life. I would always tell myself that I'd get it together next week. And literally, those three years went by in a blink. Like a total time warp. Time wasn't linear then—it was just like a sidebar from life. Looking back, I realize I was hurting so much inside and that stuff was just to numb the pain.

Jeff found construction work in the high desert of San Bernardino County, and without the responsibility of his son to temper him, he started using speed again. He became a fixture on the "speed scene" after work, hanging around bikers and gang members. One day, Jeff's propensity for fighting was tapped again when he heard about a guy who had "punched out my home girl and pulled a knife on her teenage daughter."

> I did have a mean streak, I guess, because I would say to myself that it's okay to prey on the predator. There were times I'd fight five, six, seven people at a time and I wouldn't even get hit. There's a certain kind of adrenaline—where time slows in the situation after you've done it a few times to where there's a calm about it. But not in this particular situation with that guy, because I was scared out of the dickens. Because I knew what he was and I knew what he'd done.

Jeff confronted the guy who had hurt his friend alone and, to ensure that he would never come after Jeff or his friend again, Jeff did enough bodily damage that the guy had to be hospitalized; Jeff was arrested two days later. He was assigned a public defender who, Jeff would later learn, lost more than 80 percent of his cases. Jeff was sentenced to seven years to life for aggravated mayhem, plus three years for great bodily injury and a drug possession charge that he had previously dodged. He was thirty-seven years old, and it was his first time in prison.

PRISON: HOPE LOST

The last time Jeff would get in a fight was in 2008 while awaiting sentencing in county jail. After that, Jeff looked into developing other coping strategies. "I had to find another way to resolve conflict because I wasn't going to spend five more minutes in there [prison] than I had to, because those conditions were so detestable." Jeff had used speed for the last time in July 2008, the day before he was arrested. In the bowels of county jail in November 2008, Jeff drank pruno (prison wine), which he describes as "like the Devil's own hot piss," and never drank it again. Even though he had cellies who regularly indulged in front of him, Jeff had lost all temptation. He eschewed drugs, violence, illegal cellphones, racial politics, and anything else that would interfere with his "1,000 percent commitment" to not spending more time in prison than he had to.

Jeff spent his first two years in county jail and at Tehachapi prison, where his entire physical and mental focus was on survival. He grappled to make sense of his situation.

> I struggled because on the one hand, I felt like there's no way in the deep-down depths that this was my ultimate destiny. Some type of intuition from God [was]

telling me that there was a way out of this. But also, there was overwhelming anecdotal evidence from people [telling me otherwise]. I ran into a cranky old bastard at Lancaster who had a seven-to-life sentence just like me, but he was on year forty-one! I also found out that with previous California governors, nobody got out. Even if they'd made a complete transformation.

I heard about someone who wrote to the parole board and basically said, "Look—let's just spare us all." He asked to be euthanized, basically. I honestly thought about that—I didn't want to waste food or air or bed space. I considered it not out of depression, although I was depressed. I just thought about what's the noble thing to do? Like, if I'm done—if it's over—I don't want to waste whatever resources on the planet or be a burden to taxpayers.

Jeff had lost hope.

Then one day, he suddenly pushed himself to make a change and committed himself to running the track, getting sunshine, eating lots of veggies (including the ones his friends didn't want to eat), drinking water, and focusing on his spirituality. He decided that he would "manifest mental positivity."

His improving attitude and good behavior got him transferred to Lancaster's A Yard. During his first few minutes on the famed Honor Yard, he spied men sunbathing, practicing yoga, and walking around barefoot: a carceral environment unlike anything he had ever seen before. He took a few months to acclimate and to "get the lay of the land" before he started talking to some of the men on the yard. Among them, he befriended mentors, role models, and sages who encouraged him to be "the best version of myself I could be."

I was just trying to make sense of what I could do with what was left of my time on earth. It wasn't until I got to A Yard that I realized I could live like a human being to some degree. I saw there was an infrastructure for me to take a path where maybe I'd never get out of prison, but I would die closer to who I was supposed to be than who I was. And that was worth the journey.

There were many men on the yard who helped and inspired him, but he remembers Dortell Williams's encouragement and grace more than anyone else's. Jeff tears up with affection when he reflects on the gifts that "D" gave him:

Looking back—I wasn't from his neighborhood. I wasn't his paint job. But he took the time and he had nothing to get out of it other than make a positive difference by helping me to get on the right path.

The right path included pursuing higher education. From Dortell, he learned that college was on that yard, so he enrolled in some classes from Coastline

Community College. He borrowed someone's textbook and got an A in his class on mass communication. With the encouragement of Dortell and the other men around him, Jeff was determined to "extract the positive" out of his time in prison, including earning his associate of arts degree.

In his third year of incarceration, Jeff reached a fork in the road. His latest appeal had been denied, and he had an opportunity to file yet again. Jeff looked over at the men who were hunched over in the prison law library, desperately trying to find some kind of loophole for themselves, and frantically filing papers and briefs in an attempt to get themselves free. Jeff asked himself if he, too, wanted to invest all of his time into finding some way to wriggle out of his predicament. Or, he figured he could take as many self-help and college classes as he could to be "the best version of me."

> Either way, if I was going to get any action or any kind of break in my sentence, it would coincide with the minimum amount of time I had left to serve. I still had seven and a half years before I would be parole eligible. I had to ask myself, "Am I factually innocent? Well, no . . ." The bottom line was that I just wished I was in less trouble. So I decided to take the path of self-growth and trust God that it was going to work out.

Figure 10.1 Jeff Stein accompanies cohorts 1 and 2 on guitar as they perform at California State Prison Los Angeles. Photo: R. Huskey, 2019. Courtesy of California State University, Los Angeles.

TRANSFORMATION

Jeff availed himself of the peer-to-peer self-help classes that were abundant on the Honor Yard at the time, surprised by how helpful they were in addressing addiction, the roots of criminality, and trauma. Jeff found a silver lining in his long incarceration, admitting that prison took him "off the hamster wheel" of everyday life and gifted him some time and space to focus on his self-awareness and healing.

Shortly before Jeff completed his associate's degree with Coastline, a trusted leader on the yard, Ken "Horse" Hartman, told him that the Cal State LA's bachelor's degree program was starting and he should get his application in to join the first cohort. Jeff jumped at the opportunity.

> For me, it was vindicating. That little Coastline degree was the first positive thing I started and finished in maybe my whole adult life. That degree was the first thing I worked hard on over a long period of time from start to finish. I completed a cycle. And now I'm gonna have a chance to possibly leave with a bachelor's degree? It was huge because my parents didn't graduate high school. And I knew this would help transcend my status as someone who had contact with the justice system if I ever did get out. And deep down, I always knew—I always had this intuition—we're getting out. We're going home.

It was challenging at first. Most of his classmates had taken the majority of their classes via correspondence courses, and they immediately noticed that face-to-face instruction was more rigorous, especially in writing. Jeff and his cohort were undaunted.

> I knew this new version of me finishes what I start. I was more concerned with the externals—the guards stonewalling us or the administration killing it or something. But the degree of what was within my purview? I knew that I could do it. I knew that I could finish. It just took a lot of coffee and a lot of commitment.

Jeff's defining, transformative moment happened during one of the first Cal State LA classes. While reading James Baldwin, a quote resonated deeply with him: "People pay for what they do, and, still more, for what they have allowed themselves to become. And they pay for it very simply: by the lives they lead" (Baldwin 1972, 55). Jeff infused his personal values and decision-making, both inside and outside prison, with its substance. Jeff decided he would live a life that leads by example and in service to others.

On a practical level, Jeff is confident that the class readings and discussions helped him and his classmates improve their communication and problem-solving skills. To this day, he says different readings "permeate and roll around in my brain," providing a mental toolbox that he can access to successfully engage with students, faculty, friends, family, and the public alike.

TRANSFORMATION AND HOPE

Jeff often says, however, that the most impactful element of the bachelor's degree program was the "humanness, decency, kindness, and empathy of the instructors." From them, he learned that he, too, could be an empathetic ally. The connections that were cultivated in the classroom between the cohort and faculty were made more powerful because of their shared experience.

> That helped me on an overall human level. I kind of noticed that I had a feeling of disconnect from the rest of society and humanity because I had a fucked-up upbringing that I thought was rare or unique. I felt like a stowaway—just disenfranchised and not part of it all. So I worked on that and emotional intelligence and on cultivating empathy, and that helped me feel more connected to everyone everywhere.

Jeff notes that the presence of Cal State LA faculty at Lancaster created a positive ripple effect that stretched well beyond the students themselves. He would often overhear other men on the yard talking about Macbeth even though they weren't enrolled in any classes, an example of how college was permeating the culture of the prison.

> The bachelor's degree program manifested itself into reality, in a space and time when hope was either gonna bloom or perish because of trends within the corrections world. So, the very existence of the program and that people could wake up and see people attending classes and events related to it . . . [i]t ruptures the narrative, the limiting narrative of what it means to be a justice-involved person. It absolutely expands their horizon beyond being a number and defined as the worst thing they ever did. (J. Stein, pers. comm., March 9, 2020)

There has been a ripple effect within his own family, as well. Although his siblings have not continued beyond high school, Jeff's niece-in-law from Florida is looking at going to nursing school in the near future. His brother-in-law is awed by the accomplishments of Jeff and his classmates, inspired and surprised by "how much positivity there was in a freakin' Level 4 prison" (J. Stein, pers. comm., 2019). Jeff anticipates there will be more long-term ripple effects down the road.

> Besides being the first person in my immediate family to have a college degree, I [also have the opportunity to] put something on the family tree besides

addiction, or being an orphan—all this bad shit. Now, I'm starting to put some other leaves on the tree. In just one generation, we can mitigate or erase the dysfunctionality of the prior generations.

GRADUATE

Shortly after earning his bachelor's degree in December 2019, Jeff was asked how he felt about the accomplishment.

> I mean, I have a beautifully framed degree that I can look at and stuff, but I hate to say it—I'm not satisfied with that. I want to move on to get a master's degree and maybe even a PhD program. It's taught me to not rest on my laurels. Yeah, that was accomplished and yeah, that was a monumental effort. Probably 20- or 30,000 pages of textbook reading and probably 100 papers written. Dozens of presentations, PowerPoints in public speaking events and conferences and panels. All that's done is make me a well-trained person ready to keep at it. (J. Stein, pers. comm., March 9, 2020)

In fact, Jeff did not rest on his laurels at all. Jeff was immediately accepted into Cal State LA's master's degree program in communication studies, which he completed in spring of 2022. He held part-time jobs with Cal State LA's Project Rebound and Amazon, and he was a graduate teaching assistant as well as a Comms instructor while he juggled a demanding, full-time graduate program. At times, he would stumble into the office, bleary-eyed and exhausted, but never once did anyone ever fear he would not excel or not finish the program. Those days are long behind him.

After earning his master's, he started working full-time for Cal State LA's Project Rebound program as the outreach coordinator. He tirelessly visits prisons, juvenile halls, nonprofit organizations, and community colleges to tell formerly incarcerated individuals that a bachelor's degree is within their reach and to support them along their journey. When necessary, Jeff will whip out one of his favorite mantras with potential students who may be battling their own anxieties and insecurities about college: "Your new life is gonna cost you one thing—your old one. And that's the best trade you'll ever make."

He's networking with other partners in the field and constantly seeking opportunities for collaboration. He's presenting at conferences and submitting articles for publication in journals. He won an award for innovation in the field of reentry. On a personal note, he says he's closer to his siblings than he ever was before, and he's slowly reconnecting with his son again. He recently married someone who is also a leader in the field of reentry and education.

Not until he was in prison in his forties would Jeff recognize the traumas that were rooted behind all of his behaviors.

Figure 10.2 Jeff Stein hooded, Master of Arts in Communication Studies, 2022. Photo: E. Flores, 2022. Courtesy of California State University, Los Angeles.

I have a protective nature . . . probably being the eldest of four and also being in an environment I couldn't control or protect my siblings or friends. I finally realized that all I ever wanted in my life was to be safe and happy, right? So to be safe, if someone presented to me as dangerous, I would uncork all I had on him. To be happy, I self-medicated because I didn't have the coping skills yet.

Figure 10.3 Dr. Nina O'Brien, Jeff Stein, and Dr. Cynthia Wang. Photo: S. Kellis, 2022.

Jeff sees more education in his future, but he also thinks about financial security and retirement. For now, he's taking things one step at a time. ·

> It's just been a huge blessing to have a redo because when I was younger, I always knew that I could do this but I didn't have the discipline or enough belief or faith in myself. . . . [Now I know] that I have what it takes and everything I've done prior has prepared me for anything coming next, even an EdD or PhD. I have the credentials on paper and the skill set within to do a lot of things. Including write a book or even a screenplay and stuff like that, which I'm kind of mulling over.
>
> I'm finally the big brother and the good example I should have always been; you know, it just took me a while to get here.

NOTE

1. All quotes in this chapter are from this interview, unless otherwise noted.

Chapter 11

Thomas Franklin Wheelock

Name:	Thomas Franklin Wheelock
Age:	Forty-six
Race/Ethnicity:	White
Sentence:	Life without parole
Years Incarcerated:	Twenty-three
Released:	August 14, 2020
Year Graduated:	2021
Date of Interview:	May 14, 2023[1]

Tommy was released during the COVID lockdown after serving twenty-three years in prison. The entire campus was shuttered, but I would often meet Tommy and a few other recently paroled students in the office, just so that they could have some sense of normalcy and connection as they transitioned into their new lives.

Tommy, Allen Burnett, and Tin Nguyen arrived to an eerily quiet and unpopulated campus. They had to navigate their final classes on a computer via Zoom, a stark contrast from the previous four years in face-to-face classes with professors and a strong support network in prison. Tommy completed his bachelor's degree on campus but elected not to participate in the graduation ceremony, which included nine of his cohort members. He started the Rehabilitative Counseling graduate program at Cal State LA but paused his studies after the first semester.

Tommy, who had a difficult and lonely childhood, is ecstatic when he describes the pleasure he finds in simple things such as family game nights or social outings. He recently celebrated his birthday with his fiancée and her children at Universal Studios, where they all donned Harry Potter costumes and playfully modeled their Hogwarts style throughout the park. Tommy has a new job doing reentry work with Paws for Life in a position that aligns with his skills and lived experience. After many hardships, challenges, and trial and error, he is finally finding his groove.

When Tommy arrives on campus for his interview, he looks around my office as I fiddle to get the computer and recording devices set up. He barely glances at the huge red-and-black afghan that adorns my wall, perhaps because he knows it so well. It was given to me as a gift from Cohort 1 in 2017, but it is widely known that Tommy took the lead on designing and crocheting the majority of the blanket. Instead, he is focused on a huge, poster-sized photo that is leaning along a shelf, a relic from a photo shoot with the California State University Chancellor's Office in 2019. It is a beautiful photo of the Cohort 1 students joyfully hugging each other, stunning in the raw openness of their emotions and the diversity of the men who are so freely holding each other.

"I love that picture," he remarks casually, as if he may have forgotten that he is in the middle of that huddle and it was his story that moved them all to embrace.

EARLY EDUCATION

Tommy struggled in school from the very start, describing his time in the first and second grade as "hell." He remembers that the letters on the chalkboard confused him and that he was constantly fidgety. His teachers sent notes home about his behavior, and sometimes he was sent to the principal's office. The kids teased him relentlessly so he attempted to deflect the negative attention by being the class clown.

In the fifth grade, Tommy was identified with a learning disability. What he remembers most about the diagnosis is how upset his mother was when they told her that he was going to be put in special education classes. She was, in his view, ashamed and embarrassed of her youngest son, whose two older siblings had a reputation for excelling in school and were extremely well behaved.

Tommy did not believe he belonged in fifth-grade special education classes either. The class was geared toward children with severe physical and mental disabilities, and the social isolation from his friends left him deeply ashamed. Tommy continued to flounder academically. He was moved to a parochial school at the end of the fifth grade, where they assessed his performance at a third-grade level. The nuns, frustrated with Tommy's classroom disruption, regularly delivered punishing raps on his hands and knuckles, scars from which still mark his fingers today.

Tommy began to rebel and act out at home, too. He remembers that he broke a lot of household items in fits of anger, and once thought nothing of smashing a television against the wall. He began a long pattern of self-abusive behavior, cutting and burning himself deeply. Around this time, Tommy's mother forbade him from coming into the house. She banished him to the backyard, where he slept and ate between the fifth and ninth grades.

Tommy does not recall doing any homework at this time, and although he felt that no one was willing to help him or cared about his schoolwork, he does remember that the only time he was allowed in the house was when report cards came. His siblings were straight-A students and were duly celebrated by his mother. Tommy failed all of his classes. He says he can still hear her screaming, "How can you do this to us?"

Tommy says, "I can still hear my mom's voice in my head, saying I was unwanted and unloved. I felt worthless. I felt like the child hidden beneath the stairs." The analogy of "the child beneath the stairs" is what has attracted Tommy to Harry Potter all along. "I instantly related with him."

> From the fourth grade until my sophomore year in high school, I didn't even try to learn, which is why I received failing grades. These feelings plagued me, causing me to develop a self-loathing image of myself. I dropped out of high school and eventually received a GED; I made a promise to myself to never have anything to do with school again, that's how bad of a taste school had left. I thought I would be happy being a blue-collar worker, but what I did not realize is that all of those years of being a quitter and having negative self-esteem issues would taint everything in my life. I lost jobs and I gave up on almost everything that was good, or too hard in my life. (T. Wheelock, pers. comm., 2017)

Tommy was too ashamed to tell anyone about his living situation, lying to friends about his circumstances. Tommy describes the period as "normal but abnormal" when he was sleeping unsheltered in the backyard, but he was deeply touched when his father helped him build a shack that provided him some shelter when he slept in his sleeping bag at night. The sheriff, who lived next door, would later tell investigators he had no idea that the neighbor boy was living in the backyard. Many years later, Tommy learned that his mother suffered from postpartum depression and mental illness, which would partially explain why he was treated so differently from his older siblings. He found out that his aunt and uncle recognized the hardships he suffered and tried to adopt him when he was five years old. His mother refused. He internalized her anger and abuse.[2]

TEEN YEARS

When he was in the eighth grade, his father (the only shield he had from his mother) got a job in northern California. He planned for the rest of the family to join him after he established himself and settled in. During the first six months of his father's absence, Tommy tried to commit suicide four times. His self-destructive behaviors, the burning and the cutting, became progressively worse. When Tommy was in the ninth grade, the entire family joined their father in northern California, and for the first time in many years, Tommy was included inside the house with his own room, although he remembers that it was difficult to stay in bed because he had become so accustomed to sleeping on the firm ground.

School still sucked. He got all Fs except for earning an A in art history. The art history teacher took an interest in him, recognizing Tommy's dyslexia and learning challenges. The teacher gave him simple but useful tools to help him remember key points in the class. The art history class was an anomaly, however, and Tommy cannot recall any other teachers, mentors, or anyone else who took an interest in him.

By the middle of the tenth grade, Tommy dropped out of high school and struck a deal with his father: if he got his GED, his father would give him a job in the bakery where he worked. Tommy enrolled in continuation school and, within a few weeks, secured his GED. He landed the promised job at the bakery, which Tommy describes as a wonderful job opportunity—a union position that paid $19.00 an hour. "But, within six months, I messed up and lost the job," Tommy says bleakly.

In fact, Tommy admits that before the age of twenty, he'd probably had at least fifteen to twenty jobs, all of which he messed up and lost.

> I was so insecure. I developed an issue with anyone who criticized me. I'd say, "You're out to get me!" and I'd quit. I was so touchy. I took any kind of criticism as saying, "You're worthless." I'd translate homelife to work. Then I'd mess up and feel criticized.

Tommy did not use drugs, get involved in gangs, or have any previous brushes with the law during these years. Instead, he internalized his insecurity and self-loathing, a practice that has continued to challenge Tommy throughout his life and even after his release from prison. He had vague dreams of becoming a police officer or joining the military so that he could be respected and revered as a hero. At seventeen and a half, he tried to enroll in the military but was told he was too overweight. He became despondent again and began cutting and burning himself even more deeply.

When asked if he felt any kind of positive emotions or hope during this juncture in his life, he says he *almost* had a life-changing experience at eighteen, when his girlfriend at the time became pregnant and had a baby boy they named Brandon. For the first two weeks of Brandon's life, Tommy's girlfriend remained in the hospital suffering from spinal meningitis. For those two weeks, Tommy was the primary caretaker, and he got to be the hero he always imagined he could be. But their relationship was rocky, immature, and verbally abusive. The girlfriend retained lawyers who insisted that if Tommy signed away his parental rights, his father would at least be able to continue visiting the baby. Tommy agreed. "I said, 'It's alright. I'm dead inside anyway.'" Tommy had little hope that his life would ever change for the better.

THE CRIME

At twenty years old, Tommy was at another low. He was homeless and lived on the floor of his friend's bedroom. He was overwhelmed with debt and dwelled in his victim's mentality. "I thought everyone was out to get me. That I was a failure. That I would never succeed. That I'm trying, but everything I do fails." He had taught himself to leverage this sense of victimhood to justify his poor choices and bad behavior throughout his entire life.

Tommy got a job with an armored car company. He now recognizes this was one of the worst kinds of work situations a grossly immature and insecure person could get himself into. "It was a very macho environment. Everyone teased each other," Tommy says of the corporate culture. Not only was it a negative work environment for someone with low self-esteem and high sensitivity, but the job also issued him a .38 handgun and provided access to hundreds of thousands of dollars.

In his young mind, Tommy thought money would solve all of his problems. Tommy explains that he was "future-thinking, but in a negative way," focusing only on short-term gains and his own hardships while having callous disregard for others. He imagined that money would allow him to run away from his situation and would help him to be more liked and accepted. In a funk, he watched two movies, *Heat* and *The Jackal*, and was inspired to draw up a detailed plan where he would rob his armored truck employer and escape during Thanksgiving weekend, when he could disappear unnoticed for at least twenty-four hours.

But things did not go according to plan for Tommy. Three days before Thanksgiving, Tommy had a stressful day at work. He made careless mistakes on the route that caused delays and frustration between him and his partner. At the end of the day, desperate and angry, Thomas Franklin Wheelock murdered his partner with three shots to the face and neck.

Mr. Rodrigo Cortez was survived by his wife and a four-year-old son.

By the time they caught up with him Thursday, officers say, Thomas Wheelock seemed resigned to capture, calmly surrendering during a traffic stop on Interstate 15 near Centerville, Utah, after leading authorities on an intense two-day manhunt.

"Here's a guy, he's young and scared. Whatever plan he might have had may have changed because of all the information that was out there," Oakland Police Capt. Pete Dunbar said Friday. (*Los Angeles Times* 1997)

LWOP

Until he was finally caught in Utah, Tommy imagined committing suicide on several occasions but says he was too cowardly to pull the trigger. Instead, he told the arresting officers that he wanted the death penalty because then "the state could do what I was too afraid to do to myself."

On November 1, 2001, Thomas Franklin Wheelock was sentenced to life without possibility of parole. He was sent to New Folsom State Prison and began to come to terms with his early life and what he had done, although he tried to hide his past among other inmates. One day, another inmate called bullshit at Tommy's fabricated life story. He pointed Tommy in the direction of self-help books and told him that he was not there to judge, but to care. It was not until Tommy was in prison that he encountered people who cared about his well-being.

Tommy resigned himself to his LWOP sentence and spent his days merely existing in prison. He became an avid reader, plowing through three or four books a week. Tommy describes his prison life as very square; he didn't use drugs, drink, or have gang involvement. He had zero write-ups and stayed out of trouble by getting prison jobs in maintenance and plumbing. He enjoyed fixing things and created a side hustle fixing fans, typewriters, lamps, and three-way electrical outlets for other inmates. Tommy described his early years of his LWOP sentence in prison this way:

When you come to prison you lose yourself. You become a non-person. You are no longer trusted, There is no hope, There is no future, There are so many things that you wish you could change, but you are powerless to make that change. It is very easy to give in to hopelessness and despair. I liken it to being on a rowboat, without any oars, in a storm-crossed sea. (T. Wheelock, pers. comm., 2015)

A SMALL CHANGE WITHIN

In 2013, Tommy was up for transfer, and his friend Jack persuaded him to come to Lancaster, saying it was unlike any other prison he had seen before. Tommy ended up on Lancaster's A Yard, although his first choice had been Pleasant Valley State Prison because, Tommy admits with a sardonic grin, "It sounded pleasant." Although his friend Jack had warned him that Lancaster's A Yard was a unique place, Tommy was still shocked to see inmates in bare feet on the dry grass (he'd never seen anyone walk around with their feet exposed in prison before), the interracial friendships on the yard, and the warm greeting he received upon his arrival. Soon enough, Tommy acclimated to A Yard and began walking laps with a group of ethnically diverse men who encouraged him to better himself by attending self-help groups and pursuing education.

Tommy was admittedly reluctant at first. "What was the use? I had life without. I was going to die in prison. It's not going to go toward anything." The founder of Lancaster's Honors Yard, Kenneth Hartman, argued otherwise: "It is going towards something. It is going toward being a better person. And the ability to help someone else."

> I came to prison for the first time with a sentence of Life Without the Possibility of Parole. Years passed me by and soon I realized I had to pick up the pieces of what was left of my life, and try to make what I could of a life for myself in prison. I wanted to change everything about myself that led me to be in prison, I wanted my time and my life to mean something. Like T. S. Elliot [sic], "I did not want to go quietly into the night." So I went to self-help groups and started to become the person that I wanted to be, finally I could look at the man in the mirror and not despise the person looking back at me. (T. Wheelock, pers. comm., 2015)

Tommy's new friends consistently encouraged, harassed, and cajoled him to pursue an education. The group guided Tommy toward correspondence courses with Coastline Community College. When he said he couldn't afford it, they told him they had a book club, and he wouldn't need to buy books. He enrolled in two classes and failed them both. But unlike the Tommy of his youth, this Tommy had encouragement from the sidelines. Charlie Praphatananda, Robert Chan, and Kenneth Hartman let him vent when he was frustrated and offered emotional support and friendship. This Tommy picked himself up and tried again.

"Then I got a C and I was like—this is *amazing*!" Tommy laughs. He began to like the challenge rather than to avoid it. The more he did, the more he realized he had the capacity to do. Soon, he had enough credits for five Coastline AA certificates.

> I was so afraid that if I failed at school a second time, all the hard work I put into rehabilitating myself would unravel. I did not tell my parents that I was going to school, I was too afraid to let them see me fail again. After receiving an A, I finally wrote to my parents and told them I was enrolled in college. I could not believe their response; it was so positive and uplifting, my father had so many encouraging words to share with me, it meant so much to hear how happy they were. I would daydream about my parents seeing me graduate, I couldn't wait to hand them my diploma and see the pride in their faces. (T. Wheelock, pers. comm., May 26, 2017)

Then his friends nudged him toward the bachelor's degree program. He protested. "No! That's scary. I can't do that. I'm not smart enough." He says he was "scared to death" after he'd been admitted into the program, and every day, he worried that someone was going to tell him he didn't belong. He was surrounded by friends (men he would come to refer to as "brothers"), but he thought everyone was a better writer, thinker, and speaker than he was. School looked so easy for everyone else, whereas Tommy describes every classroom moment as so challenging that it was "like breaking down a brick wall."

Tommy remembers when things began to change within him. He felt good about the way the professors and staff engaged him as if he were a human being. He liked the reassurance that there were no dumb questions or statements. He says it was mind-blowing the way the Cal State LA faculty talked to him as if he were on their same level. He thrived.

THE POWER OF THE BACHELOR'S DEGREE

Halfway through the bachelor's degree program, Tommy was still certain that he would die in prison with his LWOP sentence. And yet he recalls feeling positive changes within himself. "I was calmer. A lot of the insecurity went away just by doing it." For example, he says that he was better able to hear and accept constructive criticism from his classmates in a way that he had never been able to accept feedback before.

The Prison BA students were assigned anonymous pen pals with a parallel class on the main campus. Tommy described his experience as a burgeoning college student like this:

Now we have this amazing chance to continue our education. The more that we learn, the better people we become. For me, I want to continue on with my education, I want to get a master's degree, and then a PhD. There are so many books that are inside of me, just beginning to come out. Now thanks to this course I will have the means and the knowledge on how to make my dreams happen. (T. Wheelock, pers. comm., October 15, 2015)

The young man who had spent many years of his life ardently hating school suddenly became one of the most vocal proponents for the creation of a master's degree program for incarcerated students. So impassioned was he that he brought it up every time he encountered a Cal State LA administrator, and he would write about his fantasy of earning a graduate degree in long letters, explaining his past circumstances and his dreams for the future.

Cal State-LA would be the first master's degree program ever in the California State Prison system, something that has never been done. But, the real truth is that I love college and learning new things, this experience has been so meaningful, and has had such a positive impact on my life and my fellow Cal State-LA Golden Eagles. (T. Wheelock, pers. comm., 2019)

THE CLASSROOM

Tommy admits he reverted back to being a bit of a class clown in the Prison BA program as a way to deflect his insecurities and impostor syndrome. To outsiders, he was quiet, unassuming, and very respectful. He rarely spoke in class.

In winter 2019, Dr. Kamran Afary assigned Tommy and his cohort the task of enacting a defining or traumatic childhood event and then reenacting the ending with a more desirable outcome. Tommy, with the help of classmates who assumed the role of his mother and father, performed a brief vignette depicting his mother shouting at him for having poor grades and then banishing him to live in the backyard. The performance ended with his father finally helping him to build a shed so he could have shelter during his last few years sleeping outdoors.

It was not a story widely known by his classmates, all of whom had experienced more than their fair share of traumatic life experiences, and they were stunned into silence by the end of the performance. Suddenly, Tommy was engulfed by all of his classmates in a warm and emotional group hug. They patted him on the back, squeezed his shoulders, and said they loved him.

Tommy has said on more than one occasion that being sent to prison saved his life, while at the same time recognizing that it came at the expense of someone else's. In addition to school, he looked for ways to make amends to the community, such as crocheting blankets and hats for charities. He slowly managed to redirect his self-destructive tendencies and found friendship and family with the other inmates. He found people who held him accountable without judging him.

> Other boats surround you, these like-minded individuals want to become better people. They want to make a difference. So we bring our boats together, working together, we seek out ways to change. (T. Wheelock, pers. comm., October 2015)

The same friends who pushed him to get an education encouraged him to apply to the parole board for a commutation. After serving twenty-three years of a life without possibility of parole sentence for the murder of Rodrigo Cortez, Thomas Franklin Wheelock walked out of prison in May 2020, during the height of the COVID pandemic, as a free man.

A FREE AND EDUCATED MAN

During a Zoom presentation with Pasadena High School students in 2020, Tommy said that education had changed him by broadening his life perspective. He said, "I never grew before. Education has given me the opportunity to grow" (T. Wheelock, pers. comm., 2020).

That is not to say that life on the outside has been easy. Tommy says it has taken him three years to stabilize. He still struggles with accepting feedback from authority figures, and he is afraid of disappointing others. The fear of "not being good enough" creeps into his thoughts, and an overwhelming desire to be loved and accepted is still his strongest motivator.

Tommy says coming home was stressful. It was certainly a challenge to be released after twenty-three years during the middle of a worldwide pandemic. His final class was on Zoom instead of in person. During his first few months home, he was acutely aware of having no family support system and no money. He wanted to have a meaningful career where he could use his degree. While Tommy acknowledges that college helped him to mature, gave him structure and discipline, and provide a much-needed confidence boost, he still worried that he would never find a meaningful career where he could use his degree. He was so concerned that he would be viewed as, in his words, "just an ex-con," he applied only for menial jobs at stores such as Home Depot and then as a pump technician where he could leverage the mechanical and maintenance expertise he'd gained in prison.

Finally, just a few months into 2023, he officially started a brand-new position as a reentry coordinator for the Paws for Life program—a job that was essentially written with him in mind and that required a four-year college degree. His dream of being able to help other people is finally coming true. And so is the dream of being a part of a family. He talks about family dinners and game nights with a big grin on his face. "I still get emotional when I sit with my family (Tommy's fiancée and her children) and we're playing board games. It is weird and amazing at the same time. I get texts from them all day long—asking for help fixing something or just checking in. It's great. It's a wonderful feeling."

We made the choice to change. So it is self-select[ing]. But we did it with no hopes of ever going home, right? So there was never anything saying, "If you do this, you're going to get commuted." That wasn't even in our dreams. I lived during that time knowing and being comfortable with the fact that I was going to die in prison. I was going to die alone and forgotten. And it became more important for me to fix everything that brought me here and to learn how to be a good person . . . the BA program made me free. It's hard to explain. It's coming here to this class. It's a freedom and so it changes your whole view and you start to dream and you start to plan for the future and you start to see, "Hey, how can I help? How can I do more?" Instead of just being isolated. You want to share with other people and bring other people in. It really just opens up your horizon and then you start to dream.

Figure 11.1 Thomas Wheelock (left) discusses his early childhood experiences living in his backyard. Photo: P. Record, 2019.

NOTES

1. All quotes in this chapter are from this interview, unless otherwise noted.

2. Tommy's mother is still alive and has severe dementia. His father passed away from cancer. Tommy's siblings and mother have refused to see him since he came home.

Chapter 12

Daniel Whitlow

Name:	Daniel Whitlow
Age:	Forty-three
Race/Ethnicity:	White
Sentence:	Life without parole, resentenced to twenty-five-to-life in 2017
Years Incarcerated:	Twenty-two years, one month
Released:	February 2020
Year Graduated:	2021
Interview:	April 11, 2023[1]

Two weeks after Daniel "Moody" Whitlow was released from prison in February 2020, he and three of his free classmates came by my office to feast on hamburgers and french fries while having a rambling and thoughtful discussion about the transformative impact of higher education in prison. Bradley Arrowood, Charlie Praphatananda, Jeff Stein, and Daniel Whitlow were all deeply introspective, impassioned about the positive influence college had had on their lives, and excited about their futures. They had each spent ten or more years together at Lancaster, and when I recently replayed the recorded discussion, their mutual affection and admiration was clearly evident in the ways they joked fondly with each other or listened quietly and without interruption as each "brother" took his turn to speak.

It would be fair to describe Daniel as both a philosopher and a poet. His prison moniker, "Moody," he says, is also an accurate description of who he was as a youth—emotionally unregulated and deeply empathic. The ideas he strings together may sound both persuasively conceptual and allegorical, but the ideas he presented in my office in 2020 are consistent and just as compelling three years later when we have a one-on-one Zoom interview in April 2023.

On this day, Daniel is cracking jokes and struggling with his video camera while conducting our virtual interview from a cramped and stuffy bedroom in Arizona, from which he explains he has been forced into a frustrating and momentary pause in his studies. He was one semester away from earning his master's degree in communication studies from Cal State LA when he was called away by an ailing grandmother and elderly aunt who needed his help. Daniel is married, too, to a German citizen who has been unable to obtain her green card for permanent residency in the United States, and during this waiting period, which has extended three years now, they rarely see each other in person. Daniel finished his undergraduate degree in communication outside of prison on the Cal State LA main campus after having his LWOP sentence reduced. His final semesters as a bachelor's degree student also coincided with the surreal time of the COVID pandemic, so much of his educational experience outside of prison was very different from what he had once day-dreamed about while still incarcerated.

Things may not be going as planned for Daniel, and yet he finds sparks of comedy in the darkness and manages to wrap his brand of wry and dry humor into his rapid-fire commentary and observations.

EARLY EDUCATION

Daniel grew up in San Diego as an only child with a single mother and his grandmother. Daniel does not recall many memories of his father, other than his mother's awkward attempts to forge a relationship between father and son during occasional weekend visits to Phoenix to visit with his father's side of the family. Daniel has half-siblings from his father's side, but he is not in contact with any of them. From what he knows of them, he's fairly certain that they have conservative, "redneck" values that he does not share.

Daniel is not the first in his family to have a college education. His father has a college degree and was a teacher. His mother, who did not earn her bachelor's until after Daniel was arrested, graduated from California State University, San Marcos, with a degree in microbiology and statistics. Nor is Daniel the first in his family to have been incarcerated. Daniel describes two of his uncles on his maternal side as "installment plan crooks," men who were in and out of prison for misdemeanors, mostly related to drugs, and who still struggle today.

Daniel's recollection of his early years in elementary school is that they were boring. He remembers reading the assignments assiduously because he enjoyed knowing the answers in class and took pleasure in answering on behalf of others. Daniel says he knew he was smart, and he wielded his knowledge around his classmates because he wanted attention. He got As on tests, but he never did the homework. Daniel recalls getting penalized in math class for not showing his work, as his teacher had instructed, because he could solve the problems in his head. He argued with his teacher during class and considered them "a fucking idiot" when the teacher wrote out the math problem on the board and still got it wrong.

Still, Daniel says, the other kids knew he had the right answers, and many of them jostled to be with him because he would share the answers. He loved the popularity.

> I had a lot of friends that weren't really my friends that were just hanging out with me because I seemed to have all the answers at the time. That was amazing. Especially as a teenager—having that level of respect from others was a huge part of how I defined myself and my self-worth.

Daniel notes that when he didn't have the right answers, it was a huge blow to his self-esteem and sense of self-worth. "I felt like I had an obligation to be right all the time," he says.

Daniel enjoyed the validation and respect he earned from other students, which helped him fulfill a constant need for social inclusion and acknowledgment. Daniel says that affirmation from his classmates was especially rewarding because he never felt that anyone else at home really cared about his academic success. Daniel surmises that his mother always knew that he was intelligent and capable, and she had high hopes that he would go to college and get a good job, although she was rarely involved in his studies.

By his own account, Daniel has struggled with emotional regulation throughout his life and was diagnosed with attention deficit disorder (ADD) as a child. In his teens, a therapist suggested he presented as bipolar, which made sense to Daniel but angered his mother. In Daniel's mind, the dual diagnosis provided justification for his teenage anger, outbursts, and behavior.

> While I screamed and yelled and acted like a fool, I could say, "I'm bipolar. I'm ADD. What do you want from me? I can't regulate my emotions! The doctor said I have a problem! This is a condition. I'm just being myself." All this fucking stupid shit. But that's where I went in my head.

By middle school, Daniel says his need for social acceptance and attention from his peers was the most important thing he thought about. He admits that he spent a great deal of his young teen years worrying about "Who likes me? Who doesn't? How do I get others to like me?" He started hanging around the "wrong" people in middle school, and his grades plummeted. He started stealing. He ditched classes and caused problems at school. His principal commented that he had never had a student who ditched more classes in a single week than Daniel. Today, Daniel observes that at the time, what he probably really needed was a kind of intervention or a strong demonstration that someone in his life really cared about his future and his well-being.

> My mom's and my relationship has always been good, but she's always been more of a friend to me [than a mother]. Because for many years, she didn't really believe in punishing me at all because she felt super guilty for everything and all that stuff. So my mom and my grandma really took their foot off the pedal in terms of discipline. And I really wish they hadn't done that. They really should have been on my ass. If they'd been on my ass, I probably would not have been ditching. I probably would have focused on school a bit more—even if it needed to be like some sort of intervention, you know? Where was that somebody that comes in and helps me to get back on the right page? Whatever the case is, however, it would have been a better ending than the one that happened.

As a high schooler, Daniel had amorphous plans for his future. He fully expected that he would enroll in the local community college after graduating and would pursue his love of music by studying sound engineering or music production. It was the same community college his mother had attended, and he could imagine himself being there. Daniel recalls that he felt there were implicit expectations that he would continue on to college after high school, although he didn't find them very persuasive.

> My mom told me for a long time, "If you do really well in school, you'll have a great job." That was the message. But that wasn't very interesting to me. I thought, "If you do really well in school, then everybody will tell you that you've done really well in school and you'll have this really flashy degree that you could put on your wall. And then you can just go and play music all day once you've impressed everybody with your work—you can go on and just do the shit that you actually want to do."

According to Daniel, though, his mother was quietly concerned about his academic well-being in middle school. By high school, she had "completely disconnected from her expectations." Daniel says he was not abusing alcohol or drugs at the time, but instead, "I hung around the hundreds of people that wanted to go and steal shit."

Among these young people who stole, ditched classes, and smoked cigarettes while Daniel would play Pink Floyd for them on his guitar was Henry, the young man who would become Daniel's closest friend and codefendant.

CRIME

Daniel was sixteen when he met Henry, and he felt an instant connection. "He was the ice to my fire," Daniel explains, referring to Henry's stoic and quiet mannerisms whereas Daniel was emotional and impulsive. Henry claimed to have had an extremely traumatic childhood and was living with foster parents at the time. Together, they shared many deep and heartfelt conversations, wallowing in their shared hurt and resentments. Daniel empathized with his friend's pain, noting that:

> We were young, maudlin, wannabe-Goth teenagers. Like, we were very emo and very much edgy in our own way. And that's kind of the way we wanted it to be. So these conversations were as pretentious as you probably can imagine they were, but at the same time, we were really sharing a lot of deep hurt.

Daniel says that Henry had a rudderless understanding of how his traumatic and troubling past was affecting him at the time, yet Daniel felt so strongly protective of his friend that he easily succumbed to the idea that he needed to be a part in avenging Henry's pain, without even thinking about the consequences to his own future. Henry hatched an elaborate plan to kill his foster parents, and Daniel went along with it.

> Well, from my perspective, at the time I don't think I was aware of the ramifications of my actions. If I was, I either didn't care or it was not something that ever registered. It was not important on my list. Being there for my friend who had been there for me? Who I felt was unjustly treated, and tortured, and who needed somebody to fight for him? Yeah, [I thought] that's exactly what he wanted.

Together, they murdered Henry's foster parents. Henry was eighteen years old. Daniel was seventeen. Daniel was sent to juvenile hall, where he earned his high school diploma while he awaited trial. In January 1999, he was sentenced to life without parole.

PRISON

When Daniel reflects on his first years of incarceration, he recognizes now that he did not fully grasp how an LWOP sentence would impact him. He trusted his lawyers, who assured him that he would get out on a technicality. Daniel says it wasn't until five years into his sentence in 2004, and after undergoing an unsuccessful second trial and second conviction, that he finally understood his life was over. He was twenty-four.

Daniel was transferred to Lancaster. He concedes that he was mired in bitterness and resentment until he was confronted by an older man on the yard who was also serving an LWOP sentence. During our interview, Daniel, a prolific poet and writer, read this passage from his poem about their conversation, which gave him the push to assume accountability and responsibility for the choices he had made in his own life.

I began to give up.
  I looked around at the depressing, austere grayness of walls and buildings and fences and thought,
  "I will die here."
  I looked at the anonymous deadness of the faces of the men around me and thought,
  "I am them now."
  And when I saw my reflection in a mirror, I thought,
  "I am dead too."
  I began to unravel
  to succumb to the septic spiritual abyss
  of complete existential forfeiture.
  If I had nothing to live for, why live?
  Dissolving thoughts of collapse merrily danced in the falling ruins of my disassembling mind.
  Color no longer came to my eyes.
  Life no longer felt alive.
  I was in need of something. Anything.
  One thing was for sure, I had to choose how I wanted to live my life
  for better or worse.
  One day on the way back from evening chow, a friend asked me how I was.
  "I feel like shit," I responded.
  We both stopped walking.
  "Why?"
  "Because I'm in prison for the rest of my life. Dude, the fucking state took my life," I said to him, scoffingly.
  He must be mad to ask such a stupid question.
  He paused.
  "Well, whose life did you take?"
  I felt as though he had slapped me.
  "What?" I sputtered.
  "Stop lying to yourself." His face was adamant as stone.

"If you keep believing you did nothing wrong, nothing will change. These walls will continue to draw closer and the suffocation of your suffering will continue to grow until it bends you and breaks you in half.

"My advice. Just be honest with yourself. Accept who you are. Accept what you did and go from there." He gave me a small reassuring smile and patted my shoulder as he moved on.

I stood there for some time
Considering his words
Until the Tower Guard interrupted my reverie with a firm suggestion that I "keep walking." (D. Whitlow, pers. comm., 2023)

Daniel spent a year on Lancaster's D Yard, a general population yard that was devoid of programming, activities, or opportunities. He struggled with drug addiction, boredom, and stagnation.

I think part of the problem on D Yard—as unattractive as it may sound—is just straight up boredom. It's just there is nothing to do on D Yard. The only thing that you could really do there is the same shit that everybody does, which is all the same prison crap that doesn't really do anything for you. I did work out. I got books from the library and read books. I occasionally went to the chapel if I just wanted to get away from everything. I had a job 90 percent of the time while I was there. Yeah, [I'd] go to work, type shit, go home. But that's it. And that only took up a certain number of hours in my day, the rest of the hours were devoted to nothing.

Resigned to his LWOP sentence and lethargic from the monotony, Daniel pushed his way to Lancaster's A Yard—the Progressive Programming Facility—and his daily routine and sense of purpose immediately changed. Not only was it a much safer environment without the racial politics that are so pervasive on general population yards, but the culture on Lancaster's Honor Yard encouraged a "positive, abundant mindset." Daniel says he immediately found opportunities to explore "enjoyment, friendship, publishing, and ultimately—hope." Whereas on D Yard he could not have access to a guitar or any musical equipment, the moment he stepped on A Yard, he was immediately recruited into the band program.

In the rich and bustling environment of Lancaster's A Yard, Daniel began to find himself again.

As a young man, I didn't have any respect for my sentence because I thought that it was temporary. After I realized it wasn't temporary, it hit me so hard that I felt like I was crumbling inside. And then when I found A Yard, I felt reborn, like there was something restoring itself inside of me. Something that I had, at that point, already put inside of its own little baby coffin. I had already assumed that my heart, joy, my music, and everything would be a forever dead part of me.

In short time, Daniel became the chairman of the band, a position he served in for ten years, and equipment manager. He was an active participant and facilitator of self-help groups. He participated in the art program (although he confesses art is not one of his strengths) and was a Paws for Life dog trainer for three years. He took numerous correspondence courses through Coastline College and was pursuing an associate's degree in business.

And it was here on this yard that Daniel found that a bachelor's degree program was about to start.

GOLDEN EAGLES

Daniel had been taking correspondence courses through Coastline Community College, and he enjoyed one of his first classes, astronomy, immensely. He was encouraged by other potential students on the yard, especially Jimmie Gilmer, Woody Arrowood, Robert Chan, and Charlie Praphatananda, all of whom had been actively recruiting and supporting potential college students on the yard for years. With them as his mentors, he became a successful college student. He learned how to enroll in community college courses, shared textbooks, and was ushered onto the waiting list for the Cal State LA Prison BA Graduation Initiative.

Although he had been a poor and uncommitted high school student, Daniel found himself caught up in the excitement and the buzz of possibility that an in-person bachelor's degree program could bring. He felt encouraged by the camaraderie of a small and intimate cohort made up of men he knew well and considered his friends. He also could not deny the palpable enthusiasm of his mother and grandmother, who, he grimly admitted, "hadn't really been excited for shit [about me] for a long time."

According to Daniel, even before the bachelor's degree program officially started, there was cautious optimism on the yard about what a college program could mean for their future: this motley, diverse group of men who all had cobbled together associate's degrees through mostly correspondence community college; who all had struggled in school as children and teens well before they were ever incarcerated; and the majority of whom had LWOP sentences. They tried to imagine what obtaining a bachelor's degree would mean for their futures.

I think that the general consensus for everybody in the classroom was that regardless of what this might mean for us on individual terms and our future, this was an *event*. It's the first of its kind that has limitless potential. Unlimited potential in terms of changing our lives for the better, changing the yard for the better. Also . . . you don't ever let a good opportunity pass you by in prison. You have to be able to be aware enough to know what good or bad is. But assuming that your compass is not totally fucked, you don't ever let a good opportunity pass you by because you don't know if those opportunities are ever going to return and chances are they won't. So don't waste them. Don't waste a chance to make a change in yourself.

As a college student in a face-to-face program with Cal State LA faculty, Daniel discovered academic discipline, a passion for studying, and excitement about achievement that he did not experience as a youth in school. Daniel credits the feedback loop with the Cal State LA professors as one of the most powerful, transformative aspects of the college degree. Unlike correspondence courses, where feedback might take a month or more to receive, if at all, Daniel thrived on the reciprocal feedback and engagement with his professors and classmates. He appreciated the constructive criticism and the exploration of new ideas. And, with the encouragement and support of the students and faculty, for the first time in his life, he could understand and "objectively see myself as a product of trauma."

TRANSFORMATION

When Daniel talks about his transfer to Lancaster's A Yard and his participation in the Prison BA Graduation Initiative, there is a notable shift. He becomes more animated. His speech quickens, and his vocal intonations are expressive and gleeful. He seems especially excited to reflect upon his own transformation and development as a result of the bachelor's degree program, and he shares a litany of benefits that he believes contributed to his overall self-awareness and development.

> The friendships that I had made, accomplishing my goals, feeling proud of myself, being proud of my accomplishments, learning from my mistakes. Forging strong friendships, creating good mental habits. I really just wanted to make myself into a better person. I know I'm an intelligent guy, but in terms of the actual information and stuff like that? I had not been a very good student. Having a lot of knowledge doesn't make you smart. It just means you know a lot of shit.

Looking back, Daniel recognizes that while he was in the bachelor's degree program, he gained a new avenue to deepen his relationship with his mother, who had returned to CSU San Marcos to earn her bachelor's degree shortly after he was arrested. They were able to connect and discuss concepts and ideas in new and deeper ways. Shortly after Daniel transferred to Lancaster's Progressive Programming Facility, he began corresponding with a woman from Germany who later became his wife. Daniel very much wanted to be able to communicate with her on an intellectual level, and he was motivated by her enthusiasm and support for his educational pursuits.

According to Daniel, the presence of Cal State LA caused a ripple effect on A Yard. Some men on the yard, who had no personal aspirations of ever going to school themselves, still appreciated the sight of students traipsing off to their classes with books in hand, saying that it helped the "whole yard feel like a college campus."

> After the program started, we started to have big conversations around the tables and buildings where there were six or seven people that were taking notes and studying and going over stuff. All that was like a whole other level of excitement too. Because now we were in the public space. And it encouraged people, and it got people to join the second and third cohort, and it got people to see that this was a viable option.

On several occasions as a Cal State LA student at Lancaster, Daniel was approached by men who, though perhaps doubting their own capacity to be a college student, were very interested in finding out how they, too, could be a part of education. Daniel describes an interaction he had with two men who had each spent time in the Security Housing Unit (SHU) at San Quentin. Even in their isolation they had heard about the success of the Prison BA Graduation Initiative, and they approached Daniel for educational guidance. They explained that they had transferred to Lancaster just so that they could be closer to programming opportunities. Daniel also recalls an old cellie of his who, though deeply troubled and someone who had made many terrible mistakes before and throughout his prison sentence, began to ask Daniel to read some of his Cal State LA assignments to him. He borrowed textbooks so that he could read them himself. And every day Daniel came back from class, he would ask what they talked about that day. Daniel doubted that this man would ever pursue a college degree himself, but Daniel believes that in his own way, he was trying to expand his mind and better himself.

COMMUTATION

Although it was not at the forefront of Daniel's mind when he enrolled in the program, he and the other students could see clear benefits to being in the BA program for parole board hearing meetings.

So, I guess in the grand scheme of things I feel like I wouldn't be where I'm at, with the dreams that I have, with the potential that I have, if I didn't have the BA degree because that was the thing that opened the door. I can't even imagine what my life would look like or whether I would be free or not [without the program]. It's hard to tell. I take solace in knowing that doesn't matter. Without sounding melodramatic I think the program saved my life. I really do.

Daniel is thoughtful about what he feels he gained from earning a bachelor's degree in prison and notes that it is more expansive than a specific theory or lecture or activity in any one class. The transformational experiences happened by being in relationship with Cal State LA faculty and being accountable to each other in the classroom. It included challenging themselves to be open to feedback and introspection.

It taught me that I didn't have to live my life the way that I had thought I needed to live, that I could just learn and continue to progress as a person. Continue to work toward getting out, continuing to be who I am, not hiding behind a mask or trying to convince people otherwise, I could just be me, regardless, right? But the fact that it was a college program, it was filled with so many incredible, positive experiences that helped me to redefine how I saw myself, which really is a fundamental part of getting through your parole hearing. You have to understand who you are and what you want. They ask you to talk about your past, but if you ask a commissioner independently, the parole hearing isn't about what happened. That's a given. The record exists. The past doesn't change, right? What it's about is what you've done since then. Having knowledge of the past is only important up to the point where it meets with the present. And then to have knowledge about the present and the future. The BA program gave me present awareness and future awareness. It didn't need to teach me my past. I already knew that. But it taught me about who I am now, who I want to be the next day. That was something I'd never done.

Daniel often refers to the ways that a college education helped him in his overall transformation, particularly with regard to the "expansion of self" as a concept. Daniel explains:

In the deepest, darkest, worst days of my incarceration, my understanding of self as a concept was completely barren. I had no identity whatsoever. And that speaks to my phase of addiction, too—that was definitely part of that. But the incarcerated isolation takes all of those things away from you. And to be fair, we *have* to sacrifice those things, so that's what I did. I sacrificed my concept of self. But education showed me that I had sacrificed it and then created a pathway for me to be able to reconceptualize myself. I guess I reclaimed my identity. (D. Whitlow, pers. comm. in group interview, February 2020)

The first nineteen years of Daniel's sentence were under LWOP. Then in 2017, his writ of habeas corpus based on California and US case law was granted, and his sentence was reduced to twenty-five years to life under the juvenile life without possibility of parole initiatives that had been implemented in California. On September 25, 2019, Daniel went before the parole board and was found suitable for release. He came home in February 2020. His codefendant is still incarcerated.

After Daniel was released from prison, he immediately came to Cal State LA to continue with the handful of classes he needed to graduate. He lived in the transitional housing program just up the hill from campus, but classes were all restricted to Zoom, which Daniel sums up as "really sucked."

Yet, as it has been for the other students who have had their sentences commuted and found themselves suddenly thrust upon the Cal State LA main campus, it was a long-awaited homecoming. He recalls watching movies about college life while incarcerated, and he daydreamed about having a college experience. He says he felt instantly at home at Cal State LA, although he missed the classroom intimacy of being with his "brothers." Daniel shares a laugh about what a wondrous experience it is to be on campus and to suddenly see one of the fifteen other students, backpack hitched to the shoulders, walking purposefully to his next class as a free student.

Daniel cannot reflect on this time without remembering a fellow student and good friend from Cohort 1, Terry Don Evans. Mr. Evans passed away from complications of COVID in January 2021, just before submitting the final draft of his senior capstone project. Daniel was already on the outside when Terry passed and regrets not having had a chance to say goodbye.

DREAMS FOR THE FUTURE

At the time of the interview, Daniel was struggling with some uncertainties. He didn't know when his wife would be able to get her green card to come and live with him in the United States. He doesn't know when his family situation will improve so that he can come back to Cal State LA to complete his final semester of the master's degree program. He does know, however, that he wants to leverage his education to make a difference, which he spoke to three years ago when he first got out and addresses much the same way even now.

> The difference for a person who's transformed and who becomes devoted to that idea is that they start helping others to the surface. So instead of just using all of the gifts that we have to excel in our own lives and to make something of ourselves, we excel. Make something of ourselves to help others excel and make something of themselves to help others do the same thing. (D. Whitlow, pers. comm. in group interview, February 2020)

Figure 12.1 Daniel Whitlow crossing the stage. Photo: J. Flores, 2021. Courtesy of California State University, Los Angeles.

NOTE

1. All quotes in this chapter are from this interview, unless otherwise noted.

Chapter 13

Chay Dara Yin

Name:	Chay Dara Yin
Age:	Forty
Race/Ethnicity:	Cambodian
Years Incarcerated:	Twenty-two
Sentence:	Life without parole
Year Graduated:	2021
Interview:	April 30, 2023[1]

When Dara tells me he's been home for less than six months, I pause in surprise. It feels like he's been dropping into my office for years, a fixture on the campus just like his brothers from the program before him, and his productivity in the short few months since he returned home has been astounding and impressive.

Dara had already earned his bachelor's degree in 2021 while inside Lancaster State Prison, a year before he was released. Unlike most of the other men who came home before him, Dara didn't need to worry about what his next classes were going to be, but he is very focused on having a productive postgraduate life. Fortunately, he had guidance from two very close friends who came home many months before him, and he had a strong foundation of familial support. His friends and family shopped for clothing and sneakers for him; he had a well-paying job lined up; and there were plans for someone to pass a car down to him long before his release.

Dara is always busy, and between work, grad school, volunteer activities, consulting, and family life, he has few moments to pause. Dara's first months home have been a whirlwind of activities: hockey games, escape rooms, skydiving, parasailing, volunteering, and a trip to Las Vegas. He's been invited to Washington, DC, as a guest speaker and is consulting on the development of a trauma-informed curriculum for teens. He has a wife and stepchildren in another city, and he was submitting grad school applications within days of coming home so as to not miss any deadlines. His friends and I often encouraged him to slow down, to take a moment to pause and appreciate the world outside that is twenty-two years different from when he went inside, but he himself admits that he is singularly driven and feels like there is a lot of catching up to do. Most of all, he is propelled, he says, by a need to give back.

He started his master's degree program in educational technology at the University of Southern California (USC) in the fall of 2023.

EARLY YEARS

Dara's mother fled Cambodia after the father of his three older half-siblings, a brother and two sisters, was killed in the genocide. Family legend is not rich in details, but Dara's understanding is that his mother managed to get herself and her three children to a refugee camp in Thailand. She was sponsored by people in Florida, where she met Dara's father. Dara was born in Florida but never knew his father.

Dara grew up in Southern California, and he remembers very little of his early childhood education. He was a shy and quiet kid and describes himself as intimidated in the kindergarten classroom.

Dara's siblings were considerably older than him, all three by at least a decade, so they had lives separate from him. His siblings' lives were tumultuous. He had thought for years that they were all high school dropouts; only recently did he learn that his brother has a college degree. After Dara's brother moved out of the house, he remembers a lot of loud and violent arguments between his mother and his sisters. His younger sister ran away from home at fifteen. He says he felt disconnected from his family and hated his mother for arguing with his sisters, although he never understood the roots of their disagreements.

His mother was uneducated and worked long hours in a sweatshop, sometimes completing her sewing at home. Dara remembers that she struggled to keep the family afloat. She would often say that she "lost" their welfare checks, but Dara is vaguely certain that she was an alcoholic and had a gambling addiction. He also suspected that her erratic behavior and the questionable friends she occasionally brought into the home suggested she had a drug problem, but Dara was never able to say for certain.

Dara did well in his early years in school, although he doesn't remember receiving any kind of support for his early learning, nor was there anyone at home who could help him with his homework. He was quiet and socially awkward, but academically, he wasn't bad at it. Dara remembers being aware that he was bright and capable.

Dara recalls that he began stealing at the age of six. He always stole two of everything, one for himself and the other to give to someone else. The first thing Dara ever stole were two water guns, and he remembers gifting the other to a kid in the neighborhood in the hopes that they would play together. By the fifth grade, Dara confesses he was "stealing at a high clip." He and some other kids would ride the bus to the mall just to see what they could take. Dara, small and unassuming, was rarely suspected. Looking back, Dara recognizes his compulsive stealing was a way for him to connect with others and to garner positive feedback, which he felt was missing from his life. Today, Dara is very aware of how much he craved attention and companionship. Dara was also teased by neighborhood kids who taunted him with a Khmer slur that Dara translates as "Chinese eyes," which was hurtful and alienating. Dara assumed that if he stole things for the kids, they would be more accepting and might actually grow to like him.

The stealing escalated in the sixth and seventh grades, but he still managed to do well in school. He knew, in fact, that school was not inherently difficult for him. He told himself, "I can do this if I really want to." But in his young mind, Dara could not reconcile the value of school compared to the social and emotional reinforcement he received in the neighborhood. Even now, he is nostalgic thinking about the neighborhood streets he wandered as a kid: playing games at the video store after school; learning how to outrun and outmaneuver someone if he was being chased; and how to sell the goods he was stealing. By pocketing the money he received from selling stolen items, he was free from asking his mother or siblings for money. Dara was a sensitive kid, and deep down, he was aware that he feared rejection, so he carefully avoided situations when a loved one would have the opportunity to tell him no.

When Dara was eleven, his mother surprised him by bringing his birth father and his family to the house to visit. It would be the first and only time Dara would meet him.

I didn't know they were coming and I was outside playing around, dirty as shit, and then she called me into the house. I come up here and here's this man, right? And he's got his son and his daughter with him. His son looked just like me. Like I was looking in a mirror. At that moment . . . I think that was the lowest I've ever felt. I felt like he'd just moved on—made another son and another daughter, and I'm the oldest obviously—but like, he didn't even think back. It was awkward as hell and I was numb. I went downstairs and sat on the stairs. Just kind of like in shock. And then they left and as he saw me, he came by and pulled out some fucking money and gave it to me. I remember having the money in my hand, looking at him, and he was like, "Listen to your mom" and he walked off. I threw the money over the fence.

In fact, the paternal warning from his birth father had the opposite effect on Dara's relationship with his mother. Dara says, "Everything she said after that just didn't register even though she was saying all the right things. 'Stay out of trouble and go to school.' Like, she's saying all the classic lines that should register but don't because I'm emotionally distraught." The interaction with his father also further complicated the way Dara viewed money, which would affect him and his relationship with others for many years to come.

Instead, Dara focused even more on establishing himself in the neighborhood. Dara had realized that his skills at stealing provided him with some protection. For example, he stole junk food from the local markets and gave it to older gang members in the neighborhood. One day when he was only seven or eight, he was almost jumped by a Hispanic gang, but the Cambodian gang members he had been feeding stepped in.

Dara was also exposed to gang life through the younger of his two sisters, who was gang-involved and pregnant at a very young age.

> Going to her house was traumatic. Seeing the gang members there—I started to hate her and their gang because of the way they treated my nephew and nieces and me. I became a babysitter for them, as well. By the time I was in the sixth and seventh grade, I was getting my nephews and nieces ready for school while I was going to school, too.

Dara says that he despised his sister's gang so much that he deliberately joined a smaller rival gang at the age of sixteen. He was very aware that he was living a dichotomous life. He was still going to school and doing well, but he was also stealing and had joined a gang. His family did not speak to him in Khmer, so he wasn't accepted as entirely Cambodian, nor was he accepted as purely American. He started sleeping at friends' houses because he didn't want to be around his mother, but it didn't appear she noticed when he was gone, which angered him further. He felt that there was a familial expectation that he should do well in school and go to college, but he can't recall the message ever explicitly delivered. Dara dropped out of school in the ninth grade.

> By the time I was in the ninth grade, I wanted to be a full-fledged gangbanger. Hustling. Selling drugs. I wanted to be in organized crime—that's what all of my attention started to think about. I didn't think about schooling. I didn't care about finishing [school]. The only reason I even went to the ninth grade was so I could sell drugs.

His relationship with his mother had deteriorated, and she kicked him out of the house. He occasionally stayed with his older sister (who, he says, always represented a mother figure to him), but more often, he slept on the couches and floors of other gang members. During this time, Dara says his priorities centered around money and the relationships and recognition that money provided him.

> Money was important, but it wasn't the most important because when I joined the gang, their acceptance of me was most important. Money made them love me. I needed to be special. I wanted to be revered. I wanted my older gang homies to point to me as the model—just having that value and acceptance. So money played a part in that I was willing to do whatever it took to get that.

Dara says that, while still sixteen, he had outgrown his first gang and joined a larger one where he could get more recognition. He smoked marijuana and drank alcohol, but did not use the hard drugs he sold. He gave the money away by helping his homies buy guns and rent houses for parties. Although Dara was enveloped by the gang, he describes himself as angry and distant from others during this time.

When Dara reflects on this moment of his life, he says that he is quite sure his younger self's vision of the future was simple: that he was going to jail.

> I had homies who went to jail. It's almost like it's inevitable. I was out there hustling and thinking, "I'm going to do some time." In my mind, I'm like, how much money can I make before I get locked up?

What he did not know at the time is that he would land in more than just jail. He would be party to a crime that would give him life without parole.

CRIME

When Dara was eighteen, one of his closest friends was jumped by a rival gang. Upon recalling this moment, Dara's voice takes on a hard edge: "After that, it was just, especially from the older part of the gang: Anytime. Anywhere. It didn't matter." I ask for clarification, "So do you mean then, in your mind, the intent was 'anytime, anywhere' to commit murder?" Dara responds, "Absolutely. That's why we had a gun. Absolutely. Like—hell, yeah."

Dara recognizes now that the reflexive reaction after his friend was jumped was emotionally fraught and twisted with insecurity and male ego. He describes his thinking in a video, *A Lost Child Among Lost People* (Yin and Moncada 2020), cocreated with animation students at Cal State LA. He says that the gang's public declaration of revenge became a commitment they could not relinquish even if they had doubts, because their reputations were on the line among all of the other neighborhood gangs. When Dara imagined their rival gang members celebrating their successful attack on his friend, he was convinced that it had to be remedied.

Dara says that in his youthful naivete and arrogance, he believed he was invincible. He thought that because he was smart and savvy, he was skillful enough to avoid negative consequences. After all, despite his drug dealing and other antisocial behavior, he had successfully avoided any serious discipline or punishment.

Dara and three of his homies, including the one who was jumped, were obsessed with the need for revenge. Weeks after Dara's friend was jumped, they cornered the rival gang members in the local DMV parking lot. One of the rival gang members was shot in the head but survived with serious injuries. Another person was murdered.

Dara somberly admits that, in the moment, he is sure his younger self was elated and without regret.

> [I thought] He deserved it. No doubt about it in my mind. If anything, you signed up for this. I became a gang member. I knew I could die. They should know that too. You signed up for it [long pause] . . . Obviously, at the time, you don't understand environmental factors. You don't understand distresses and traumas that may be impacting you. You don't know what mental health is. You don't understand any of that. You think you're a grown man making these decisions but really, we were all just kids.

From afar, Dara saw his friends get arrested in front of their homes the day after the shooting. He fled to Texas and avoided arrest for a year and a half. There, he lived with extended family and was introduced to a younger cousin who instantly idolized him. Dara taught him everything he knew about living a criminal lifestyle, from selling drugs to stealing cars. Dara taught his cousin how to instill fear in others and to use violence to engender respect.

> My cousin followed in my footsteps. . . . He's in prison in Texas now for double murder. And he's like a kid from the suburbs. . . . I know what I did. . . . I don't think he wanted for anything—I mean, maybe he did emotionally? But when I got there, man! He looked at me like he instantly had a bigger brother. And I just—I just taught him what I knew. And it was the most horrible thing I could teach anybody.

Dara says the negative influence he was on his cousin is one of his most painful regrets.

PRISON

After hiding in Texas for almost two years, Dara ventured back to California and was soon arrested. He received a sentence of life without parole just a few weeks before his twenty-first birthday. In the moment, he says he knew the sentence meant he was supposed to die in prison, but he laughed it off at the time, not realizing the enormity of it.

He didn't have time to worry about the meaning of an LWOP sentence because he needed to focus all of his energies on survival. At the time of his sentence, Dara guesses that Asians were outnumbered a hundred to one in the California State Prison System, and he had a reputation that he needed to transfer from the streets into the prison to preserve his own safety. Just as it was when he was a gang member on the streets, his priority in prison was to be respected and feared. He hustled, selling drugs or taking part in "whatever illegal criminal business was available."

Dara spent his first seven years in Pelican Bay before transferring to Corcoran. At Corcoran, he was sent to the hole, and when he emerged a year later, he realized he hadn't seen his family in years. He asked to be transferred to Lancaster to be closer to them, a lengthy process that was successful only with the assistance of a special correctional officer, Mrs. Craig, who facilitated the transfer and helped him restore his family visiting rights.

TURNING POINT

Dara successfully transferred to Lancaster and, after ten years of distance between them, scheduled a family meeting. Dara recalls that he was hypervigilant and panicked throughout the first visit.

> I'm not really talking because I'm seeing them and it's like I don't even know them and they don't know me. But at the end of the visit, my mother told me, "I love you," in English. I had never heard her say that in *any* language to me before. It didn't even register at first but when I went back to the cell, I kind of played back the visit. I saw her frail, four-foot-ten body walking through that prison visiting door. Just ninety pounds and small . . . and it was just this . . . immense shame.

Dara says he began to question and take a hard look at himself after that visit. His voice catches as he reflects:

> I'm thinking . . . I didn't do shit for her. I did all this shit for everybody else . . . but I didn't do shit for her. But one thing I did remember was that she wanted

me to go to school. You know, amongst all the negative things that she would say to me, she would always say that I was smart. And I decided—I was still in all of that prison gang shit and all—but I decided I was going to go to school, too. I was going to get my GED. And I went and did it. Easily.

He sent his GED certificate to his mother. He remembers seeing the piece of paper hanging on the wall behind her during one of his illegal cellphone video calls with her. "And I was like, 'What fucking else can you do now??'"

Dara was still certain he would die in prison, but his thinking began to change. He asked himself *how* he wanted to die in prison. *What* would he be doing? *What* would his legacy be? Dara was on Lancaster's B Yard, a general population yard, but he had heard about the college programming on Lancaster's A Yard and knew that the men there had started a book-sharing club so that college could be more affordable. For the first time in his life, Dara stopped worrying about what the homies would think of him. He was exhausted from thirteen years of negotiating the constant tension of prison politics and skirmishes, and he was slowly getting ready to disassociate himself from that life. Dara started to imagine what it would be like to see his college degrees hanging on his mother's wall.

He asked to be transferred to Lancaster's Honor Yard. Many of the prison staff openly expressed their doubts that Dara, a heretofore active gang member, would be able to find success on a yard that focused on rehabilitation and the absence of prison politics. Still, his counselor, Ms. Black, pushed him through. In short time, not only did Dara find success on the Honor Yard, but he became a leader.

> The Honor Yard—you know, it just broke it down. It broke down what my [former] sense of loyalty was and what love is and what love should look like. It was never really told to me before. Yes, college started it, the pursuit of education started it—but the social and emotional education that I received there were, bar none, the reason why [I'm here today].

On A Yard, Dara's life changed. In addition to pursuing his associate's degree from Feather River's correspondence program, Dara participated in self-help classes facilitated by other men on the yard such as Lee Gibson, Justin Hong, and Allen Burnett. He appreciated hearing human stories similar to his own, which made him feel understood and less alone. He began to understand the complicated relationship with his mother and the role his father's abandonment played in his life. He realized that he had spent much of his life seeking acceptance and validation from the outside rather than from within himself. Through deep and unrelenting group work led by his peers, Dara began to assume responsibility for his actions and accountability for the harm he had caused. He no longer celebrated the death of his victim, but felt the full burden of regret and remorse. By learning from and "standing on the shoulders of giants" on A Yard, Dara began to change from someone who viciously took from the community to someone who wanted to help repair the community.

Dara confesses that for a long time, he was skeptical about the outside programs that came to Lancaster's A Yard, including the bachelor's degree program. He was, he explains, accustomed to viewing everything as transactional, and so he wondered what Cal State LA was getting for putting incarcerated students through college. He didn't trust it.

In 2018, under the tutelage of Professor Kamran Afary and his partner, Elizabeth Malone, Cohort 2 students wrote and produced a narradrama performance based on their life experiences titled *Imagine That!* Dara says it wasn't until then that he began to trust Cal State LA. He recalls his first reaction to Professor Afary's assignment: "Eh?? You want us to do a paper *and* a performance?" But the camaraderie and closeness that was developed among his cohort after that first skit created an unbreakable bond.

> Working together at first . . . it was odd, you know? And then it became like this energy that just fed all of us. And you know, now those guys will always be my brothers. . . . The conversations that were spurred by the assignments. How we stuck together and graduated together and helped each other all the way through. And it was the professors who really nurtured that and encouraged that along with the curriculum. There was selflessness from the professors. They cared about us as individuals as opposed to the work. That's when I really felt like the bachelor's degree program was what it said it was going to be.

Not only did Dara find that pursuing a bachelor's degree was deepening his relationship with others, he discovered that he was experiencing a profound shift in his mindset and values as well. Dara submitted the following reflection after the students performed *Imagine That!* in front of hundreds of friends and family:

> I am changing my negative mindset . . . being able to seek higher education. . . . I want better for myself now. I want better for the community that I helped destroy. (C. D. Yin, pers. comm., 2018)

While pursuing a bachelor's degree, Dara could see his understanding of relationships and connection changing. Whereas in his earlier years, he was more focused on his own ego and self-aggrandizement, his Cal State LA classes helped him understand both the macro and the micro ways that larger societal issues directly impacted him and the choices he made. With education and a better understanding of himself and his motivations, he was able to deliberately choose a different path.

Good or bad, when I say I'm gonna do something, I'm gonna do it. So when education came to prison, I was like, "Let's do it. I want to do that. I want to be a part of that." At some point, we all have egos in a certain way, right? But now, [I'm doing this] because I don't want to just be known as "that guy in prison." I don't want my mom to just think I'm in prison wasting away. I want to be able to say, "Yeah, I could have done this if I was out of prison, but the opportunity came to me in prison." And that's my chance. It was my job to continue to do it and show myself that I can do it and be happy on my own terms.

Dara's mother passed away from cancer in 2019, before he graduated from Cal State LA. Although he does not think she understood the enormity of him pursuing a bachelor's degree in prison, he knew she bragged to his siblings about him being in college. His mother never knew that he had an LWOP sentence; Dara says neither he nor his siblings wanted to "crush her spirit." Instead, when she would ask him on the phone when he was coming home, Dara would simply answer that he did not know and change the subject.

On October 6, 2021, students from Cal State LA's Prison BA Graduation Initiative celebrated thirty-seven graduates with a groundbreaking commencement ceremony on the hot and dusty A Yard. Dara was selected by his peers to present the keynote for his cohort, Cohort 2. This is what he said:

I am humbled to have the opportunity to speak with you all today. Thank you, Cal State Los Angeles, for your forward thinking and for believing in us. Thank you all for taking the time to come here today and join us in what we all will remember one day as "The Beginning." Though my graduation signifies an accomplishment, for me this is so much more. My mother could not read or write. A single mother escaping the jungles of Cambodia during its genocide. Making it to America, raising four kids and countless grandchildren, without an education. She knew the importance of an education, even when I did not. In 2019, during the fall semester, my mother passed away due to stage-four lung cancer. My educational journey was because of her.

Today, an education to me means freedom, redemption, and opportunity. The freedom to create better lives. A redeeming quality in the sense that we can step out of an identity that was destructive and into the person our mothers always meant for us to be. The opportunity to show that we are not our worst decisions, that we crave to be a part of the larger society so that we can put to use our unique combination of lived experience and education.

To the 2021 Cal State graduating class of the Progressive Program Facility: I challenge you to show our effort, determination, and accountability in the next steps of our lives, for we are the lucky, blessed, we are the representation of the incarcerated that must succeed. We already have. We help create legislation: [Billy G.], Samual Brown; we've written books: Jason Keaton, Terry Evans; we help at-risk youth: Terry Bell, Deon Whitmore, Larry Torres; we help others find their voices: Dortell Williams, Allen Burnett; we train dogs: Aaron Benson,

Gustavo Tamayo, [J. H.], Thaisan Nguon, paws up! All of this success from behind the walls of prison.

Imagine what else we could do? Find the answers to poverty? Homelessness? Help rebuild our K–12 schools? Put an end to kids joining gangs? Impossible? Not if you ask us. Imagine if those answers are here among the positive standing with society. Imagine that it starts today. Right now, dream the possibilities and build those dreams into reality. Imagine that. (C. D. Yin, pers. comm., from the speech he delivered October 6, 2021, at California State Prison, Los Angeles County, A Yard)

Because Dara thought he was never coming home, being "happy on my own terms" meant, in part, seizing opportunities like the bachelor's degree program or self-help classes, even if he didn't believe he would ever be able to employ those skills on the outside. When California's laws began changing in 2012, such as SB 9, which provided youthful offenders sentenced to LWOP with an opportunity for the court to take a "second look" (Harris 2013), Dara said it was a game changer for California's prisons. Dara figured that applying for a commutation was not unlike playing the lottery: one could never win if they didn't play. And though Dara recognized his record was far from "squeaky clean," he submitted an application for consideration. His LWOP sentence was commuted by Governor Gavin Newsom, and he came home at the end of 2022, a year after earning his bachelor's degree in communication.

Figure 13.1 Dara after his keynote speech at the Prison BA Graduation Initiative, October 6, 2021. Dara is being hugged by his classmate, Deon Whitmore. Photo: R. Huskey, 2021. Courtesy of California State University, Los Angeles.

THE RIPPLE EFFECT OF A FREE COLLEGE GRADUATE

Dara talks about what it is like, meeting new people on the outside as a free person.

> Man, I feel so prideful when I talk to people and they be like, "Oh, you're going to school? You're going for a bachelor's?" And I'm like, "No, I'm going for a master's degree." And they be like, "Oh? But you just got out?" And I get to say, "Cal State LA, baby!"
>
> You know, that pride I had in there with [Cal State LA]? It's not just in there. It transfers. It comes out *with* you. Education is that important; it's definitely part of rehabilitation. It is a holistic approach. It's not all education, but it is definitely a piece of it. I mean, to me, education is the crown jewel of rehabilitation. All kinds of education: social and emotional learning, emotional intelligence, and the academics.

Today, Dara says that his life is more than he could have ever imagined. He thinks about all of the things he gets to do now. He gets to appreciate the view from his transitional home's balcony. He gets to stress about traffic jams. He gets to hug his sister and kiss her on the forehead before she goes to work. He gets to tell his nieces and nephews that he loves them.

And, he has an opportunity to try to make amends.

> I feel so humbled and undeserving because you know I took someone's life. I know that family will always be grieving. I hope they will know that I am working in his name to help change and stop that cycle of violence.

Figure 13.2 Dara Yin (second from left) celebrates his graduation with family and friends at CSP Los Angeles County in Lancaster, CA, October 6, 2021. Photo R. Huskey, 2021. Courtesy of California State University, Los Angeles.

THE FUTURE

In fall 2023, Dara began attending the University of Southern California to pursue a master's degree in educational curriculum development. He is interested in translating his lived experiences and knowledge to bring social and emotional learning to our school systems. After working part-time in a financial advisement office, he started another part-time job working for an arts collaborative that serves at-risk youth. Working with youth is a passion project for Dara, largely because he relates so much to the kids he interacts with: "Academics are important. But students can't do work if they're distraught emotionally. It doesn't matter what you're teaching."

Most recently, Dara started working as a community organizer for API Rise, a nonprofit based in Los Angeles dedicated to lifting up the voices of Asian Pacific Islanders impacted by the California industrial prison complex. For Dara, everything in his life is coming around in a full circle. He says, "I believe education is the answer to ending poverty, systemic racism, and violence." Dara is a living example of the change that education can bring.

NOTE

1. All quotes in this chapter are from this interview, unless otherwise noted.

Chapter 14

Reflections

On my most recent birthday, I decided to throw a taco party for myself at the Cal State LA office. I invited all of the students and alumni who started their Cal State LA journey as part of the Prison Graduation Initiative and who are now home—twenty-three people strong and counting—as well as other Project Rebound members.

We also had a news reporter from ABC7 unexpectedly in the mix. The network wanted to interview some students for a story they planned to air about a new grant we had just received, so it was a happy coincidence for ABC to come on taco night. The grant was from the Bureau of Justice Assistance to fund a new program dubbed the "Prison to Career Equity Pathway"—a program to help incarcerated and formerly incarcerated college graduates with their professional development and leadership skills in order to find meaningful careers that blend both their lived experience and academic expertise.

The reporter got the footage he needed for the two-minute piece but ended up staying for three hours. He ate tacos, filmed the group as we sang "Happy Birthday," and patiently obliged us when we asked him to take group photos.

He stayed, he said, because he was fascinated by the group dynamic and the familial feel that flowed around the buffet table. He noticed that the students fondly refer to me as "Mama Taff" or "Mama T," a nickname I had long resisted but finally succumbed to. He observed how eager the men were to catch up with each other, the good-natured ribbing, their warm exuberance and support for each other. The reporter had more than enough footage, but still he let his camera roll while everyone moved their chairs in a big circle to tell stories about their growth after spending decades together on the same prison yard, then as a college cohort, and now, as free people with expansive opportunities and exciting futures ahead of them.

Having more than half of our students now living and thriving on the outside as college graduates was once unfathomable. That we would be gathered together eating tacos to celebrate my birthday was never imagined. The reporter did not think to ask me about *my* transformation as a result of this college in prison experience, although there is much to share both professionally and personally. Higher education in prison has been ambitiously resurrected across the country over the past ten years, and most prison education administrators have been learning on our feet as we go. Everything I have learned, especially about transformation and hope, has been from the students. If the reporter had asked, there is a litany of favorite topics that I enjoy expounding upon at length.

Among them is my belief that the most important benefit students receive from a face-to-face bachelor's degree program in prison is not about reducing recidivism or securing well-paying jobs, but it is about the resonance of hope, humanity, and lasting transformation. I would add, too, that these benefits are not one-sided but flow reciprocally between scholars, professors, and staff. Through my regular and ongoing interactions with our students and alumni, I have reevaluated everything I thought I once knew about what it means to be human and the purpose of mass incarceration, which, before this program, I honestly never thought much about before.

I have come to believe in second chances (and third, and fourth) and that there is no one beyond redemption. My own evolution and transformation is ongoing and never-ending.

I would invite the reporter to delve into the concept of the ripple effect by listening to the men who had been historically viewed as the black sheep of their family, but who, as striving college students in a carceral facility, became venerated mentors, peer leaders, role models, sages, and inspiration for family members, yard mates, and their community. LWOP students, who by definition were not expected to ever be released from prison, created a continuous ripple effect that motivates their children, siblings, and cousins to go to college.

I am convinced, too, that it is the ripple effect from a college education in prison that will interrupt the intergenerational cycle of incarceration. Over time, we will see how our pioneering scholars are able to influence the generations that follow them to choose a new path that prioritizes meaningful goals and societal contributions rather than falling into the well-worn rut of losing hope and succumbing to painful histories marred by trauma, low expectations, and violence.

Finally, after almost a decade in the field of higher education in prison and reentry, I've come to acknowledge that, while there are intrinsic values of a college education in prison, a degree alone does not remove all societal limitations. A college degree—even magna cum laude—means very little to graduates who emerge from prison clutching a diploma but who have been incarcerated for decades since their early teens without previous work experience. Our students are seeking opportunities to blend their lived experience with their academic achievements, and we need to guide students to view the possibilities that await them by helping them to develop their resumes, tie their classroom experience to potential work experience, and introduce career options. Our students and graduates need to learn about leadership, and to embrace the skills and assets they bring to work situations, guidance for which they will gain through coaching, mentoring, and networking. Additionally, we need to encourage the corporate, public, and nonprofit sectors to seek out and embrace the talents and skills of systems-impacted graduates.

TODAY

In July 2024, Jimmie Gilmer came home after serving thirty-six years of a life without possibility of parole sentence. He had entered prison a high school dropout, a drug dealer convicted of double murder. He came home with his GED, multiple associate of arts degrees, and a bachelor's degree in communication from Cal State LA. Jimmie was a star football player in high school, and he still carries his impressive height and imposing figure with athletic grace. His teeth sparkle, and his eyes crinkle at the corner when he smiles. His mother-in-law marvels that everywhere they go, there will be someone somewhere who recognizes him.

In many ways, Jimmie's homecoming brings the Prison Graduation Initiative full circle. The men he had helped prepare for the GED and encouraged to participate in the textbook sharing program had come home well before him. Many of the students interviewed in this book attributed their academic achievements to Jimmie's constant encouragement, cajoling, and support.

Now, Jimmie and seventeen of his former classmates from Lancaster are in the next phase of their lives. Jimmie is in our inaugural cohort of the Prison to Career Equity Pathway Program, which provides paid training, coaching, mentorship, and a career-oriented fellowship. He joins the rotation of students who regularly visit my office four or five deep to dig through my candy bowl, exchange gossip, or introduce me to someone new who just came home and is thinking about college. We snap pictures on each other's phones and then post them on a group text thread along with goofy memes and emojis.

They are published authors, keynote speakers, and sought-after experts on incarceration, trauma, and reentry. They have family dinners on weekends. They have become homeowners and invested in small ventures. They frequent the Cal State LA Credit Union and Trader Joe's. They drive brand-new Teslas and motorcycles. They have pursued graduate degrees, have opened their own businesses, have full-time jobs, and travel the world. They go to Disneyland, Chuck E. Cheese, and the beach. They have gotten engaged and married. They've become fathers. They give back to the community to leave it better than they found it, just like they promised.

And, just by living their lives in the best way they can, these college grads are creating a powerful ripple effect among their friends, family, and community. They are role models and mentors who are keeping the commitments they made to the parole board and to themselves. They inspire others to pursue a bachelor's degree or even a PhD and to dedicate themselves to serving others. There are, too, other ripple effects that may have been unexpected, but they are no less meaningful in their impact. I see this in the way that total strangers celebrate their achievements on social media or how a video journalist none of us knew was compelled to stick around just to engage with the students and talk to them as human beings.

The ripple effect within myself was unexpected and unparalleled. I have learned that change and transformation is always possible and that embracing educational opportunities is freeing. I now know that we *all* can rise above the worst decision we've made in our lives to be agents for positive change.

READER REFLECTIONS

- How has this book affected your understanding of higher education in prison and its value?
- Did you find common themes across these stories, and if so, what were they?
- What role do you think higher education plays in recognizing one's own humanity?
- If you were to choose one student's story, what would you identify as the turning point at which he shifted from a criminal mindset to that of a scholar?
- Do you think people who are incarcerated should be allowed to pursue a college degree in prison? Why or why not?
- These incarcerated scholars often refer to traumatic experiences and unresolved trauma as having a major influence in their lives. What could we do in our communities and society to better address trauma? Why would we make this effort?

Figure 14.1 ©The California State University 2019; Photographer: Patrick Record.

Glossary

A Yard: Location of Cal State LA's Prison Graduation Initiative at Lancaster State Prison. Interchangeably referred to as the Honor(s) Yard or Progressive Programming Facility by interviewees.

Cal State LA: California State University, Los Angeles. One of the California State University's twenty-three campuses across the state and a comprehensive public university of approximately 26,000 students in Los Angeles.

CDCR: California Department of Corrections and Rehabilitation.

Cellie: Person with whom one shares a prison cell.

Chrono: An informational note documenting behavior that is placed in an individual's permanent file.

Cohort: A group of students engaged in the same course of study who complete classes and the program together. A cohort often becomes a learning community.

Corcoran: California State Prison, Corcoran. Also referred to as Corcoran State Prison.

Drama therapy: Drama therapy uses play, embodiment, projection, role, story, metaphor, empathy, distancing, witnessing, performance, and improvisation to help people make meaningful change.

GED: The general education equivalency test offers a credential equivalent to a high school diploma.

Green-lighted: Marked or targeted for assault by other inmates.

Hole: Administrative segregation in prison to prevent further violence or to exert punishment. A prison within a prison.

Honor Yard (or **Honors Yard**): Kenneth Hartman and other incarcerated men on Lancaster State Prison's A Yard established it as an Honor Yard for individuals who wanted to focus on rehabilitation and positive programming. Individuals who came to live on the self-governed yard agreed to leave behind ethnic and racial politics, gang affiliations, violence, and drugs. Simultaneously referred to as A Yard and Progressive Programming Facility by interviewees.

Kite: A message or a letter. A handwritten note that could be for staff or other incarcerated individuals, sent between cells.

LAC: California State Prison, Los Angeles County in Lancaster, California. Also referred to as Lancaster State Prison or Lancaster.

LWOP: The sentence of life without the possibility of parole, or a person with an LWOP sentence. As an alternative to the death sentence, incarcerated individuals with this sentence assume they will die in prison unless they receive a commutation or their case is reconsidered because of the age at which they were convicted.

Narratherapy: A style of therapy that helps people become—and embrace being—an expert in their own lives. In narrative therapy, there is an emphasis on the stories that a person develops and carries with them through life.

OG: Original gangster. A term of respect within a gang for an older, more experienced member.

Pers. comm.: Personal communication.

PGI: Cal State LA's Prison Graduation Initiative, a face-to-face bachelor's degree completion program for incarcerated students. Previously known as the Prison BA Graduation Initiative.

Progressive Programming Facility: See A Yard and Honor Yard.

Recidivism: In this book, it refers to previously convicted and/or incarcerated persons reoffending and reentering the prison system.

SHU: Security Housing Unit at Pelican Bay Prison in northern California. Occupants in the solitary confinement units spend 22.5 hours per day alone in seven-by-eleven-foot windowless cells. Also, Security Housing Unit at San Quentin.

Three Strikes law: A law that imposes a mandatory life sentence for repeat offenders with three serious or violent felonies. California voters approved an initiative for a Three Strikes law in 1994.

Suggested Reading

Alexander, Michelle. 2010. *The New Jim Crow: Mass Incarceration in the Age of Colorblindness*. New York: The New Press.

Anderson, Annika, Roberta Fox, Paul Jones, Rigaud Joseph, Wendi Witherell, and Ashley Adams. 2023. "Reentry and Transition into College Life: A Study of Formerly Incarcerated Individuals in Southern California." *Journal of Human Behavior in the Social Environment* 34 (2): 268–89. doi:10.1080/10911359.2023.2244019

Binda, Hilary, Jill Weinberg, Nora Maetzener, and Carolyn L. Rubin. 2020. "'You're Almost in This Place That Doesn't Exist': The Impact of College in Prison as Understood by Formerly Incarcerated Students from the Northeastern United States." *Journal of Prison Education and Reentry* 6 (2): 242–63.

Buckley, Annie, ed. 2024. *Higher Education and the Carceral State: Transforming Together*. New York: Routledge.

Castro, Erin L., Rebecca K. Hunter, Tara Hardison, and Vanessa Johnson-Ojeda. 2018. "The Landscape of Postsecondary Education in Prison and the Influence of Second Chance Pell: An Analysis of Transferability, Credit-bearing Status, and Accreditation." *The Prison Journal* 98 (4): 405–26.

Conway, Patrick Filipe. 2023. "Beyond Recidivism: Exploring Formerly Incarcerated Student Perspectives on the Value of Higher Education in Prison." *The Review of Higher Education* 46 (4): 453–83.

Corbett, Erin S., ed. 2024. *The Bloomsbury Handbook of Prison Education*. New York: Bloomsbury Publishing.

Davis, Lois M., Robert Bozick, Jennifer L. Steele, Jessica Saunders, and Jeremy N. V. Miles. 2013. *Evaluating the Effectiveness of Correctional Education: A Meta-Analysis of Programs That Provide Education to Incarcerated Adults*. Santa Monica, CA: RAND Corporation. https://doi.org/10.7249/RR266

Gellman, Mneesha. 2020. "Higher Education Access and Parity: The Emerson Prison Initiative's Bachelor of Arts Program." In *Higher Education Accessibility Behind and Beyond Prison Walls.* Hershey, PA: IGI Global. doi: 10.4018/978-1-7998-3056-6.ch003

Gellman, Mneesha, and Justin McDevitt, eds. 2024. *Unlocking Learning: International Perspectives on Education in Prison.* Waltham, MA: Brandeis University Press.

Ginsburg, Rebecca, ed. 2019. *Critical Perspectives on Teaching in Prison: Students and Instructors on Pedagogy Behind the Wall.* New York: Routledge.

Hughes, Emma. 2016. *Education in Prison: Studying Through Distance Learning.* New York: Routledge.

Johnson, Hans, Eric McGhee, and Marisol Cuellar Mejia. 2024. "Fact Sheet 2024: California's Population." Public Policy Institute of California. https://www.ppic.org/publication/californias-population/.

Karpowitz, Daniel. 2005. "Prison, College, and the Paradox of Punishment." In *Crime and Punishment: Perspectives from the Humanities (Studies in Law, Politics, and Society* vol. 37). Leeds, UK: Emerald Group Publishing Limited.

Kleinstuber, Ross, Jeremiah Coldsmith, Margaret Leigey, and Sandra Joy. 2022. *Life Without Parole: Worse Than Death?* New York: Routledge.

Lagemann, Ellen Condliffe. 2017. *Liberating Minds: The Case for College in Prison.* New York: The New Press.

Mukamal, Debbie, and Rebecca Silbert. 2018. *Don't Stop Now: California Leads the Nation in Using Public Higher Education to Address Mass Incarceration. Will We Continue?* Stanford, CA: Stanford Criminal Justice Center and Corrections to College California. https://perma.cc/F6ZN-UJKW.

Mukamal, Debbie, Rebecca Silbert, and Rebecca M. Taylor. 2015. *Degrees of Freedom: Expanding College Opportunities for Currently and Formerly Incarcerated Californians.* Stanford, CA: Stanford Criminal Justice Center. https://law.stanford.edu/publications/degrees-of-freedom-expanding-college-opportunities-for-currently-and-formerly-incarcerated-californians/.

Murillo, Danny. 2021. *The Possibility Report: From Prison to College Degrees in California.* Campaign for College Opportunity. https://collegecampaign.org/wp-content/uploads/imported-files/Possibility-Report.pdf.

Quach, Khoi, Michael Cerda-Jara, Raven Deverux, and Johnny Smith. 2022. "Prison, College, and the Labor Market: A Critical Analysis by Formerly Incarcerated and Justice-Impacted Students." *ANNALS of the American Academy of Political and Social Science* 701 (1): 78–97. https://doi.org/10.1177/00027162221112772

Roy, Bidhan Chandra, Tiffany Lim, and Rebecca Silbert. 2020. "We Are Cal State LA: The Prison BA From a Mission and Values Perspective." In *Higher Education Accessibility Behind and Beyond Prison Walls.* Hershey, PA: IGI Global. https://doi.org/10.4018/978-1-7998-3056-6.ch004

Torres, Anacany. 2020. "Watering the Roses That Grew from Concrete: The Support Services for Formerly Incarcerated Students on a Community College Campus." California State University, Long Beach. https://www.proquest.com/docview/2465753809.

Van der Kolk, Bessel. 2014. *The Body Keeps the Score: Brain, Mind, and Body in the Healing of Trauma.* New York: Viking.

Bibliography

Baldwin, James. 1972. *No Name in the Street*. New York: The Dial Press.

Barajas, Julia. 2022. "Write a Different End: How Building Community Can Take Students from Prison to College Degree." *LAist*, May 19, 2022. https://laist.com/news/education/hidden-curriculum-csu-project-rebound-re-entry

Brown, Samual Nathaniel. 2018. "Eden Is No More." In *Disconnected-Reconnected: Writing from Lancaster Prison*, edited by Bidhan C. Roy, 17–28. Brick of Gold Publishing Company.

Burnett, Allen D. 2017. "An Irreparably Good Man." In *Words Uncaged: Human*, edited by Bidhan C. Roy, 19–28. California State University, Los Angeles. https://static1.squarespace.com/static/5d81a718b33c0b468acbe5b9/t/5e35d9942eda975 27117adf4/1580587452362/human-book-pages-final.pdf

Davis, Lois M., Robert Bozick, Jennifer L. Steele, Jessica Saunders, and Jeremy N. V. Miles. 2013. *Evaluating the Effectiveness of Correctional Education: A Meta-Analysis of Programs That Provide Education to Incarcerated Adults*. Santa Monica, CA: RAND Corporation. https://doi.org/10.7249/RR266

G., Billy. 2017. "Butterflies." In *Words Uncaged: Human,* edited by Bidhan C. Roy, 86–91. California State University, Los Angeles. https://static1.squarespace.com/static/5d81a718b33c0b468acbe5b9/t/5e35d9942eda97527117adf4/1580587452362/human-book-pages-final.pdf

Harris, Michael. 2013. *California Law Gives Youth Sentenced to Life Without Parole Another Chance*. National Center for Youth Law. January 1, 2013. https://youthlaw.org/news/california-law-gives-youth-sentenced-life-without-parole -another-chance#:~:text=In%20a%20key%20policy%20shift,to%2025%20years %20to%20life

Harvey, Antonio R. 2023. "Wilson Seeks to Remove Slavery Language from California's Constitution." *LA Sentinel*, February 23, 2023. https://lasentinel.net/wilson -seeks-to-remove-slavery-language-from-californias-constitution.html

Human Rights Watch. 2023. *"I Just Want to Give Back": The Reintegration of People Sentenced to Life Without Parole.* https://www.hrw.org/report/2023/06/28/i-just-want-to-give-back/reintegration-of-people-sentenced-to-life-without-parole

J. H. 2017. "The Longest Ride." In *Words Uncaged: Human,* edited by Bidhan C. Roy, 10–13. California State University, Los Angeles. https://static1.squarespace.com/static/5d81a718b33c0b468acbe5b9/t/5e35d9942eda97527117adf4/1580587452362/human-book-pages-final.pdf

J. H., and Stephann Lalanne. 2018. *Being Reasonable About Unreasonable Decisions.* https://www.lettersfromtheetui.com/visual-letters

J. H. 2018. "Daisies." In *Disconnected:Reconnected: Writing from Lancaster Prison,* edited by Bidhan C. Roy, 81–83. Brick of Gold Publishing Company.

Keaton, Jason. 2018. "The Second Cohort Introduce Each Other." *Prison BA Journal* 1: 4–5. https://www.prisonbajournal.org/issues-1

Keaton, Jason. 2020. *Rough Around the Edges: My Journey.* Self-published.

Kübler-Ross, Elisabeth. 1969. *On Death and Dying: What the Dying Have to Teach Doctors, Nurses, Clergy, and Their Own Families.* New York: The Macmillan Company.

Lamar, Kendrick. 2009. "Uncle Bobby & Jason Keaton." Track 8 on *The Kendrick Lamar EP.* Top Dawg Entertainment.

Lim, Taffany S. 2020. "The Prison to College Pipeline: The Transformative Impact and Ripple Effects of Hope on Incarcerated Students, Other Inmates, and Their Families." EdD dissertation, California State University, Fresno. *Proquest* 28023551.

Los Angeles Times. 1997. "Armored Car Guard Confesses to Slaying, Police Say." November 29, 1997. https://www.latimes.com/archives/la-xpm-1997-nov-29-mn-58825-story.html

Maxson, Cheryl L., Malcolm W. Klein, and Lea C. Cunningham. 2006. *Street Gangs and Drug Sales in Pasadena and Pomona, California, 1989–1991.* Inter-university Consortium for Political and Social Research [distributor], January 12, 2006. https://doi.org/10.3886/ICPSR06255.v2

Mukamal, Debbie, and Rebecca Silbert. 2018. *Don't Stop Now: California Leads the Nation in Using Public Higher Education to Address Mass Incarceration. Will We Continue?* Stanford, CA: Stanford Criminal Justice Center and Corrections to College California. https://perma.cc/F6ZN-UJKW

Mukamal, Debbie, Rebecca Silbert, and Rebecca M. Taylor. 2015. *Degrees of Freedom: Expanding College Opportunities for Currently and Formerly Incarcerated Californians.* Stanford, CA: Stanford Criminal Justice Center. https://law.stanford.edu/publications/degrees-of-freedom-expanding-college-opportunities-for-currently-and-formerly-incarcerated-californians/

Nguon, Thaisan, and Nathaniel Trias. 2018. "From Letters to Visits in Prison: A Past Relationship Becomes Present Again." *Letters from the Etui.* https://www.lettersfromtheetui.com/visual-letters

Nguyen, Tin. 2017. "An Educational Journey." In *Words Uncaged: Human,* edited by Bidhan C. Roy, 62–65. California State University, Los Angeles. https://static1.squarespace.com/static/5d81a718b33c0b468acbe5b9/t/5e35d9942eda97527117adf4/1580587452362/human-book-pages-final.pdf

Outhyse, Tessa. 2022. "A Year After Graduating, Jason Keaton Is Helping Others." California Department of Corrections and Rehabilitation. https://www.cdcr.ca.gov /insidecdcr/2022/10/28/a-year-after-graduating-jason-keaton-is-helping-others/

Rose-Aminifu, Risala. 2017–2018. Unpublished performances.

Roy, Bidhan Chandra. 2018. "Locked-up Vietnamese California: A Boom Interview with Tin Nguyen." *Boom California.* University of California Press. https://boom-california.org/2018/04/11/locked-up-vietnamese-california/

Sawyer, Wendy. 2019. "Since You Asked: How Did the 1994 Crime Bill Affect Prison College Programs?" Prison Policy Initiative. https://www.prisonpolicy.org/ blog/2019/08/22/college-in-prison/

Schatz, Brian (Office of US Senator). 2019. "The Restoring Education and Learning (REAL) Act." https://ajcunet.edu/wp-content/uploads/2024/03/Higher-Ed-letter-in -support-of-legislation-to-repeal-the-prohibition-on-Pell-Grants-for-incarcerated -individuals-April-2019.pdf

Stallworth, Leo. 2021. "Inmates at Lancaster Prison Earn Bachelor's Degrees." *KABC-TV,* October 6, 2021. https://abc7.com/prison-inmates-college-degree-cal -state-la-lancaster/11086787/

Van der Kolk, Bessel. 2014. *The Body Keeps the Score: Brain, Mind, and Body in the Healing of Trauma.* New York: Viking.

West, Kanye. 2007. "Can't Tell Me Nothing." Track 6 on *Graduation.* Def Jam Recording and Roc-A-Fella Records.

Yin, Chay Dara, and Marco Moncada. 2020. *A Lost Child Among Lost People.* https:// vimeo.com/showcase/7155653

Index

Page references for figures are italicized.

About the Author

Taffany Lim, Ed.D., is the founding Executive Director of Cal State LA's Center for Engagement, Service, and the Public Good where she oversees university initiatives that engage the campus and community in the promotion of the public good.

Under her leadership, the Center for Engagement, Service, and the Public Good established the first face-to-face BA degree completion program for incarcerated students in the state of California, which has received funding from the Second Chance Pell program, the Andrew W. Mellon Foundation, Bureau of Justice Administration, and the Renewing Communities Initiative. The Prison Graduation Initiative began at California State Prison – Los Angeles County, a maximum-security facility for men located in the high desert of Los Angeles County. Since the Prison Graduation Initiative's inception in 2016, more than 50 men have earned bachelor's degrees in Communication, almost half of whom are now home from prison. The Prison Graduation Initiative recently expanded to the California Institute for Women where they offer a bachelor's degree in liberal studies. She also oversees Cal State LA's Project Rebound, modeled after San Francisco State University's program of the same name to help matriculate and graduate formerly incarcerated students, and in 2023, Taffany created the Prison to Career Pathway program to help formerly incarcerated college graduates leverage their academic achievements with their lived experiences into meaningful careers.

Prior to her appointment with the Center for Engagement, Service, and the Public Good in January 2014, Taffany served as the Associate Director for the Pat Brown Institute for Public Affairs (PBI) where she developed and managed PBI's signature Community Policing Training Program, providing training and technical assistance to dozens of police departments in California.

Taffany specializes in program development, project management, planning, training and facilitation. She has spent more than 25 years of her career working with public sector and nonprofit organizations including United Way, KCET Public Television, the Los Angeles Department of Mental Health, and the City of Pasadena's Public Health Department. She was also an independent consultant for many years and served with a team of facilitators offering a two day workshop on Influencing through Communication. The team worked through the Los Angeles County Workforce Development Office, providing training to thousands of nurses and staff who worked for Los Angeles County health care organizations.

Taffany has a BA in psychology and social welfare from UC Berkeley, a master's in public administration from USC, and her doctorate in educational leadership from Fresno State.